Textual Intercourse proposes that the language and practice of writing plays in early modern England were inextricably linked to languages and practices of eroticism, sexuality, and reproduction. Jeffrey Masten reads a range of early modern materials – burial records, contemporary biographical anecdotes, and theatrical records; essays, conduct books, and poems; the printed apparatus of published plays, and the plays themselves – to illustrate the ways in which writing for the theatre shifted in the seventeenth century from a model of homoerotic collaboration toward singular authorship on a patriarchal–absolutist model. Plays and collections of plays by Shakespeare, Shakespeare and Fletcher, Beaumont and Fletcher, Margaret Cavendish, and others, are considered.

Masten thus brings together disciplines and interests that have traditionally worked in isolation: he shows how the history of the book can also be the history of sexualities; and he illustrates the ways in which methods attuned to sexuality and gender can illuminate more traditional questions of authorship, attribution, textual editing, and the history of literary and intellectual property.

Cambridge Studies in Renaissance
Literature and Culture 14

Textual intercourse

Cambridge Studies in Renaissance Literature and Culture

General editor
Stephen Orgel
Jackson Eli Reynolds Professor of Humanities, Stanford University

Editorial board
Anne Barton, *University of Cambridge*
Jonathan Dollimore, *University of Sussex*
Marjorie Garber, *Harvard University*
Jonathan Goldberg, *Duke University*
Nancy Vickers, *University of Southern California*

Since the 1970s there has been a broad and vital reinterpretation of the nature of literary texts, a move away from formalism to a sense of literature as an aspect of social, economic, political, and cultural history. While the earliest New Historicist work was criticized for a narrow and anecdotal view of history, it also served as an important stimulus for post-structuralist, feminist, Marxist, and psychoanalytical work, which in turn has increasingly informed and redirected it. Recent writing on the nature of representation, the historical construction of gender, and of the concept of identity itself, on theatre as a political and economic phenomenon and on the ideologies of art generally, reveals the breadth of the field. Cambridge Studies in Renaissance Literature and Culture is designed to offer historically oriented studies of Renaissance literature and theatre which make use of the insights afforded by theoretical perspectives. The view of history envisioned is above all a view of our own history, a reading of the Renaissance for and from our own time.

Recent titles include

Men in women's clothing: anti-theatricality and effeminization, 1579–1642
Laura Levine, Wellesley College

Shakespeare and the theatre of wonder
T. G. Bishop, Case Western Reserve University

Anxious masculinity in early modern England
Mark Breitenberg

Seizures of the will in early modern English drama
Frank Whigham, University of Texas at Austin

The emergence of the English author: scripting the life of the poet in early modern England
Kevin Pask, McGill University

A complete list of books in the series is given at the end of the volume

Textual intercourse

*Collaboration, authorship, and sexualities
in Renaissance drama*

Jeffrey Masten

Harvard University

CAMBRIDGE
UNIVERSITY PRESS

Published by the Press Syndicate of the University of Cambridge
The Pitt Building, Trumpington Street, Cambridge CB2 1RP
40 West 20th Street, New York, NY 10011–4211, USA
10 Stamford Road, Oakleigh, Melbourne 3166, Australia

First published 1997

Printed in Great Britain at the University Press, Cambridge

A catalogue record for this book is available from the British Library

Library of Congress cataloguing in publication data
Masten, Jeffrey.
Textual intercourse: collaboration, authorship, and sexualities in
Renaissance drama / Jeffrey Masten.
    p.   cm. – (Cambridge studies in Renaissance literature and culture:14)
Includes bibliographical references and index.
ISBN 0 521 57260 6 (hardback) – ISBN 0 521 58920 7 (paperback)
1. English drama – Early modern and Elizabethan, 1500–1600 – Criticism,
Textual.   2. Newcastle, Margaret Cavendish, Duchess of, 1624?–1674 –
Dramatic works.   3. Homosexuality and literature – England – History – 16th
century.   4. Homosexuality and literature – England – History – 17th
century.   5. English drama – 17th century – Criticism, Textual.   6. Drama –
Authorship – Collaboration – History.   7. Authorship – Sex differences.
8. Shakespeare, William, dramatic works.   9. Sex in literature.
10. Beaumont, Francis, and John Fletcher – dramatic works.
I. Title.   II. Series.
PR658.T4M37   1997
822′.309–dc20   96–2949   CIP

ISBN 0 521 57260 6 hardback
ISBN 0 521 58920 7 paperback

CE

Contents

Illustrations

Illustrations in the text

Acknowledgments

The process of writing this book has also been the process of imagining an institutional structure in which an acknowledgment page could be a title page. In the absence of that possibility, I want to affirm here that certain collaborations function throughout the pages that follow. There are, as is our custom, notes throughout this book that acknowledge particular debts, borrowings, and rearticulations, but here I cite other collaborations: how might I fully separate out these contributions, or know who is speaking a given word or sentence or method, so as to mark it?

This project was first conceived and supported at the University of Pennsylvania, through the teaching of a dynamic Renaissance studies group, including Rebecca Bushnell, Margreta de Grazia, Maureen Quilligan, Phyllis Rackin, Peter Stallybrass, and Robert Y. Turner, each of whom will, I hope, see his or her particular gifts of thought and method reflected here. The knowledge and expertise of Georgianna Ziegler (then curator of the Furness Shakespeare collection) stands behind many of this book's early modern citations. This project owes a great deal to the encouragement, hospitality, and example of Stuart Curran. From the moment of its first and most unconvincing articulation, Margreta de Grazia and Peter Stallybrass have read, directed, and encouraged this work, and to put my gratitude all too minimally, I'm thankful that I can count them as advisors, teachers, and friends. In different and complementary ways, they have made this work enjoyable, and possible.

Also beginning at Penn, and now dispersedly, a group of colleagues supported this work with friendship, citations, conversation, and critique: Rebecca Bach, Sara Beasley, Will Fisher, Juliet Fleming, Teresa Goddu, David Golumbia, Andrea Henderson, David Herman, Lisa Myers, Craig Smith, Max Thomas. Among her many other gifts, Wendy Wall has helped me to finish, and begin.

At Harvard, particular chapters were constructively questioned by friends and colleagues: Doug Bruster, Dan Donoghue, Philip Fisher,

Elizabeth Fowler, Marjorie Garber, Scott Gordon, Roland Greene, Phil Harper, David Hirsch, Barbara Johnson, Barbara Lewalski, Derek Pearsall, David Perkins, Elaine Scarry, Marc Shell, Werner Sollors, and Helen Vendler. For particularly enabling gifts of collegiality, critique, and/or song, I want to thank Chris Cannon, Phil Harper, Meredith McGill, D. A. Miller, Wendy Motooka, Michael Prokopow, and Lynn Wardley. I'm grateful for the resourceful research assistance of Nick Hoffman and Eric Wilson, who have also been attentive readers and contributors. Thanks too to Doug Trevor, who ably produced an index from a somewhat reluctant text. The staff of the Houghton Library reading room has been an indispensable help to my research and teaching of early printed editions. I am grateful to the Houghton Library for permission to reproduce many of the photographs in this book, and to the Hyder E. Rollins Fund, Fred N. Robinson Publication Fund, and Clark Fund at Harvard for material support of research and publication.

Parts of this book have had the benefit of discussion in a number of contexts: the Lesbian and Gay Studies Seminar at the Harvard Center for Literary and Cultural Studies; seminars and sessions of the Shakespeare Association of America; the Renaissance Seminar at Wesleyan College; English departments at Ohio State University, Ohio University, and Swarthmore College; the International Elizabethan Theatre Conference on collaboration; a 1991 conference on authorship and intellectual property at Case Western Reserve University organized by Martha Woodmansee and Peter Jaszi; the Fellows seminar at the Newberry Library. An NEH Fellowship at the Newberry helped me in the final stages of this project.

I want especially to thank a group of scholars and friends, present at these and/or other discussions, who have, with suggestions, encouragement, and productive resistances, contributed generously to my understanding: Henry Abelove, Peter Blayney, Lee Edelman, Margaret Ferguson, Paul Gehl, Suzanne Gossett, Stephen Greenblatt, Ann Jones, Michael Keefer, Andrea Lunsford, Carol Mason, Julie Mulroy, David Norbrook, John Norman, Patricia Parker, Elizabeth Pittenger, Richard Rambuss, Mary Beth Rose, Marc Schachter, Anne Shaver, the late Gary Spear, Gary Taylor, Nancy Vickers, Paul Werstine, Martha Woodmansee. In particular, the work and encouragement of Jonathan Goldberg, David Kastan, Karen Newman, and Valerie Traub have helped to write this book. I'm grateful to Stephen Orgel for the example of his work and for his generous attention to this project from an early stage.

I want to thank Linda Bree, Audrey Cotterell, Josie Dixon, and Ann Rex for their work on this book at Cambridge University Press.

I'm grateful to the teachers in my family, and in particular my parents,

James and Janice Masten, who started this whole process by teaching me to read and write. Since then, never anticipating how the story might turn out, they have seen it through with indefatigable support and understanding.

As I write this, I can hear Jay Grossman asking me, with characteristic humor, to be done with it already. Soon, but not without first recording my gratitude to and affection for him: with notable endurance, he has read, written, disputed, distracted, humored, waited, supported, realized.

I am grateful to the Johns Hopkins University Press for permission to publish a revised version of chapter 1, which first appeared in *English Literary History* 59 (1992); and to Duke University Press for permission to publish a revised version of material in chapters 2, 4, and 5, first published in *Queering the Renaissance*, Jonathan Goldberg (ed.), 1993.

Introduction: Textual intercourse

'I'll tell you what I did yesterday! I got the sexton, who was digging
Linton's grave, to remove the earth off her coffin lid, and I opened it. I
thought, once, I would have stayed there, when I saw her face again – it
is hers yet – he had hard work to stir me; but he said it would change, if
the air blew on it, and so I struck one side of the coffin loose – and
covered it up ... and I bribed the sexton to pull it away, when I'm laid
there, and slide mine out too. I'll have it made so, and then, by the time
Linton gets to us, he'll not know which is which!'

'You were very wicked, Mr Heathcliff!' I exclaimed; 'were you not
ashamed to disturb the dead?'   Emily Brontë, *Wuthering Heights*[1]

It was once in my thoughts to have Printed Mr. *Fletcher's* workes by
themselves, because single & alone he would make a *Just Volume*: But
since never parted while they lived, I conceived it not equitable to
seperate their ashes.

Humphrey Moseley, "The Stationer to the Reader," *Comedies and Tragedies
Written by Francis Beavmont and Iohn Fletcher Gentlemen* (1647)[2]

I begin with the desire to sleep with the dead. Not my own desire –
though figuratively there will be more to say about this – but rather the
desire that might be said to be inscribed in the words of Sir Aston
Cokain, playwright and friend of playwrights, writing of his close friend
Philip Massinger, in his 1658 poem "*An Epitaph on Mr*. John Fletcher,
and Mr. Philip Massinger, *who lie buried both in one Grave in St*. Mary
Overie's Church *in* Southwark":

In the same Grave *Fletcher* was buried here
Lies the Stage-Poet *Philip Massinger*:
Playes they did write together, were great friends,
And now one Grave includes them at their ends:
So whom on earth nothing did part, beneath
Here (in their Fames) they lie, in spight of death.[3]

Cokain's account, so far as we can check it, agrees with the other bits of
text that survive: both Fletcher and Massinger are recorded in the church
registry as having been buried in the parish graveyard – Massinger for a

1

fee of £2, the exorbitancy of which may reflect *his* desire (for he was buried last) to be interred with Fletcher in the church itself.[4]

Nevertheless, as I will have occasion to remark a number of times in this study, the facticity of such an account – whether Fletcher and Massinger actually shared a grave – is not the point of this recounting. For such knowledge is, I take it, unretrievable at this distance, and even were we to know it, what would it then tell us about the relation of Massinger to Fletcher, or of Cokain to either, or (as is more to the point in this investigation) about the cultural meanings of collaborative play-wrighting, dramatic authorship, and attendant sexualities in early modern England? What is striking about Cokain's poem is, first, the terms in which it discusses the living and writing arrangements of early modern dramatic collaborators ("great friends ... whom on earth nothing did part" – terms that, as we will see, intersect with other discussions of early modern collaboration and male relations), and second, the alterity of this configuration to more modern eyes.

To unearth what such a configuration might have signified, we might begin by thinking about funeral rituals in early modern England, and David Cressy's suggestion that these rituals functioned to "aggregat[e] the deceased to his ancestors and [to] reintegrat[e] the survivors into the everyday world of the living" (p. 116).[5] It was typical, Cressy notes, for people to request burial beside or near their relatives or spouses: "near to the place where my wife lieth" (p. 110), or "in the [church] where my mother, brother, and kindred lie" (p. 111). For this reason (and because burial ground was scarce), it was not unusual to have multiple inhabitants of the same grave – though the practice of burying perfect strangers together seems to have been common only in plague-time.[6] In general, burial requests, along with church registries, suggest that burials reflected a certain version of early modern English social order; they were structured along lines of family and social class.

I want to interpret Fletcher and Massinger's burial together as a part of this *general* sense that the arrangement of the dead reflects the society of the living – Fletcher and Massinger *continue* to lie together, the poem emphasizes, *"in spight* of death." However, as the readings that structure much of this book will demonstrate, this double interment of friends reflects another aspect of early modern English social order: the socially sanctioned bonds among men within the institutions of the theatre and (as we will see in chapter 2) the more widespread bonds in this culture among those who were, or desired to be, English gentlemen. (The full contextualization of the homoerotic meanings of Cokain's language will have to wait until that chapter's discussion of social class, collaboration, and the discourse of male friendship;[7] even in passing, however, we can note the brief sodomitical resonance of the rhyme "friends" and "ends.") These arrangements may look quaint or odd, exaggerated or suspect, under the current dispensation. But we are looking at this material from the vantage point of a culture that has since invented and naturalized "companionate marriage";[8] we read with eyes that have also read *Wuthering Heights*, eyes trained to see post-mortem heterosexual union as the height of romantic attachment, even if, like Nelly Dean, we purport to find the details of coffins, corpses, and burials a bit shocking.

Returning to Cressy's formulation, we might notice how Fletcher and Massinger's double burial "reintegrat[es] the survivors into the everyday world of the living." This is, as we will see, an everyday world suffused with, structured by, collaborative textual practice, and Sir Aston Cokain (himself a survivor, playwright, gentleman, and friend) writes of Massinger and Fletcher's collaboration and friendship, and produces, or re-produces, his own writing out of this collaborative arrangement. This cycle of generative copying, gentlemanly reproduction, and the distinctly non-privatized property of words and identities is reproduced by another, more familiar, aspiring gentleman and playwright, writing presumably to another gentleman in a volume of sonnets published in 1609: "Thou shouldst print more, not let that coppy die."[9]

Fletcher and Massinger are said to be buried together in a church on the Bankside, and there is another account – John Aubrey's, to be read in detail in chapter 2 – in which Fletcher and another of his collaborators, Francis Beaumont, lay there together (alive), in a house "not far from the Play-house" that they shared, along with their clothes and bed, their writing, and a "wench."[10] As both Steven Mullaney and Scott McMillin have demonstrated, the cultural geography of the theatre in early modern England is important, and in G. E. Bentley's studies of players and dramatists we have the beginnings of a sociology of this Bankside culture that may explain the living arrangements, writing arrangements, acting arrangements, and funeral arrangements of these men and the institutions they worked within.[11] Like so many of their colleagues, Fletcher and Massinger's lives and deaths are recorded in a local parish;[12] as Bentley notes, the wills of the players often inscribe the bonds of this culture on the Bankside, as in the case, for example, of the acting-company sharer Augustine Phillips:

Item, I give and bequeath to my fellow William Shakespeare a thirty shilling piece in gold; to my fellow Henry Condell one other thirty shilling piece in gold ...to my fellow Robert Armin, twenty shillings in gold ...
Item, I give to Samuel Gilborne, my late apprentice, the sum of forty shillings, and my mouse-colored velvet hose, and a white taffeta doublet, a black taffeta suit, my purple cloak, sword and dagger, and my bass viol.[13]

These are dying arrangements, reflecting living arrangements that often existed, as we shall see, not to the exclusion of, but alongside, marriage;[14] these are also the living conditions that produced the highly collaborative texts we now call Renaissance drama. Like the arrangement of corpses, wills as a social practice seek to preserve affiliations beyond the grave – to reproduce social alliances through the distribution of objects, space, property. The languages in which these practices are described and inscribed now appear to us to be somewhat unusual ("Playes they did write together, were great friends, / And now one Grave includes them at their ends ... "); it is nevertheless the argument of this book that, reading the languages of collaboration and authorship attentively, we will begin to see some signal differences of our culture from that of these dead men, in both their textual relations and their sexual ones.

This project, then, emerges from a pair of related perceptions about early modern England. First, in a way that has not been fully recognized or conceptualized by scholars trained to organize material within post-Enlightenment paradigms of individuality, authorship, and textual property, collaboration was a prevalent mode of textual production in the sixteenth and seventeenth centuries, only eventually displaced by the mode of singular authorship with which we are more familiar. This is especially true, as I will emphasize, of texts associated with early modern theatres,[15] and chapter 1 attempts to expand and complicate our understanding of the ways in which those theatres produced collaborative texts. Though drama is this book's predominant focus, it is important to stress that it is only one of many collaborative discursive sites and genres in a period in which textual property was typically not assigned to authors by law or custom; J. W. Saunders, Arthur Marotti, Wendy Wall, and others have persuasively demonstrated, for example, the collaborative construction of meaning in Renaissance poetic manuscripts.[16] Second, whether collaborative or authorial, textual production – that is, the writing, performance, collection, publication, and circulation of plays, and the ways in which those processes were understood to function – occurred within the context of conflicting and contested "sex/gender systems."[17] This is not to say simply or only that theatres and publishing houses were predominantly male concerns,[18] but also that these texts emerged within larger rhetorics of sex/gender that were both reflective and productive of their culture and its institutions. This project thus traces the correspondences between, on the one hand, models and rhetorics of sexual relations, intercourse, and reproduction and, on the other, notions of textual production and property. The first line of Fletcher and Shakespeare's *The Two Noble Kinsmen* proposes one resonant formulation of this relation to which we will return in detail in chapter 2: "New Playes, and Maydenheads," they write, "are neare a kin."[19]

Studies have been done in both textual and sexual areas, but they have until very recently tended to operate by mutual exclusion, with bibliographic/textualist work ignoring the production of texts within the discourses of a sex/gender system, and sex/gender studies often eliding the conditions and conventions of textual production.[20] As I hope the catachresis of my title suggests, this study situates itself, instead, at the intersection of the textual and the sexual; it insists upon relating the material conditions and cultural representations of sex/gender and of textual production. My chiastic assumption throughout is that any reading of these materials must address the fact that texts are produced within a particular sex/gender context and that gender and sexuality are themselves in part produced in and by texts. At this conjunction, the project necessarily attempts a revision both of our assumptions about sexual/social relations among men[21] in the Renaissance – and among men and women, as my references to Gayle Rubin's and Eve Sedgwick's formulations suggest – and of our approaches to textual production, circulation, and property. Indeed, as the accumulated readings of this evidence will show, it is difficult in this period to separate out what now appear to us to be the distinct rhetorics (even "disciplines") of the sexual and the textual; much of the work of this book is an attempt to excavate and contextualize these languages and rhetorics in a historically attentive way.[22]

Any discussion of these issues in the early modern period must necessarily acknowledge the centrality of Michel Foucault's assertion that "homosexuality," as a sexual identity or orientation central to the conception of individuality, was a cultural production of the nineteenth century in the West.[23] David M. Halperin has further stressed that "heterosexuality" (again, as the articulation of an identity) came into being *after* "homosexuality" and is, equally, a historically contingent development.[24] As Jonathan Goldberg's *Sodometries* has recently argued in compelling detail, and as the work of this book will support, neither of these terms adequately accounts for the relations and representations we encounter in early modern texts.[25] Chapter 2 in particular will demonstrate that a reinvestigation of the discourses of male friendship, individuality (in the now-obsolete sense of "indivisibility"), and collaboration has much to tell us about the sexual terms we have traditionally used to investigate and taxonomize the past and will suggest the difficulty of imposing our own terms on the early modern culture we are in the process of exhuming.[26]

There is a risk here, of course, of seeming to deny homosexuality in the past and seeming to erase the traces of a "gay history" that has only recently begun to speak this name.[27] It is true that this study will not "homosexualize" Renaissance collaboration or argue simply that the writers under consideration are "homosexual" in anything like the modern sense of that word, but it will insist upon the crucial (but different) sexual valences of texts written about and between men in this period. While eschewing a historical methodology that finds only versions or expressions of itself in the past,[28] this study nevertheless acknowledges its genesis within the modern discourse of homosexuality, which makes possible (or rather, *necessitates*, in an anti-homoerotic culture) this archaeological endeavor. Like any historical investigation, mine will not cease to be shaped by contemporary interests, and it will necessarily draw upon discourses that have a sexual charge legible to modernity, but, as Halperin has noted, we must "suspend our projects of identification (or disavowal, as the case may be) long enough to devise an interpretation of erotic experiences ... that foregrounds the historical and cultural specificity of those experiences."[29]

Thus, the impossibility of sleeping with the dead. Or, to phrase this more chastely and less figuratively: the impossibility, even as it figures as an intractable curiosity or desire, of searching the annals of the past for erotic subjects motivated by our desires and living our practices, with the cultural and political meanings we associate with these desires and practices. This is perhaps an impossible project even for Cokain – as contemporaneous a historian of a collaborative erotics as he might seem to be – for, as the final chapters of this book will demonstrate, a more modern configuration of sexualities begins to emerge even in the years that separate Cokain's poem from the lives of those he memorializes.

In a way that will be congruent with this book's rethinking of collaboration, authorship, and associated notions of individuality/subjectivity, my discussions of sexuality thus focus not on individuals and their presumed sexual identities, but on the textual representations of sexual acts and systems. This is not an investigation that seeks to answer whether, say, Massinger, Beaumont and Fletcher, Shakespeare, or (more fictively) Palamon and Arcite were "gay." Rather, it examines the relation between what we have tended to view as two distinct discourses: of sexuality and eroticism, and of writing and authorship. This book attempts to reintegrate those discourses by reading together the "rhetorics" of sexuality and the "apparatus" of printed play-texts. Not, I hope, at the expense of what we sometimes call actual, lived experience, but because I take rhetoric and apparatus – no matter how far removed a shared title page may seem to be from a shared bed or grave – to be inseparable from the ways in which that experience may have been structured for those living it.

Moreover, identifying Renaissance figures as gay – "outing" them – seems the mildest of possible claims one might make on the basis of the evidence we will read, because it locates gaiety only in specific individuals, working effectively to quarantine other dramatists and writers of the period from the perceived threat of homosexuality. In a largely heterosexist economy of literary value, Beaumont and Fletcher would become sexual suspects, but Shakespeare, Middleton, Webster, and Ford would seem to profit from their labeling. Instead, by making a *discursive* argument – by emphasizing that these were the *discourses* through which collaboration and authorship were understood – I want to claim a much larger effect for the languages we will encounter within Renaissance English culture. By denaturalizing authorship and common-sense notions of writing, we are beginning to recognize the prevalence of collaboration, as a practice, in the Renaissance theatre; by training ourselves to read the (sexual) discourses that both inscribed and reproduced that practice, we will begin to notice its prevalence elsewhere in the culture: in conduct books, essays, letters, commonplace books, plays (written in collaboration or alone). We might take as a figuration of this disseminative process Fletcher's own wide-ranging textual practice; he wrote alone, with Beaumont, with Shakespeare, with Massinger, with, perhaps, Middleton and others. The point, then, is not to bring the Renaissance out of the closet, but to bring the closet out of the Renaissance – to account for the abiding differences in the ways this period represented sexuality and its connections with modes of textual production.[30]

The book begins by "Seeing double" – by intervening in what has become the normative critical treatment of collaboration and authorship in Renaissance dramatic texts. The chapter urges both that we no longer regard collaboration as an aberrant form of textual production in a period and genre in which it in fact predominated, and that we forego anachronistic attempts to divine the singular author of each scene, phrase, and word. By looking carefully at play-texts as printed artifacts (in particular, early editions of *The Knight of the Burning Pestle*), the chapter introduces a detailed material(ist) approach to collaboration and authorship that relies upon but also revises Foucault's idealized renunciation of the author.

With this retheorization of collaboration, authorship, and textual property as its point of departure, the book proceeds to an analysis of the intersection of sexual and textual discourses in the production and publication of play-texts. Chapter 2, "Between gentlemen," demonstrates the mutual implication of discourses of male friendship, eroticism, and textual collaboration in conduct books (*The English Gentleman*), essays (Bacon's and Montaigne/Florio's "Of Friendship"), and two plays, *The Two Gentlemen of Verona* and *The Two Noble Kinsmen*. Chapter 3, "Representing authority," outlines, in a number of play-texts from the early decades of the seventeenth century, the emergence of presiding authorial figures like Gower in *Pericles* – figures that appear on stage as "authors" of a theatrical event – and traces this emergence in relation to discourses of patriarchal absolutism in the *Workes* of James I and others. These developments are contemporaneous with the increasingly frequent publication of play-texts in impressive folio format, organized around authorial figures; chapter 4, "Reproducing works," begins by analyzing these dramatic collections (particularly the earliest Jonson and Shakespeare folios). The chapter concentrates upon the 1647 Beaumont and Fletcher folio – a book that may, as Aston Cokain later argued, include collaborative work not only by Beaumont and Fletcher, but also by Massinger.[31] Said in its commendatory poems to have been "Got by Two Fathers," the textual offspring of "two Masculines espous'd,"[32] this volume engages both patriarchal–absolutist and homoerotic modes of textual reproduction, and it inscribes the contestation of authorship and collaboration at a decisive moment in English political history.

As these chapters demonstrate in their particular analyses, the concentration on relations between men and the construction of an authorship initially gendered male will include centrally a consideration of the position of women. In fact, an analysis of period attempts to control, appropriate, and/or erase women, as well as their real and imagined resistances, is closely related to the consideration of male textual reproduction. This project thus attempts to avoid reproducing in its own practice the marginalization of women often inscribed and enacted in the material it reads. With few exceptions, the genre at the center of this study *does* exclude writing by women,[33] but these rereadings of collaboration and authorship nevertheless suggest new perspectives on the situation of women attempting to locate themselves in a textual economy normatively transacted between men. Comprehensive answer(s) to this query are beyond the scope of the present project, but from the perspective outlined here the problem confronted by women writers in this period could be articulated as follows: in a discursive world where men often figure texts as compliant women ("New Playes, and Maydenheads, are neare a kin"), how does a woman make the transition from being written to *writing*? Proceeding from chapter 4's analysis of dramatic folios and the contested emergence of patriarchal authorship in the seventeenth century, this book's final chapter considers the publication, in elaborate folios, of Margaret Cavendish's plays in the 1660s, and their positioning (critically unremarked) within/against the folio tradition of Jonson (1616, 1640), Shakespeare (1623, 1632, 1663–64, 1685), and Beaumont and Fletcher (1647, 1679).

"What strange Production is at last displaid," John Berkenhead writes, describing the publication of Beaumont and Fletcher's collaborations,[34] and, in a more critical fashion, this book thus attempts to make strange (or rather, to demonstrate how the texts of this period themselves make strange) our own normative conceptions of textual production and property, and of essential sexuality and modes of eroticism; it calls into question the relation between what to us now appear to be self-evidently distinct categories.[35] If, on the one hand, post-structuralism has argued for the death of the author in theory, this book attempts to demonstrate the implications of the absence of the author (and the presence of more corporate forms of textual production) at a given point in history. If, on the other hand, we are beginning to realize the implications of the nineteenth-century construction of homo- and heterosexualities, this study attempts to sketch some of the possible configurations that preceded those particular discursively constituted options. How will we read, interpret, conceptualize, organize, and edit texts written before the birth of the author in its modern (self-possessed and sexually orientated) incarnation?

For reasons that are related to these questions, much of the material in this book is associated with the figure of Shakespeare, for it is here that there is the most to be realized through revisions of textuality and sexuality in the study of early modern drama. As we will see more particularly in chapter 2's analysis of *The Two Gentlemen of Verona*, there has traditionally been much at stake (critically, canonically, institutionally) in attributing to Shakespeare either homo- or heterosexuality in their modern forms.[36] While not failing to acknowledge the homophobia that has motivated attempts to protect Shakespeare from the stigma of homosexuality, this project attempts to disengage this homo/hetero binarism. In the critical climate that has prevailed for much of this century, the question "Was Shakespeare gay?" has had provocative, evocative power,[37] yet the more useful work (historically, politically) is, as I have already suggested, to demonstrate not that Shakespeare or any of his less canonical contemporaries was definitively "gay" *or* "straight," but that he, like other playwrights in the period, wrote within a paradigm that insistently figured writing as mutual imitation, collaboration, and homoerotic exchange.

Shakespeare, furthermore, is a prime location for a reconsideration of collaboration and the emergence of authorship, for it is in that particular canon that the Author, anachronistically applied, is most powerful and tenacious in the study of Renaissance texts and history. Since the eighteenth century, Shakespeare has been viewed as *the* individual Author and the author of individuality[38] – the very anti-type of collaboration. "His" texts have been read as chronologies of personal/generic development, as material for authorial psychoanalysis, as the organic efflux of the singular mind of genius, as maps of a peculiarly individuated language and imagery. Even the recent influential studies positing revision in certain Shakespearean texts are careful always to situate Shakespeare as the agent of revision, pre-empting the possibilities of diachronic collaboration.[39] The most rigorous new historicist revaluations of Shakespeare – for example, Stephen Greenblatt's analysis of the "collective production of literary pleasure and interest" – have largely adhered to an individuated, non-collaborative Shakespeare.[40] We thus have much to learn from a (re)consideration of collaboration in the texts of the Shakespeare canon.[41] Foucault has argued that "the author is ... the ideological figure by which one marks the manner in which we fear the proliferation of meaning";[42] by demonstrating a thematics of collaboration in some "Shakespearean" texts and by illustrating the emergence of the author as contemporaneous with (not prior to) those texts and their publication, the present study will attempt to detach their significations from the domain of the anachronistic author. To do so, of course, is to argue implicitly the inappropriateness of an authorially based canon in this period.[43] My examination of texts associated with this most canonical of authors thus results not from a desire to maintain the privilege and privileging of Shakespeare in literary studies, but rather from a sense that it is over his dead authorial body/corpus that we have the most to learn by reconceptualizing both collaboration and sexuality.[44] This book does not attempt, then, to provide a comprehensive reading of all Renaissance instances of dramatic collaboration, or of authorship, or of sexuality. Rather, it seeks to intervene in conventional critical practice by analyzing certain significant discursive sites.

Finally, a few words (but by no means the last) about the particularity of those sites – about texts and citations. One of the corollary arguments of this book is that we cannot separate our understanding of period notions of textual production and property from the documents and particular languages in which those texts first circulated; the idea of authorship – the necessity of knowing "who is speaking," as I will suggest in the first chapter – is in part produced by the textual configurations that supply that information. For this reason, I attempt throughout this project to read texts not as they have been edited and author-ized for modern consumption, but in their sixteenth- and seventeenth-century incarnations. Throughout, I retain early modern spelling, both as a reminder of historical otherness – these texts were produced in a culture that lacked (without knowing it) our insistence on consistency, uniformity, and prescriptive grammar – and because, as I hope to demonstrate in the course of my argument, the routine standardizations of modern editing are often at odds with a historicist critical practice. (To the extent possible, I have also retained the original emphases in the texts I cite.[45] In printed book titles, early modern capitalization has been followed where possible in the notes and bibliography, though not in the text proper; original typefaces in citations of titles, authors, and publishers have not been replicated.) To attach a name to a book that did not bear one, to modernize, standardize, repunctuate, and emend in our own image the texts of another period, to elide or rewrite, often silently, the apparatus in which a text originally circulated – all of these acts relinquish and/or ignore important evidence of the culture we read.

Reading that culture, as I have been reminded at almost every stage of researching, writing, and citing this book, is often at odds with many of the fundamental structures of literary research. *The Short Title Catalogue*, the reference tool with which all work on Renaissance printed texts must begin, for example, arranges its entries by author (or postulated author).[46] *The Library of Congress Subject Headings*, an index that controls the configuration of card- and computer-catalogs in libraries throughout the U.S., lists "collaboration" as a subject only under the larger rubric of "authorship." The list of author-based research systems in the humanities, of course, also includes the citation procedures prescribed by the Modern Language Association and the *Chicago Manual of Style*. Since I draw upon a number of collaborative and/or anonymous texts, and since I insist on the fact that authorial attribution is itself a historically contingent development, "it was once in my thoughts," as Beaumont and Fletcher's publisher Humphrey Moseley might say, to print a conventional bibliography for this book, arranging it by author, and simply noting the difficulty and irony of such an arrangement. This procedure would, among other deformations, necessitate the usual approach to collaborative texts, placing texts produced by Beaumont and Fletcher among the B's (with Beaumont's, but away from Fletcher's, other texts). But since never parted while they lived, I conceived it not equitable to separate their ashes. The bibliography is a compromise, arranging early modern texts by year (and within years, by early modern authorial attribution, if any); the historical movement from undifferentiated collaboration to the imperative of the author-centered bibliography forms the structure of this book.

1   Seeing double: collaboration and the interpretation of Renaissance drama

> It were ... wisdome it selfe, to read all Authors, as *Anonymo's*, looking on the Sence, not *Names* of Books ...[1]

" ' "What does it matter who is speaking," someone said, "what does it matter who is speaking." ' "[2] It is perhaps writing against the grain of the chapter that will follow to begin by quoting Foucault's quotation of Beckett in his essay "What Is an Author?," elaborately framed by the technologies keeping in place the Author whom Foucault critiques – the quotation marks, the citation. To follow this genealogy of quotation back further is to reach Beckett's ambivalent "someone," though even here I would want to note the attribution of these words to an authorial presence. *Someone*, like *anonymous*, denotes the insistence of the author-ship question; though it does not identify, it marks a space for identity, a need to know "who is speaking."

The historicity of that need is registered in the word *anonymous*, which supports Foucault's contention that the author has a particular point of emergence as a cultural fiction. *Anonymous* does not take on its recogniz-ably modern sense in English ("bearing no author's name; of unknown or unavowed authorship") until the late seventeenth century; earlier, around 1600, the word signifies "a person whose name is not given, or is unknown," but does not connect persons with texts (*OED*).[3] Beginning around 1676, however, *anonymous* begins to signal the author-ization of a text, the importance of someone, anyone, speaking.[4] The author's emergence is marked by the notice of its absence.

My *its* here remarks on the author's singularity, for as modern usage makes clear, *anonymous* emerges with the author as a singular entity; *anonymity*, the *OED* notes, is a property of "*an* author or *his* writings" (my emphasis). There is a moment in history, in other words, when it becomes important to know not only that someone is speaking, but also that some *one* is speaking. In contrast to the *OED*, my use of *its* also avoids (for the moment) the normative seventeenth-century gendering of authorship; subsequent chapters of this book will demonstrate the

12

inextricability of the question of authorship from patriarchy's interest in the identity of the father.[5]

The singular author and its twin, anonymous, are in a sense my subject, but I am most interested in what preceded and accompanied that double "birth." There was, as the epigraph from 1654 suggests, a period of transition in early modern English culture – a time when both reading "Names" and reading "Sence" existed as interpretive methodologies – preceded by a time when interpretation often proceeded without an author. My project here is thus the genealogist's: to trace back beyond the impasse of Beckett's pronoun the seemingly natural connection between the author and the text – the some/one and the speaking – in order to demonstrate that interpretation has not always proceeded on the basis of that relation (and thus need not always do so). Barthes famously noted the author's "death,"[6] and what I hope to elaborate here is the author's "birth." I hesitate over these metaphors deliberately, for (as I think Barthes would appreciate and as I hope to demonstrate in the work that follows) "birth" naturalizes and makes inevitable an event – or rather, a complicated *set* of events – that were contingent and by no means biological, transcultural, or even uniformly distributed across discourses and genres within a given culture.

The site of this analysis is a set of texts that consistently defy our modern sense of both authorship and anonymity, play-texts generated in the predominantly collaborative dramatic practice of early modern England. Most of these texts began as productions in the theatre, where their writers were not known, and many of them first appeared in print without ascription of authorship (or anonymity); they are thus "pre-anonymous" – that is, "anonymous" only in a sense that existed before the word itself emerged with the author to describe their condition. *Anonymous*, in other words, only assumes its textual associations as a marking of difference from a new concept of authorship. These texts also defy modern anonymity in another crucial way, for their authorlessness is often plural and collaborative.[7]

Collaborative dramatic texts from this period thus strikingly denaturalize the author–text–reader continuum assumed in later methodologies of interpretation. Located both at a historical moment prior to the emergence of the author in its modern form and as a mode of textual production that distances the writer(s) from the interpreting audience, collaborative play-texts disperse the authorial voice (or rather, our historically subsequent notion of the authorial voice). Read in the forms in which they initially circulated, these texts instead exhibit the different configurations of authorities constructing, re-forming, and controlling texts and (as we shall see) constraining their interpretation. In such a

context, interpretation – and here I mean both our methods for interpreting a play-text and our sense of what an interpretation is – can be
radically different.

Refiguring collaboration

In a scholarly field dominated by the singular figure of Shakespeare, it is
easily forgotten that collaboration was the Renaissance English theatre's
dominant mode of textual production. In his ground-breaking study of
the profession of dramatist from 1590 to 1642, Gerald Eades Bentley
notes that nearly two-thirds of the plays mentioned in Henslowe's papers
reflect the participation of more than one writer. Furthermore, of all the
plays written by professional dramatists in the period, "as many as half
... incorporated the writing of more than one man." Printed title-page
statements of singular authorship "tended ... to simplify the actual
circumstances of composition" when compared with other records.[8]
There is also ample evidence of the frequent revision of play-texts, itself a
diachronic form of collaboration. It was common practice for the
professional writers attached to a given theatrical company to compose
new prologues, epilogues, songs, characters, and scenes for revivals of
plays in which they did not originally have a hand – *Doctor Faustus* and
Sir Thomas More are famous examples. Thus "almost any play first
printed more than ten years after composition and ... kept in active
repertory by the company that owned it is most likely to contain later
revisions by the author or, in many cases, by another playwright."[9]

In a broader sense, theatrical production was itself a sustained
collaboration, "the joint accomplishment of dramatists, actors, musi-
cians, costumers, prompters (who made alterations in the original manuscript) and ... managers."[10] That is, the construction of meaning by a
theatrical company was polyvocal – often beginning with a collaborative
manuscript, which was then revised, cut, rearranged, and augmented by
book-holders, copyists, and other writers, elaborated and improvised by
actors in performance, accompanied by music and songs that may or
may not have originated in a completely different context.[11]

Furthermore, the larger theatrical enterprise, situated in the marketplace, was the highly lucrative, capitalist collaboration of a "company"
of "sharers," in commerce with themselves (as their terminology suggests) and with their audience – in Jean-Christophe Agnew's useful
phrase, "a joint venture of limited liability."[12] Plays' prologues and
epilogues, the liminal speeches situated between the play and the play-
house, often stage the intersections of acting company and audience in
the language of a collaborative commerce; the prologue to *Romeo and*

Iuliet (1597) emphasizes this trans/action when it speaks of "the two howres traffique of our Stage."[13] Human hands – hands that applaud, but also the hands that pay to see the play, the hand-shaking that seals the bargain, the collaborating hands of exchange and commerce – make repeated appearance in this framing material: "Do but you hold out / Your helping hands," the prologue to *The Two Noble Kinsmen* asks, "and we shall ... something do to save us."[14]

Including theatrical production in a discussion of "collaboration" may risk an excessive broadening of the term, but it is important to suggest (as I think the play-texts themselves do) the inseparability of the textual and theatrical production of meaning in a context that did not carefully insulate the writing of scripts from the acting of plays. (Actors William Shakespeare and William Rowley can serve as figures for this convergence.) The commonplace editorial concern over a play's "date of composition," which assumes a relatively limited amount of time during which a text was fully composed and after which it was merely transmitted and corrupted, is obviously problematic in this broader understanding of collaboration. What does "composition" include in such a context? (Re)writing? Copying? Staging? The addition of actors' gestures on stage? Typesetting (which, after all, is called "composing")? When is (the writing, staging, printing of) a text complete?

Censorship – in Annabel Patterson's extended sense, an activity that both silences discourses and generates others[15] – is a further participant in the production of theatrical meaning in this period. To choose two familiar examples: in *Sir Thomas More*, the censor writes in the manuscript along with the collaborating writers, making changes and demanding others. The suppression of *A Game at Chesse* from the public stage occasioned the proliferation of widely variant printed and manuscript versions of the play.[16]

Despite this broad range of figures and forces collaborating in play-texts, later considerations of Renaissance drama have nevertheless worked to construct an authorial univocality. Viewing these texts as literature in the library rather than as working documents in the playhouse, criticism has read them primarily as written communications between writers and readers.[17] Such an approach privileges "writer" and "reader" according to their value in modern literate, literary culture and elides both the prior textual exchange(s) among writers and actors *and* the oral/aural transaction between actors and audience, the more prominent participants in the initial and most prolific form of these texts' public/ation. Theatrical practice reserved no place for the writer in performance except as an actor in the company, and these texts were generally made accessible to readers only as an afterthought capitalizing on their theatrical popularity. It is crucial, in other words, to consider the social production of different genres and the ways in which they reach print. *The Faerie Queene* and, say, *Romeo and Iuliet* may both appear to be texts designed for reading (especially as edited and formatted for modern consumption); however, the former exhibits the apparatus of both the book and the author, while the latter (in quarto form) presents itself not as a communication between writer and reader (or even as a book, in the modern sense), but rather as a representation/recapitulation of a theatrical experience, a communication between actors and audience – the text "*As* it hath been often (with great applause) plaid publiquely."[18] Only by eliding or ignoring the theatrical as a mode of (re)production can these texts can be read from the post-Enlightenment perspective of individual authorship, the now-hegemonic mode of textual production and the site of Foucault's critique.[19]

Traditionally, criticism has viewed collaboration as a mere subset or aberrant kind of individual authorship, the collusion of two unique authors whom subsequent readers could discern and separate out by examining the traces of individuality and personality (including handwriting, spelling, word-choice, imagery, and syntactic formations) left in the collaborative text. The work of Cyrus Hoy, to choose the most prominent and influential example of such studies, attempts to separate out the collaborators in "the Beaumont and Fletcher canon" on the grounds of "linguistic criteria"; however, there is a recurrent conflict in Hoy's project between his post-Enlightenment assumptions about authorship, textual property, and individuality of style, and the evidence of the early modern texts he analyzes. Hoy wishes "to distinguish any given dramatist's share in a play of dual or doubtful authorship" by applying a "body of criteria that, derived from the unaided plays of the dramatist in question, will serve to identify his work in whatever context it may appear."[20] His studies thus begin with the presumption of singular authorship ("unaided plays") and proceed to collaboration (tellingly glossed as "dual or doubtful"). Furthermore, his results assume that a writer's use of *ye* for *you* and of contractions like *'em* for *them* is both individually distinct and remarkably constant "in whatever context."

These assumptions are challenged by evidence Hoy himself adduces. Problematically, as Hoy realizes, "there is no play that can with any certainty be regarded as the unaided work of Beaumont,"[21] and he admits that "Beaumont's linguistic practices are themselves so widely divergent as to make it all but impossible to predict what they will be from one play to another."[22] Beaumont's presence will thus be ascertained as that which remains after Fletcher, Massinger, et al. have been subtracted. Further, because he finds *The Faithful Shepherdess*, though "undoubtedly Fletcher's own," linguistically at odds with his other unaided works, Hoy omits it from his tabulation of evidence establishing Fletcher's "own" distinctive style.[23] Whatever the other problems of method and evidence, this astonishing moment of deliberate omission seriously undermines Hoy's project, and may alert us to the theoretical issues inherent in using evidence of "linguistic preferences" and "language practices" in the pursuit of essential and stable identities. These terms, indeed, may expose a problem now more fully legible through the lens of sexuality-theory: is Fletcher's style chosen or innate? An act or an essence? Are his characteristic practices preferred or performative?[24]

Hoy's results are, furthermore, rendered problematic by the frequency of revision in these texts and the mediation of copyists, actors, compositors, and their "linguistic preferences" between Hoy's hypothetical writers' copy and the printed text he actually analyzes.[25] Additional questions arise when we consider the complexities at the outset of collaborative writing, which may have included, in the words of Sheldon P. Zitner, "prior agreement on outline, vetting of successive drafts by a partner, composition in concert, brief and possibly infrequent intervention, and even a mutual contagion of style as a result of close association."[26]

The last item in Zitner's series highlights the extent to which he remains in Hoy's paradigm, in which one writer's healthy individual style must be protected from infection by another's. Zitner thus exhibits Hoy's problem at a more theoretical level. We might note that the presumed universality of individuated style depends on a network of legal and social technologies specific to a post-Renaissance capitalist culture (e.g. intellectual property, copyright, individuated handwriting).[27] Furthermore, the collaborative project in the theatre was predicated on *erasing* the perception of any differences that might have existed, for whatever reason,[28] between collaborated parts. Moreover, writing in this theatrical context implicitly resists the notion of monolithic personal style Hoy presumes: a playwright im/personates another (many others) in the process of writing a play-text and thus refracts the supposed singularity of the individual in language. At the same time, he often stages in language the *sense* of distinctive personae, putting "characteristic" words in another's mouth. What Hoy says of Beaumont –

His linguistic "preferences" – if they can be termed such – are, in a word, nothing if not eclectic ... it is this very protean character which makes it, in the end, quite impossible to establish for Beaumont a neat pattern of linguistic preferences that will serve as a guide to identifying his work wherever it might appear

– might well apply to all playwrights in this period.[29] Indeed, the playwright of this era often thought to be most individuated – Shakespeare – has likewise been characterized by the diversity, protean quality, and expansiveness of "his" language.[30]

A more detailed critique of Hoy's attributions is required and might investigate the extent to which his specific linguistic criteria (the pronominal forms *ye/you*, for example) are, as the *OED* suggests, actually class-related differences – that is, the extent to which they reflect not an individual's linguistic preference or habit, but rather a subject inscribed in and constituted by specific linguistic practices. (This is an issue of some complexity, for *ye* rather than *you* may announce the writer's own inscription in class-coded language, and/or may be the writer's ascription of that language to characters within the text.) Or a further critique might consider in detail the methods and evidence Hoy uses to produce a layered composition (Beaumont revising or revised by Fletcher, Massinger revising Beaumont and/or Fletcher) out of a two-dimensional printed document. I cite here some of the more general difficulties of Hoy's work because he is considered both an exemplary pioneer of, and a reliable model for, twentieth-century considerations of collaboration.[31] He illustrates both the distinctly modern notions of individuality and authorial property underlying such considerations, as well as the corresponding sites for a post-structurally informed historicist critique. Above all, we can see in Hoy's work the insistence with which modern scholarship has asked the author question; the ultimate object of this quest is to know "who is speaking" each and every word of the canon.

That a historically inappropriate idea of the author here effectively constrains interpretation is best illustrated by the modern bibliographical fact that Hoy's authorial attributions in the Beaumont and Fletcher canon, a series of seven articles published in *Studies in Bibliography* from 1956 to 1962, prepared the way for, and are the basis of, the "standard" edition of those texts, *The Dramatic Works in the Beaumont and Fletcher Canon*, which began to appear in 1966 under the general-editorship of Hoy's adviser Fredson Bowers (who also edited *Studies*).[32] The collaborative plays in this influential edition, Bowers remarks, "have been grouped chiefly by authors," and Hoy himself argues elsewhere that "[s]cholarly investigation of the authorial problems posed by collaborative drama is ... a *necessary precondition* to critical and aesthetic considerations of such drama."[33] Collaborative texts must submit to an editorial apparatus founded on singular authorship, their "authorial problems" solved, before interpretation is permitted to proceed.[34]

What I seek to demonstrate here is that Hoy's mode of reading collaboration in early modern English drama merely as a more *multiple* version of authorship – a mode reproduced in editions and criticism of plays not only in the Beaumont and Fletcher canon, but also in the intersecting canons of Shakespeare, Massinger, Middleton, et al. – does not account for the historical and theoretical challenges collaboration poses to the ideology of the Author. Collaboration is, as we shall see, a dispersal of author/ity, rather than a simple doubling of it; to revise the aphorism, two heads are different than one.[35]

Such a reconceptualization of Renaissance dramatic collaboration has profound implications for the way we interpret these plays. As we have seen, bibliographical attention to a text is often considered to be necessarily prior to interpretation – establishing a definitive, authoritative set of words for subsequent explication – but shifting the focus from authorship to collaboration demonstrates the extent to which twentieth-century textual criticism has itself been an elaborate interpretive act framing all its efforts with Foucault's constraining author.[36] Bowers's prefatory words describing his general editorship of *The Dramatic Works in the Beaumont and Fletcher Canon* suggest, furthermore, that modern textual criticism reproduces in its own practice the privileging of author-based interpretation over collaboration:

The texts ... have been edited by a group of scholars according to editorial procedures set by the general editor and under his close supervision ... We hope that the intimate connexion of one individual, in this manner, with all the different editorial processes will lend to the results some uniformity not ordinarily found when diverse editors approach texts of such complexity. At the same time, the peculiar abilities of the several editors have had sufficient free play to ensure individuality of point of view its proper role; and thus, we hope, *the deadness of compromise that may fasten on collaborative effort* has been avoided.[37]

As in Zitner's rhetoric of collaborative "contagion," Bowers in this remarkable statement seeks to protect from the deadly grasp of collaboration the "peculiar abilities" of the individual working in its "proper role." The danger collaboration poses to this editorial paradigm is likewise figured in the notion of "corruption" so important to twentieth-century editing of Renaissance texts, for "corruption" – the introduction of non-authorial material into a text during the process of "transmission" – is "collaboration" given a negative connotation. If the making of play-texts and theatrical productions was a collaborative enterprise, how can we edit out of the 1623 folio version of *Hamlet*, for example, the "corruption" of actors' "interpolations"?[38] To do so is to deploy authorship as a constraint on interpretation in a way the text itself warns against:

> *Ham.* And could'st not thou for a neede study me
> Some dozen or sixteene lines,
> Which I would set downe and insert?
> *players* Yes very easily my good Lord.[39]

This exchange, which I quote from the first quarto, is itself "set downe" and "inserted" differently in the folio and second quarto versions of the play – the latter described on its title page as "enlarged to almost as much againe as it was," without ascription of the augmenting agent.[40]

Though more self-consciously interpretive than bibliography, critical readings of these plays continue to rely implicitly on the assumption that texts are the products of a singular and sovereign authorial consciousness, and a reconception of collaboration thus has manifold implications here. Dwelling on collaboration in this period demonstrates at the level of material practice the claims of much recent critical theory; the production of texts is a social process. Within Hoy's paradigm of collaboration, language is fundamentally transparent of, because it is produced by, the individual author; the language one uses is (and identifies one as) one's own. But if we accept that language is a socially produced (and producing) system, then collaboration is more the condition of discourse than its exception.[41] Interpreting from a collaborative perspective acknowledges language as a process of exchange; rather than policing discourse off into agents, origins, and intentions, a collaborative focus elaborates the social mechanism of language, discourse as intercourse.[42] "If literature were as original, as creative, as individual, as unique as literary humanists are constantly saying it is," Morse Peckham has noted, "we would not be able to understand a word of it, let alone make emendations."[43] A collaborative perspective also forces a re-evaluation of (and/or complicates) a repertoire of familiar interpretive methodologies – most prominently, biographical and psychoanalytic approaches – based on the notion of the singular author. Other traditional critical categories policing the circulation of language become problematic as well – for example, "plagiarism," "borrowing," "influence" (and its "anxieties"), "source," "originality," "imagination," "genius," and "complete works."

Double vision

The collaborative production of play-texts, as I have begun to suggest, was manifold, and it is important to note that collaborations between (or among) writers had differing valences. Further investigation might detail both the differences and the similarities of collaborations (between Beaumont and Fletcher, and, say, Middleton and Rowley, or Chapman,

Jonson, and Marston) that resulted from different positionings within the institutions of the theatre and outside it; crucial to such an analysis are Bentley's distinctions between "regular attached professional" playwrights and those like Jonson situated between the theatre and a patronage network with significantly different socio-economic inflections.[44] My point here, however, is to call for a revision in the way we have read Renaissance dramatic collaboration *generally*, and the ways we have deployed it in our readings of Renaissance dramatic texts. That is, I am contending that collaborative texts produced before the emergence of authorship are of a kind different (informed by differing mechanisms of textual property and control, different conceptions of imitation, originality, and the "individual") from collaborations produced within the regime of the author. I want to show more fully the implications of a collaboratively attuned (rather than authorially based) interpretation by examining a particular text in the Beaumont and Fletcher canon, a text of which the author-question has been often asked and (ostensibly) answered definitively: *The Knight of the Burning Pestle*.

We can take as a guide to a collaborative reading the sustained ambivalence the early printed texts of *The Knight of the Burning Pestle* demonstrate toward authorship. *The Knight*, probably initially performed between 1607 and 1610, was first printed in a 1613 quarto, the title page of which mentions no writer(s). The dedicatory epistle, however, notes:

This vnfortunate child, who in eight daies ... was begot and borne, soone after, was by his parents ... exposed to the wide world, who for want of iudgement, or not vnderstanding the priuy marke of *Ironie* about it (which shewed it was no offspring of any vulgar braine) vtterly reiected it ...[45]

The play, apparently unparented on its title page, is here the offspring of both a singular "braine" and plural "parents." (Further, it bears publicly a "priuy" birth-"marke" of this ambiguous lineage.) This situation is only complicated by the second and third quartos of the play (both dated 1635); these title pages announce that *The Knight* was "Written by Francis Beaumont and Iohn Fletcher. Gent.," but they include a different prefatory letter, "To the Readers of this Comedy," which cites a singular "Author [who] had no intent to wrong any one in this *Comedy* ... which hee hopes will please all."[46] Finally, in these subsequent quartos there also appears "The Prologue," a speech transferred into this text from an earlier play, which explains, in the only sentence it alters from its 1584 pre-text, that "the Authors intention" was not to satirize any particular subject.[47] Most modern editors emend "the Authors intention" to "the author's intention," but we would want to note in this context the fertile ambiguity (or oblivion) of early modern orthographic practice, which does not distinguish genitive singular from plural or genitive plural – that is, it does not use another of authorship's more recent technologies, the apostrophe, to separate the writer's/writers' propriety from his/their plurality.

A look at the preliminary material of these quartos thus demonstrates that, though authorship is intermittently present, it does not appear in anything approaching a definitive or monolithically singular form; all three quartos, like many others of this period, instead foreground in their apparatus a different network of textual ownership and production. Unlike the writer(s), the publisher Walter Burre does appear on the Q1 title-page, and he also signs the dedicatory epistle (quoted above) to Robert Keysar, the manager of the Blackfriars theatre where the play was first performed and the previous owner of the text. The epistle establishes an extended filiation for this child/text, arguing that, despite "his" failure in the theatre, he is "desirous to try his fortune in the world, where if yet it be welcome, father, foster-father, nurse and child, all haue their desired end."[48] If the "father" here is the play's writer (with Keysar as foster-father and Burre as nurse), his singularity jars with the "parents" noted above – although the parents who first "exposed" the text might also be read as the (boy) players. In sum, though no author (certainly no *single* author) emerges from these initial references to the play's origins, the quartos' preliminary materials do display a complex and shifting network of other authorities: the publisher Burre, the printer N.O., the acting-company manager Keysar, the inhospitable theatre audience, the players and their royal patron (Q3 advertises the text "as it is now acted by her Majesties Servants at the Privatehouse in *Drury lane*"), the writers Beaumont and Fletcher (eventually, after both are dead), the "gentlemen" readers, and the unnamed writer of another play whose "intentions" are transferred over and now said to apply to the "Authors" or "author" of this play.

Later in the century (concurrent with the shift I earlier located in *anonymous*) the play's authorial lineage seemingly becomes more important, but it is by no means more fully stabilized. A speech that probably served as a prologue to a revival between 1665 and 1667, for example, assumes that the play is solely Fletcher's;[49] published in 1672, this prologue precedes by only seven years the ascription of the play as collaborative in *Fifty Comedies and Tragedies Written by Francis Beaumont And John Fletcher, Gentlemen* (the second folio).

I am obscuring from this textual history the fact that virtually all the recent editions of *The Knight* now place Francis Beaumont, alone, on their title pages.[50] Though the quartos situate the initially unauthored, eventually collaborated play within a collaborative network, these editions deploy an army of editorial glosses to contain the subversive ambiguities cited above, proceed to interpret the play via its relationship to Beaumont's other plays (no easy task, given the paucity of this canon) or to his class-position and family history, and separate it off from (to name some other possible contexts) other plays performed by the Children of Blackfriars, or other plays associated with the name "Beaumont and Fletcher."[51] The irony of reducing *The Knight of the Burning Pestle* to a single author is that it is perhaps the most wildly collaborative play of this period. By this point, it should be clear that I do not here mean "collaborative" merely in the usual, restricted sense of two or more writers writing together; this play exposes – in a way that we lose when we read it as the creation of particular individuals acting (as Bowers might say) in their "proper role" – the more broadly collaborative enterprise of the early modern English theatre.

From the moment the Citizen interrupts the actor speaking the prologue in his fourth line and climbs onto the stage, *The Knight of the Burning Pestle* stages the somewhat contentious collaboration of an acting company and its audience. The audience becomes, literally, a part of the play, as the boy actors reluctantly agree to improvise, at the request of the Citizen and Wife, a play called *The Knight of the Burning Pestle* – starring the Wife's serving-boy Rafe – along with their rehearsed production of *The London Merchant*. This odd juxtaposition of genres – romance-quest and city-comedy – becomes increasingly complex, as the players attempt to accommodate and fuse the divergent plots. Like the framing prologues and epilogues of other plays, *The Knight's* opening lines (as well as its sustained amalgamation of plots) suggest the general situation of acting companies attempting to sell their representations within the proto-capitalist marketplace of early modern London: they are (in a sense that is constantly being renegotiated) bound by the desires of their audience, at the same time that they participate in the construction of those desires. The economic valence of this transaction is registered at several points in the play, as in the episode where the Citizen gives money to the actor playing the innkeeper for accommodating Rafe and thus for accommodating (literally and figuratively) the audience and its desire to see a knight-errant.

The boy who speaks for the players and negotiates with the citizens, like most prologue-emissaries between acting company and audience, invariably uses the plural and collaborative "we" to represent the company (B1) and establishes joint ownership in "the plot of our Plaie" (D4^v).[52] A more comprehensive view, however, would see the entirety of the play's production (that is, the intersections of the "actors'" *The*

London Merchant and "citizens'" *The Knight of the Burning Pestle*) as the corporate effort of the players – the collaboration of actors-acting-as-actors and actors-acting-as-citizens. This negotiation in turn brings into view another, silent collaborator in the larger production, the gentlemanly audience of the private theatre where the play is presented. No representative of this audience speaks, but the Boy, and occasionally the citizens, gesture toward its ostensibly more refined tastes:

Cit. Boy, come hither, send away *Raph* and this whoresonne Giant quickely.
Boy. In good faith sir we cannot, you'le vtterly spoile our Play, and make it to be hist, and it cost money, you will not suffer vs to go on with our plot, *I pray Gentlemen rule him.* (F4ᵛ, final emphasis added)

The play here suggests the more complex task of accommodation facing the players: negotiating between the desires of the private theatre's gentlemen-patrons and the citizens eager for "something notably in honour of the Commons of the Citty" (B1ᵛ), a process with economic ramifications, as these lines make clear.

These negotiations draw into play a number of divergent discourses, as I have already noted in passing; *The Knight of the Burning Pestle* is quite literally, in Barthes' famous phrase, "a tissue of quotations drawn from the innumerable centres of culture."[53] The range of the play's "quotation," its discursive diversity, is immense in a way that I can only suggestively summarize; this is nevertheless another important way in which the play figures the collaborative enterprise of theatrical writing in this period.[54] Rafe's improvised adventures in *The Knight of the Burning Pestle* appropriate and play with the discourse of romance-epic: he reads aloud an extended passage from *Palmerin de Oliva*, a romance translated into English in 1581; his subsequent adventures gesture toward episodes of *Don Quixote*, *Arcadia*, and *The Faerie Queene*; and he trains his "squire" and "dwarf" (two serving-boys) to speak in the antique chivalric discourse of those familiar texts.[55] Rafe's adventures also draw on a genre of plays about "prentice worthies."[56] The "actors'" *The London Merchant* is a similar pastiche of genres ("prodigal" plays, romantic-comedies, city-comedies), and Jasper's appearance as the ghost of himself deploys a revenge-tragedy convention in the service of a marriage-plot. Furthermore, the play's collation of romantic comedy eventuating in marriage with Rafe's romance-quest ending in his own death may figure the emergent genre which the team of playwrights subsequently attached to this play were to make famous: tragicomedy.[57]

At a more local level, the play continually exhibits its allusive permeability. Figuring the larger theatrical practice of importing music "originating" elsewhere to fit the current production, Master Merrythought's lines are virtually all quotation/revisions of contemporary ballads and madrigals that circulated orally and/or in print. Modern editions attempt to separate these texts out of the texture of the play by italicizing them, labeling them "song," and devoting appendices to their special status as music. As Zitner, with evident frustration, notes in his appendix "The songs": "There are perhaps forty-one passages to be sung in *The Knight*. One says 'perhaps' since it is sometimes difficult to distinguish what is to be sung from what is to be spoken."[58] (A variation on the theme with which we began: what does it matter whom one is singing?)

A similar difficulty of distinguishing parts within the collaborated texture character-izes the serving-boy/hero Rafe. As already noted, he speaks in chivalric discourse as "the Knight of the Burning Pestle," and his first sustained utterance in the play is a recitation from *1 Henry IV*. Likewise, his speech at the end of Act IV parodies both the septenary meter of Elizabethan verse-narratives and May Lords' May-Day speeches. The generic attentiveness of Rafe's "tragic" death speech – about which the boy-actor complains, "'Twill be very vnfit he should die sir, vpon no occasion, and in a Comedy too" (K2ᵛ–K3) – signals Rafe's own construction out of allusion: the long narrative rewrites passages from *The Spanish Tragedy*, *Richard III*, and *Eastward Ho!* Furthermore (and potentially more subversive to an author-based notion of this text), Rafe's last words, "oh, oh, oh, &c." (K3ᵛ), are the same as Hamlet's in the Folio version of that play, where they are often presumed by modern editors to be excisable from the "author's" text as "actor's interpolations."[59] Rafe's final "&c." succinctly marks his last moments as the actor's improvisatory collaboration with, and beyond, the script.

Lee Bliss has argued that "Rafe becomes of necessity [*The Knight*'s] self-appointed dramatist: he must create dialogue and motivation that will give life and shape to ... rather skimpy situational clues" and "labors manfully to impose narrative coherence." This is, she argues, "the young playwright's own situation."[60] While we might agree that Rafe is the central improvisatory, creative figure of *The Knight of the Burning Pestle*, to construct him as a type of the "presiding dramatist" (in Bliss's view, the young Beaumont) is to impose a constraining coherence on interpretation that the text militates against. For if Rafe *is* the author, he is the author as collaborator, improviser, collator of allusion – the locus of the intersection of discourses, but not their originator. More importantly, like the musical Merrythought, he does not exist outside, or independent of, the text; he is himself a construction of those discourses, the author as staged persona, "a tissue of quotations." Furthermore, like the "text" Barthes theorizes, a "multi-dimensional space in which a variety of writings, none of them original, blend and clash" (p. 146), Rafe is without origin – as the Wife puts it in her epilogue, "a poore fatherlesse child" (K4). And to this extent he reproduces the troubled patrilineage of the text that begets him.

Reconfigurations

According to Foucault, "the author is the principle of thrift in the proliferation of meaning ... a certain functional principle by which, in our culture ... one impedes the free circulation, the free manipulation, the free composition, decomposition, and recomposition of fiction" (pp. 118–19). And though, as we have seen, a dispersal of the author in *The Knight of the Burning Pestle* may allow fiction to circulate more freely, we would be mistaken to think that the fatherless status of both the Knight (Rafe) and *The Knight* figures the freeing of fictions. "What Is an Author?" proceeds to such a visionary close, evoking a future in which fiction seems to circulate unlimited by authorial or other constraints, but Foucault himself acknowledges earlier in the essay that a culture devoid of all such mechanisms is "pure romanticism" (p. 119).[61]

This is a romanticism I do not want to reproduce in speaking of the early modern period. *The Knight of the Burning Pestle*, we remember, has an extended filiation, which includes a "foster-father" and "nurse," and the quarto preliminaries exhibit a network of constraining figures, including the previous owner of the text, the publisher, the actors, the theatre audience, and the readers of the printed texts – as well as the "author(s)," whose status is by no means fixed. Rafe may be "a poore fatherlesse child," but he is also a servant/apprentice shown quite clearly to be constrained by a particular class-position and, in his adventures (however freely they may seem to proliferate), by the desires of his master and mistress.[62] Fiction in this play is also all too obviously limited by the discourses available to the Citizen and Wife, the generic repertoire of the actors, and their location within the competitive theatrical market.

As I've argued implicitly in the interpretation outlined above, all of these constraints are more relevant to an interpretation of this text than the author(s). Even such rigorous theorizations of the author as Wayne Booth's "implied author" and Alexander Nehamas's "postulated author" are problematic when applied to the interpretation of collaborative dramatic texts from this period. Nehamas, for example, writes that "in interpreting a text ... we want to know what *any* individual who can be its subject must be like. We want to know, that is, what sort of person, what character, is manifested in it." The need to postulate such an author – even (only) as "a hypothesis ... accepted provisionally [that] guides interpretation"[63] – is specific to certain historical moments and genres. Chapters 4 and 5, focused on folio volumes organized around authorial figures, will demonstrate the extent to which this need is only beginning to become relevant to drama in the seventeenth century.

While these observations are obviously indebted to Foucault's conceptual shift, I would at the same time want to interrogate his imagination of a post-authorial "constraining figure," for it seems to register both a residue of intention left by the deceased author and a singularity that the above discussion seeks to complicate. We might speak instead of "constraining contexts" for *The Knight* and other plays of the period; as I have argued, a more appropriate interpretation is one guided and constrained by what we know about the discourses, figures, locations, and cultural practices participating in its emergence. The ambivalence of this text and this culture toward the author is itself one of those contexts.

My terms here are plural, for, as we have seen, this text defies even the ideally liberal constraint Foucault imagines, "fiction passing through something like *a* necessary or constraining *figure*" (p. 119, my emphasis).[64] It may be that we will not be able to emerge from the Enlightenment legacy of that necessary individual. However, our attempts to do so in our investigations of the past – to see figures (plural) rather than the singular reflections of our authorial selves, to note for example that my writing and citing in the present context collaborate with, among other things, a Chicago manual and a university press that prescribe "my" "style" – can be instrumental in that emergence. To revise the position from which we began, and to ask the question with which the remainder of this book will be occupied: What, or rather *how*, does it matter who are speaking?

2 Between gentlemen: homoeroticism, collaboration, and the discourse of friendship

Making acquaintance

ACQVAINTANCE is in two bodies individually incorporated, and no lesse selfely than sociably united: two Twins cannot be more naturally neere, than these be affectionately deare; which they expresse in hugging one another, and shewing the consenting Consort of their minde, by the mutuall interchoice of their Motto; *Certus amor morum est.*
"A Draught of the *Frontispice,*" *The English Gentleman* (1630).[1]

Thus Richard Brathwait glosses the figure of "Acquaintance," one of eight virtues first visualized in the frontispiece of his *The English Gentleman*, which, as it amply unfolds itself in subtitle, is a volume *"Containing* Sundry excellent *Rules* or exquisite *Observations*, tending to Direction of every *Gentleman*, of selecter ranke and *qualitie*; How to demeane or accommodate himselfe in the manage of publike or private affaires."[2] In the 1630, 1641, and some 1633 editions of *The English Gentleman*,[3] "A Draught of the *Frontispice*" literally folds out from the volume's binding as a separate and larger page; it works as a textual key opposite the map of allegorical panels surrounding the gentlemanly figure of the title, who looks out from the center of the elaborately engraved page (Fig. 1).

Brathwait's unfolding of "acquaintance" receives further elaboration in his later chapter devoted to that subject, but there is much writ small in this engraving and its textual explanation. "ACQVAINTANCE," says the gloss, "is in two bodies individually incorporated"; friendship is literally made corporeal in two bodies that are one. The friendship they embody is thus "individual" in the earlier meaning of that word, "indivisible"; Raymond Williams and Peter Stallybrass have shown that, prior to a dramatic shift in the seventeenth century, *individual* signified the opposite of its present meaning, as *OED*'s quotations illustrate: "To the ... glorie of the hye and indyuyduall Trynyte" (1425), or as Cockeram defined the word in his 1623 word-list, "not to bee parted, as man and wife."[4] That the friends of the engraving are made one flesh is further stressed in the

A Draught of the Frontispice, with all such especiall *Properties*, *Adjuncts* and *Characters*, propriated, personated and expressed, as may give clearer light to the explanation of it.

Whereto are annexed certaine exquisite *Motto's*, *Impresses*, with other *Ornaments* of *Art*, purposely devised: *and contrived, to adde more beautie and Perfection to the Worke.*

YOUTH is expressed, featured and pourtrayed with a fresh, cheerefull and amiable countenance, seated on a mount, environed with two opposite Rockes: on the right hand stands *Vertue*, with a Palme or Olive branch in her hand, illustrated by this Motto; *Virtus vincit*: On the left hand stands a *Siren*-appearing to the halfe body, with haire dishevelled; who with an attractive aspect reflecteth on *Youth*; fixing his eyes on either object; her Motto; *Vox, lene, sed amara lethi*.

DISPOSITION is displayed by a youthfull wanton, and amorous presence; about the feature grow fruits and delicacies of all sorts, as if he were seated in *Pandora's* Pavillion, and reaching to pull an Apple, he closeth this Motto; *Nitimur in vetitum. Flora & verbena*.

EDUCATION is presented with an ingenuous countenance, is included with the seven Liberall Sciences; so many Portals being shadowed, on whose Frontispice, each distinct Science is inscribed; neere to the feature are figured *Bractea* and rods: from which adjunct he deriveth this Motto; *Plura & verbena*.

VOCATION is described in a grave, civill and demure habit, a countenance constant and setled: adjoyning to which Picture appeares a ship with failes displayed, while *Vacuum* fixeth his eye on a Globe, or Marine Map: under the feature are mattocks, sledges, shovels, and other utensils; from whence he extracteth this Motto; *Passer & paruus*.

RECREATION is delineated by a fresh, flourishing, and agile Physionomie; about which portraiture are Hawkes sitting on pearches, with Spaniels lying under them: Horses likewise and Hounds ready for the Chace; remote from these are Deere, Hares, and Conies grazing; upon the other Border or Verge of the Picture, is presented a Summer Arbour, and in it Tables, Cards and Chesse-boord; where *Recreation* is expressed playing upon a Violl, with a Song-booke before him: Suiting his humour with this Motto; *Non arcum semper tendit Apollo*.

ACQUAINTANCE is in two bodies individually incorporated, and so lesse selfe than sociably united: two Twins cannot be more naturally, neere, than these individually deare; which they expresse in hugging one another, and shewing the consenting Consort of their minde; by the mutuall intercourse of their Motto; *Cernis amos mortem est*.

MODERATION is moulded after such a manner, as if a feature may expresse a tempt, not flying may be devised more absolute, to convey affection by the eye, or diction to the heart, than the representment of this Picture, reposing in a private harbour, as one secured from danger, having no other attendants to share with him in his peacefull reposture, than the *Halcyon* flying and flickering above him, and the *Torrent* crawling and creeping below him; the *Halcyon* implying calmenesse; the *Torrent* importing immensitie: having the Sea under him, shelves about him, but tranquillity within him, and the approvement of this Motto to secure him; *Moderata durant*.

PERFECTION is only shadowed, because in his native lineature hardly to be expressed; having resemblance to the Sun-reflecting *Eagle*, whose Emblem he retaines; branching his *Ayery* in the highest Spire, and scorning to stoope to any object in this inferiour Sphere: Deblazoned by a head breaking thorow a cloud, clothed or impaled with Sun-beames, to expresse his glory; and ushered by this Motto in his convoy to his Country; *Hac cælum petitur via*.

In the middle betwixt the Veines, is the Pourtraiture of a comely Personage drawne to the whole Body, representing an *English Gentleman*, with a Rod in his hand, to expresse his curiall office; with this Motto, to agnize his alliance and service; *Spe in cælis. Pe in terris.*
For other *Attributes*, *Properties*, or *Adjuncts*, from shadowes they receive their lustre, which give best life and light to any Picture.

Figure 1   Title page and "Draught" of the frontispiece: Richard Brathwait, *THE English Gentleman* (London: by Iohn Haviland [for] Robert Bostock, 1630).

gloss's twinning; the metaphor (supported by parallel syntax and rhyme) naturalizes the bond of acquaintance: "two Twins cannot be more naturally neere, than these be affectionately deare." The indistinguish-ability that is part of twinship is depicted in the engraving (Fig. 2), a mirroring image of identically dressed and positioned gentlemen. The engraving thus brings together several contemporary meanings of *near*: "Closely related by blood or kinship," "Of persons: Closely attached to, very intimate or familiar with, another," "Of friendship, etc.: Close, intimate, familiar," and "Close at hand; not distant" (*OED*). Thus, twinning "close at hand" is also *twining* (or intertwining); affection is represented by physical intimacy, expressed by "hugging one another," and the engraving depicts a courtly dance, the position of the cloaks suggesting the velocity with which the two gentlemen are moving to become "no lesse selfely than sociably united," "two bodies individually incorporated."

That the homoeroticism of "acquaintance" here relates to the textual intercourse that will be the focus of this chapter is demonstrated in both the engraving and the final lines of the gloss. The gentlemen show "the consenting Consort of their minde" (which is notably singular), and they select a motto by "mutuall interchoice." The excessiveness of these phrases – the repetition of the prefix *con-* and the "choice" that in its overdetermination is both "mutuall" and "inter" – suggests the extent to which the gentlemen are indistinguishable and their motto unattributable to either one or the other. Likewise, in the engraving, a precursor of the modern cartoon-bubble emerges from both men, figuring the collabora-tive texture of their voice. This "voice" is notably scriptive in its early-modern figuration, a scroll inscribed with a handwritten motto. The motto thus collates two strands of Renaissance practice: it is both a word (*mot*) or saying, (highlighting *motto*'s etymology from Latin *muttum*, "uttered sound"), and a visual, heraldic text, part of an extensive, eight-panel *blason* of *The English Gentleman*. The Latin text of the motto has a number of relevant translations. "*Certus amor morum est*" may mean "a secure love is a virtue" or "love of virtue is a secure thing." A further possibility is "The love [that is, the conjunction or agreement] of desires [or wills, or mores] is a secure thing," a translation that resonates, as we shall see, with Montaigne's description of friendship as the "agreement of wills."[5]

Brathwait's *English Gentleman* comes comparatively late in the history of Renaissance friendship, arriving as it does at the cusp of a companion-ate ideal of marriage that was radically to alter the sex/gender system.[6] But in glossing acquaintance, Brathwait here recapitulates in small space what was voluminously inscribed in other earlier Renaissance English

Figure 2 Detail of title page: Richard Brathwait, *THE English Gentleman* (London: by Iohn Haviland [for] Robert Bostock, 1630).

treatments of friendship. Many of the treatments emerge, like Brathwait's, in gentlemen's conduct books; *The Faerie Queene*, for example, the "generall end [of which] is to fashion a gentleman or noble person in vertuous and gentle discipline," devotes a book to the subject.[7] Other treatments – for example, Bacon's "Of Friendship" and Florio's translation of Montaigne's *"De l'amitié"* – are less obviously class-encoded. All were published during a period of remarkable social mobility, a time when the boundary between gentle- and common men was increasingly fluid and contested;[8] furthermore, as Frank Whigham has shown, they both describe gentility and allow for its replication and proliferation, often among the very members of society from whom the books' writers sought to distinguish themselves.[9] As we shall see, Renaissance theories of friendship are in fact predicated on the notion of reproducibility – they take as their basis the classical conception that friends (as Florio's Montaigne summarizes) are "one soule in two bodies, according to the fit definition of *Aristotle*" (p. 94).[10] Brathwait himself notes that friendship is "where two hearts are so individually united, as neither from other can well be severed" (p. 243); a friend is "nothing else than a *second selfe*, and therefore as individuate as man from himself" (p. 293).

Unlike Brathwait's *Gentleman*, which declares its position in its title, Montaigne's essay "Of Friendship" would not at first appear to be heavily class-inflected. Nevertheless, the title page of the *Essayes*' influential English translation announces Montaigne as *"Gentleman of the French Kings Chamber"* and the translator Florio as *"Reader of the Italian tongue vnto the Soveraigne* Maiestie of ANNA, Queene of England ... And one of the Gentlemen of hir Royall Priuie chamber."*[11] Within this context, the essay "Of Friendship" is in particular a complex negotiation of the issues at the nexus of homoeroticism, male friendship, and collaboration; in John Florio's translation, published repeatedly in the early seventeenth century, the essay both augmented and participated in English discourses of friendship.[12]

What we might call the collaborative text of male friendship is "Of Friendship"'s point of departure. The essayist begins by describing "the proceeding of a Painters worke I have" (p. 89); he writes that a "desire hath possessed me to imitate him," and compares his essays to the collages the painter creates by framing his pictures with "antike Boscage or Crotesko [grotesque] works": "what are these my compositions in truth, other then antique workes, and monstrous bodies, patched and hudled-vp together of divers members, without any certaine or well ordered figure, having neither order, dependencie, or proportion, but casuall and framed by chaunce?" (pp. 89–90). The essayist immediately illustrates the "monstrous" body of his text in a citation itself drawn from an "antike worke": "A woman faire for parts superior,/Endes in a fish for parts inferior." This misogynist aphorism – a collaboration with Horace over a monstrous female corpus – leads directly into another collaboration, one that is ostensibly source and subject of the essay, Montaigne's friendship with "*Steven de la Boitie*" (Florio's partial anglicization, p. 90). Arguing that his own "sufficiency reacheth not so farre," the essayist writes – at a structurally significant moment, the midpoint of the *Essayes*' first book – that he has "advised [him] selfe to borrow" and insert into his own book an essay ("Voluntary Servititude") by Boitie (p. 90). The collaborative texture of this friendship becomes the essay's controlling topos, for it began (and indeed is "bound") in a printed text: "To ... his pamphlet I am particularly most bounden, forsomuch as it was the instrumentall meane of our first acquaintance" (p. 90). Furthermore, the friendship eventuates in several publications: Montaigne says that he had encouraged Boitie's essay-writing while he lived, was Boitie's literary executor and publisher after his death, and writes "Of Friendship" and the subsequent piece in the *Essayes* as an introduction to, and dedication of, Boitie's work.[13]

In his dedication to the volume of translated *Essayes* in which "Of Friendship" appears, Florio links his own textual production with this essay and its collaborative process. There he addresses *his* patron in the language Montaigne uses in dedicating Boetie's work: "let me for [Montaigne] but do and say, as he did for his other-selfe, his peerlesse paire *Steven de Boetie*, in the 28. [chapter] of this first [book], and thinke hee speaks to you my praise-surmounting Countesse of *Bedford*, what hee there speakes to the Lady of *Grammont*."[14] Situating himself as *Montaigne*'s "other-selfe," Florio significantly broadens the network of collaborative, friendly relations, and his dedicating analogy further blurs, or enlarges, the "I" of the essay on friendship. Who writes "Of Friendship"? And of *which* friendship? Montaigne is "bounden" to Boetie's pamphlet and "bound" in Florio's book; Montaigne (translated by Florio) says he cannot distinguish himself from Boetie; and Florio speaks Montaigne's words (which he has translated) as his own. Translation, collaboration, and friendship intersect, undercutting the modern sense of the essay as individual utterance.[15]

Within this collaboratively textual framework, "Of Friendship" attempts to negotiate the relation of male friendship and sexual love. The "affection toward women" cannot compare with male friendship, "nor may-it be placed in this ranke," for it is "a rash and wavering fire, waving and diverse: the fire of an ague subject to fittes and stints" (p. 91). But the attempt to disengage friendship from the ostensible disease of male/female sexual love is undermined in the terms of its own explanation:

As soone as it [lustfull love] creepeth into the termes of friendship, that is to say, in the agreement of wills, it languisheth and vanisheth away: *enjoying* doth loose-it,[16] as having a *corporall* end, and subject to society. On the other side, friendshippe is *enjoyed* according as it is *desired*, it is neither *bredde*, nor *nourished*, nor *encreaseth* but in *jovissance*, as being spirituall, and the mind being refined by vse and custome. (p. 91, my emphasis)

The language of jouissance and sexual "enjoying" circles back to describe its supposed opposite, friendly love, and the denigrated "corporall end" of sexual love is re-embodied in the peculiarly corporeal breeding, nourishing, and growth of friendly "jovissance."[17]

Continuing the analysis of relations with women, the essay differentiates marriage from other sexual love of women and argues that it likewise is a relationship incompatible with friendship. "[A] covenant which hath nothing free but the entrance," marriage is "a match ordinarily concluded to other ends," and is thus, unlike friendship, immersed in the vicissitudes of "commerce or busines" (p. 91). Furthermore, women are pronounced incapable of the "conference and communication" of friendship. To be sure, the essay continues, it would be ideal to have, simultaneously, both sexual relations and friendship:

truely, if without that [women's insufficiency], such a genuine and voluntarie acquaintance might be contracted, where not onely mindes had this entire jovissance, but also bodies, a share of the aliance, and where man might wholy be engaged: It is certaine, that friendship would thereby be more compleate and full: But this sexe [women] could never yet by any example attaine vnto it, and is by ancient schooles rejected thence. (pp. 91–92)

For a moment, the essay explicitly addresses the possible conflation of sex and friendship, then discards it, citing misogynist classical authority. Further, the text immediately disallows, on different grounds, another possible configuration of gender and sexualized friendship – one, ironically, based on "ancient schooles": "And this other Greeke licence is justly abhorred by our customes, which notwithstanding, because according to vse it had so necessarie a disparitie of ages and difference of offices betweene lovers, did no more sufficiently answere the perfect vnion and agreement, which here we require" (p. 92). Notably, sexual relations between men are incompatible with friendship not because they are sexual *per se*, but because, in the only precedent example (Greek pederasty), they included "disparitie" and "difference" – whereas the essayist would require "conference and communication," or, returning to Brathwait's language, "mutuall interchoice." What appears to be the strict separation of friendship and sexuality in the essay, then, is instead a refusal of relations founded in "disparitie": of gender, of age, or of "office" (a word that brings along with its reference to a given role within a sexual act a significant class-encoded meaning, as *OED* suggests).[18]

Given this understanding of sexuality, we can begin to see in this essay another mode of eroticism in the language of an *equitable* jouissance; this discourse repeatedly circulates in the inscription of Montaigne's friendship with Boitie:

[Friendship] is I wot not what kinde of quintessence of all this commixture, which having seized all my will, induced the same to plunge and loose it selfe in his, which likewise having seized all his will, brought it to loose and plunge it selfe in mine, with a mutuall greedinesse, and with a semblable concurrance. (p. 93)

The mutuality of the passage is clear in its mirroring syntactic structure, but some linguistic excavation is necessary to recover its remarkable homoeroticism. *Will* was a capacious signifier in early modern English, referring to: "(a) 'one's will,' what one wishes to have or do ... (b) the auxiliary verb indicating futurity and/or purpose ... (c) lust, carnal desire ... (d) the male sex organ ... (e) the female sex organ."[19] Furthermore, *plunge*, as *OED* notes, meant "to put violently, thrust, or cast *into* (or *in*) a liquid, a penetrable substance, or a cavity," and *loose* could signify the meanings we now distinguish as "loose" and "lose" (the latter spelling is indeed used at this point in the 1632 edition). Taken together, these significations suggest that the essay figures a mutual interpenetration in which each friend's "will" acts as desire, penetrator, and receptacle. The chiastic structure of the sentence – culminating in a "semblable concurrance" (a running-together that is also altogether similar) – is reminiscent of the "consenting Consort" of Brathwait's gloss.[20] In fact, the *con*- which recurs in these texts is what we might call the prefix of homoerotic friendship, as another passage suggests: "In the amitie I speake of, they [friends] enter-mixe and *con*found themselves one in the other, with so vniversall a *com*mixture, that they weare-out, and can no more finde the seame that hath *con*joyned them together" (p. 92, my emphasis). Penetrator and penetrated are indistinguishable in this paradigm (there is none of Greek pederasty's "difference" or "disparitie"); indeed, the very "seame" of the interaction disappears.[21]

The "homo" of the eroticism I have located in treatments of male friendship is thus doubly appropriate, for, as our glance at Brathwait and Montaigne begins to suggest, Renaissance friendship texts inscribe an erotics of similitude that goes far beyond the modern conception of mere sameness of sex. Gentlemen friends are identically constituted, as both the rhetoric and the material production of these texts in print suggest.

Brathwait, who published copies of his *English Gentleman* three times, writes in the chapter on acquaintance that the *"absolute* ayme or end of *friendship* is to improve, reprove, correct, reforme, and conforme the whole *Image* of that man with whom they converse, to his similitude whome all men represent."[22] Brathwait speaks of friendship in the language of the print-shop ("proof," "correct," "forme"), and like the engraving that figures it, friendship (re)prints identical, homo/geneous gentlemen engaged in homoerotic self-duplication.

In the complexity with which it sets forth this relation of friendship and sex, "Of Friendship" furthermore suggests the extent to which we must distance ourselves from a modern taxonomy of sexualities in order to understand Renaissance sex/gender systems. "Of Friendship" divides erotic activity into a number of arenas, none of them exclusive designations of a subject position corresponding to the modern terms *homosexual* and *heterosexual.* The essay prohibits the "Greeke licence" of pederasty at the same time that it valorizes another, interpenetrating version of sex between men. Furthermore, in the essay's hierarchy of relations, sex between women and men (both within and outside marriage) lies below male friendship. Within this misogynist paradigm, it is, like pederasty, a relationship of "disparitie" and thus not friendship; nevertheless, it exists *alongside* eroticized friendship between men: *"Vnder* this chiefe amitie [friendship], these fading affections [desire for women] have sometimes found place in me ... So are these two passions entred into mee in knowledge one of another, but in comparison never..." (p. 91, my emphasis). In contradistinction to Montaigne's (and Florio's) celebrated humanism, these sentences also measure their distance from the modern conception of the self-generating, self-discovering individual and sexual subject, for these "passions" arise not from within but instead "enter in" from the outside. As such, they remind us of this subject's individuality (in the earlier sense of "indivisibility") from social mechanisms that only now seem to be the antithesis of essay-writing as a self-ish activity.

The essay further illustrates the extent to which what we normatively now call *homosexuality* is in English Renaissance culture dispersed into a number of discourses, each of which differently negotiates power relations. *Pederasty*, like *sodomy*, described sexual relations between men of different social categories; *pederasty* emphasized an age difference, and *sodomy*, as Alan Bray has copiously documented, often suggested sexual relations between men of differing social class.[23] Montaigne and Brathwait, however, demonstrate that these were not the only types of Renaissance homoeroticism and, more importantly, that homoeroticism was not uniformly inscribed as abhorrent or disruptive. For alongside the condemned homoeroticism of sodomy (with its attendant discourses of "disparitie" and social disruption), there was the sanctioned homoeroticism of male friendship.[24] This mode is not only sanctioned but also *constitutive* of power relations in the period; as the engraving of "acquaintance" graphically demonstrates, it figures importantly in the construction and reproduction of the entitled English gentleman.

It is my contention that late sixteenth- and early seventeenth-century dramatic writing occurs within this context of a collaborative homoerotics. By "dramatic writing" here I mean primarily two things: first, the practice of collaborative writing that predominated as the mode of textual production in early modern theatres, as we saw in chapter 1; and second, the writing in (the texts of) the plays. More simply: the collaborative writing of Renaissance drama, and the dramatization of Renaissance collaboration. Taking the Brathwait engraving as an emblem, and Florio's Montaigne as an exploration of a collaborative homoerotics, the remainder of this chapter elaborates on this chiasmus by focusing closely on two theatrical texts that raise issues of collaboration and eroticism in the context of gentlemanly friendship – as the titles within their titles suggest: *The Two* Gentlemen *of Verona* and *The Two* Noble *Kinsmen*. Negotiating the competing demands of friendship and Petrarchan love, *The Two Gentlemen of Verona* illuminates the collaborative male inscription of a social order; within the play's collaborative practice, texts and women circulate among gentlemen. *The Two Noble Kinsmen* exposes some disruptions and tensions in *Two Gentlemen's* final consolidation of friendship and marriage, and thus provides a possible critique of the collaborative practice that frames its own presentation in the 1634 quarto – a prologue in which "New Playes, and Maydenheads, are neare a kin," and a title page on which two gentlemanly playwrights are said to collaborate.[25] Thus, this chapter seeks both to rewrite the normative critical view of Renaissance male friendship, in which friendship is taken to occlude homoeroticism,[26] and to provide a cultural perspective on collaboration as a textual practice. Where the previous chapter attempted to disengage theatrical collaboration from an anachronistic notion of authorship, this chapter suggests the ways in which collaboration is itself implicated in and enabled by Renaissance discourses of eroticism, gender, and power.

Duplications

The Two Gentlemen of Verona sets male friendship within a decidedly class-inflected context; Valentine and Protheus, its title(d) protagonists, begin the play as gentlemen-under-construction, and the play works to

constitute them as gentlemanly subjects.[27] Panthino, the servant of
Protheus's father Antonio, suggests some of the possibilities for the
training of young gentlemen, in language that resonates with the
gentlemanly conduct books: some gentlemen, he says

> Put forth their Sonnes, to seeke preferment out.
> Some to the warres, to try their fortune there;
> Some, to discouer Islands farre away;
> Some, to the studious Vniuersities . . .   (TLN 309–12)[28]

Panthino – reiterating here the advice of another gentleman, Antonio's
brother – advocates travel for Protheus, noting that it "would be great
impeachment to his age, / In hauing knowne no trauaile in his youth"
(TLN 317–18), and thus connects the gentleman's travel to the advance-
ment of empire and the pursuit of humanistic study. Acknowledging that
his son "cannot be a perfect man, / Not being tryd, and tutord in the
world" (TLN 322–23), Antonio rejects the possibility of training his son
in these exclusively male preserves, but settles on Protheus's participation
in the equally homosocial[29] world of the court:

> There shall he practise Tilts, and Turnaments;
> Heare sweet discourse, conuerse with Noble-men,
> And be in eye of euery Exercise
> Worthy his youth and noblenesse of birth.   (TLN 332–35)

The emulation that constructs the gentleman – father, uncle, and servant
all agree that Protheus must be like the sons of other men and "in eye of
euery Exercise" – recapitulates the homogeneity we recognized in both
Brathwait and Montaigne's discussions, as Valentine's speeches recom-
mending Protheus to the Duke at court again make clear:

> I knew him as my selfe: for from our Infancie
> We haue conuerst, and spent our howres together,
> . . .
> He is compleat in feature, and in minde,
> With all good grace, to grace a Gentleman.   (TLN 712–13, 723–24)

And yet, although the play thus emphasizes the homosocial networks
of gentlemanly education through emulation,[30] it also seems relentlessly
to put male friendship and Petrarchan love in direct competition.[31] The
text commences in the middle of a discussion that places the two in
contention; Valentine is about to depart for court, leaving his friend, who
stays behind for love of Julia:

> Cease to perswade, my louing *Protheus*;
> Home-keeping youth, haue euer homely wits,
> Wer't not affection chaines thy tender dayes

> To the sweet glaunces of thy honour'd Loue,
> I rather would entreat thy company,
> To see the wonders of the world abroad.   (TLN 4–9)

But though the play consistently places male friendship and male–female love at odds (and this speech is proleptic of larger, subsequent disjunctions), it is important to recognize that this cannot be seen simply as a contest between eroticized male–female relations and platonic male friendship, for male friendship and Petrarchan love in this play speak a remarkably similar language. "My louing Protheus," for example, signifies in both directions; Protheus is "chained" by affection for Julia but equally bound to his male friend, to whom he speaks in similarly affectionate language:

> Wilt thou be gone? Sweet *Valentine* adew,
> Thinke on thy *Protheus*, when thou (hap'ly) seest
> Some rare note-worthy obiect in thy trauaile.
> Wish me partaker in thy happinesse,
> When thou do'st meet good hap; and in thy danger,
> (If euer danger doe enuiron thee)
> Commend thy grieuance to my holy prayers,
> For I will be thy beades-man, *Valentine*.   (TLN 14–21)

This exchange and its terms of address insert the play into a discourse of homoerotic male friendship from its first conversation. "Sweet *Valentine*" suggests the resonant historical meaning of that name, "a sweetheart, lover, or special friend" chosen on St. Valentine's Day (*OED*), and Protheus no sooner speaks than he gives himself ("*thy* Protheus") to Valentine. "Conversation" is furthermore an apt description of the exchange that opens this play, for it is also, as we have seen, the activity of the homosocial court: "There shall he … conuerse with Noble-men." Valentine's later attestation of Protheus's gentlemanliness there – "from our Infancie / We haue conuerst" – thus recalls this first moment, the infancy of these characters upon the stage in this play. *Con/versation*, moreover, has within it the prefix I have already associated with homoerotic friendship; as *OED* makes clear, the word signified both textual and sexual exchange into the nineteenth century.[32] Indeed, Protheus and Valentine's conversation immediately takes a turn in this direction:

> *Val.* And on a loue-booke [you will] pray for my successe?
> *Pro.* Vpon some booke I loue, I'le pray for thee.
> *Val.* That's on some shallow Storie of deepe loue,
> How yong *Leander* crost the *Hellespont*.
> *Pro.* That's a deepe Storie, of a deeper loue,
> For he was more then ouer-shooes in loue.   (TLN 22–27)

Jonathan Goldberg has detailed the "textual determination" of character
in this play (the way in which character is constituted by the play's many
circulating texts),[33] and here the character and relation of the friends is
introduced and produced through an erotic tale, a "loue-booke," that
again gestures in several directions. Marlowe's *Hero and Leander* features
both the relationship of its title and a significant homoerotic component;
with their punning on *deepe*, the two friends cite the poem at what is
arguably its most homoerotic moment, Leander's submarine encounter
with Neptune as he swims the Hellespont and the homoerotic trajectory
of the god's "deepe perswading Oratorie."[34]

The opening scene's competition of friendship and Petrarchan love is
in fact heightened by the topos of homogeneity we have noticed in other
texts of male friendship – the friend as "second selfe" – for after
following Valentine to court at the behest of father, uncle, and servant,
Protheus, in the play's central disruption of friendship by love, falls for
Valentine's beloved Sylvia.[35] Yet Protheus, in the first of two important
speeches attempting to negotiate these competing demands, demonstrates
the extent to which the two speak in identical terms:

> Is it mine, or *Valentines* praise?
> Her true perfection, or my false transgression?
> That makes me reasonlesse, to reason thus?
> . . .
> Me thinkes my zeale to *Valentine* is cold,
> And that I loue him not as I was wont:
> O, but I loue his Lady too-too much,
> And that's the reason I loue him so little.   (TLN 851–53, 858–61)

The speech enacts the contention of two "loues" and turns on the
currency of that word in both discourses. Protheus's next solo speech
(separated from this one by a short comic scene) again compares his
loues – "To leaue my *Iulia*; shall I be forsworne? / To loue faire *Siluia*;
shall I be forsworne? / To wrong my friend, I shall be much forsworne"
(TLN 930–32) – and in its inversion of "shall I" privileges the demands
of friendship. The speech continues to demonstrate the intersecting
discourses of love and friendship, but it also plays with and puts pressure
on the terms of friendship we have seen outlined elsewhere:

> I cannot leaue to loue; and yet I doe:
> But there I leaue to loue, where I should loue.
> *Iulia* I loose, and *Valentine* I loose,
> If I keepe them, I needs must loose my selfe:
> If I loose them, thus finde I by their losse,
> For *Valentine*, my selfe: for *Iulia*, *Siluia*.
> I to my selfe am deerer then a friend . . .   (TLN 946–52)

Florio's Montaigne writes of his friend, "If a man vrge me to tell wherefore I loved him, I feele it can not be expressed, but by answering; Because it was he, because it was my selfe" (p. 92) and this formulation demonstrates succinctly how Protheus's speech contradicts the tenets of Renaissance friendship. In making himself "deerer then a friend," Protheus doubles back on the friend "as individuate as man from himself." Losing that friend, he ostensibly finds himself: "I cannot proue constant to my selfe, / Without some treachery vs'd to *Valentine*" (TLN 960–61). Yet for all his revisions, Protheus nevertheless grounds his betrayal of his friend in the language of friendship; like the previous speech, this one turns on the use of a single word in both Petrarchan and friendship discourses: "*Valentine* Ile hold an Enemie, / Ayming at *Siluia* as a sweeter friend" (TLN 958–59). This line demonstrates the extent to which courtship is in this play constantly collapsing into friendship, and, though they would seem to be most at odds in Protheus's betrayal of Valentine for Silvia, they cannot here be entirely differentiated. Abandoning Valentine ("Sweet *Valentine* adew"), Protheus, in his duplicity, chooses Silvia as a "sweeter friend" – and thus becomes *more like Valentine*.[36] And when Valentine is later banished from court, Protheus assures him that he can address his letters to Silvia to/through him.

If, following Goldberg's argument, character in this play is constituted through the circulating Petrarchan love-letters that cross and recross the text, when we consider these scenes of writing and circulation more fully within their social context, we again find not the opposition of male friendship and Petrarchan love but rather their interdependence. But a consideration of writing also begins to suggest a more specific configuration of friendship and love, for the letters of Petrarchan love in this play move consistently within a homosocial network. Insofar as character is charactered in the letter, it is figured within the circuit of the homosocial. Early in the play, Julia writes a letter to Protheus, who, interrupted in its reading by his father, says:

> 'tis a word or two
> Of commendations sent from *Valentine*;
> Deliuer'd by a friend that came from him.
> . . .
> There is no newes, (my Lord) but that he writes
> How happily he liues, how well-belou'd,
> And daily graced by the Emperor;
> Wishing me with him, partner of his fortune.   (TLN 354–61)

The letter from the lover becomes the letter from the loving friend delivered to the father. With the response of Protheus's father, the letter eventuates in Protheus following the course of that friend to court:

> *Ant.* And how stand you affected to his wish?
> *Pro.* As one relying on your Lordships will,
> And not depending on his friendly wish.
> *Ant.* My will is something sorted with his wish:
> Muse not that I thus sodainely proceed;
> For what I will, I will and there an end:
> I am resolu'd that thou shalt spend some time
> With *Valentinus*, in the Emperors Court ...   (TLN 362–69)

Patricia Parker has noted in *The Two Gentlemen* the importance of the appropriate rhetorical trope *geminatio* or "the doublet" – the repetition of words with no intervening space between[37] – and this exchange illuminates *geminatio*'s troping of not only doubleness but also homosocial reproduction. What was called the "redoubling of a word"[38] here serves not only to send Protheus to duplicate Valentine at the Emperor's court ("what I will, I will"), but also to exhibit the extent to which all men in this play participate in the copious twinning of homosocial similitude situated there: "My *will* is something sorted with his *wish*."

The doubling of Valentine at the Emperor's court is accomplished by letter even before Protheus leaves Verona, for in the next scene of the play, Silvia causes Valentine to write a letter for her to a "secret, nameles friend of [hers]" (TLN 495), who is Valentine himself. His servant Speed explains, in a speech which culminates in elaborate gemination:

> often haue you writ to her: and she in modesty,
> Or else for want of idle time, could not againe reply,
> Or fearing els some messēger, yᵗ might her mind discouer
> *Her self* hath taught *her Loue himself*, to write vnto *her louer*.
>   (TLN 555–68, my emphasis)

"[S]he woes you by a figure," Speed says (TLN 539), alerting the audience to the rhetorical trope he speaks and its inscription in the path of a text that quite literally *circu*lates; writing to a "secret, nameles friend," Valentine makes a doublet of himself in a letter. Speed's further comment ("All this I speak in print, for in print I found it" [TLN 569]) associates the doubling letter and the rhetorical trope with the printed reproduction of the gentleman we earlier noticed in Brathwait's attempt to "improve, reprove, correct, reforme and conforme."[39] The circulating text short-circuits something in its reproduction, however; Silvia, Goldberg observes, "can only speak to her lover if he speaks for her."[40] Valentine becomes (to use Speed's terms) both Silvia's "Pupill" and her "Tutor"; a "Spokes-man" to and for himself, he is both "scribe" and recipient of a desire that cannot in this textual economy be fully denoted as "Silvia's" (TLN 529, 537, 531). This friendly letter is in a fundamental way, then, a homosocial text – a letter between *man*. As such it figures collaboration at its most homo-erotic; "I knew him as my selfe."

Another of Valentine's letters likewise exposes the homosocial circuit of writing in this play, moving not from Valentine to Silvia (its ostensible destination as Petrarchan verse) but between Valentine and the Duke her father. The Duke intercepts Valentine in the midst of his attempt to elope with Silvia; Valentine carries with him both the ladder by which he will ascend to Silvia's window and the verses describing how he will "enfranchise" her (TLN 1220). To expose Valentine's plot, the Duke doubles Valentine's desire, claiming that he wants to substitute a wife for his daughter Silvia and asking Valentine's advice in wooing a woman he describes as being in exactly Silvia's position. As the Duke suggests ("Now as thou art a Gentleman of blood / Aduise me where I may haue such a Ladder" [TLN 1190–91]), Valentine's plot is an attempt at class-climbing, and his intercepted verses to Silvia deploy conventional Petrarchan conceits to figure the class-encoded situation both of himself as would-be gentleman and of the Duke/ Emperor (would-be suitor of a woman like his own daughter) who reads them aloud:

> My thoughts do harbour with my *Siluia* nightly,
> And *slaues* they are to me, that send them flying.
> Oh, could their *Master* come, and goe as lightly,
> Himselfe would lodge where (senceles) they are lying.
> My *Herald* Thoughts, in thy pure bosome rest-them,
> While I (their *King*) that thither them importune
> Doe curse the grace, that with such grace hath blest them,
> Because my selfe doe want my *seruants* fortune.
> I curse my selfe, for they are sent by me,
> That they should harbour where their *Lord* should be.
>
> (TLN 1210–19, my emphasis)[41]

Valentine's verses figure his desire to substitute for his text; he would become, in other words, the character represented in/by the letter, a doublet of the Duke, who is (Silvia's) "master," "king," and "lord." As in the other circulating letters and verses of this play, this letter is as much about the constitution of the gentlemanly subject as it is about the trajectory of Petrarchan desire; the gentleman is written in the character(s) of homosocial emulation, through Petrarchan verse. Valentine's letter goes to and imitates the Duke; the Duke reads a letter that describes his own imitation of Valentine.

These inscriptions are supported by what we know of the circulation of Petrarchan verse in late sixteenth- and early seventeenth-century culture. The sonnet (of which Valentine's poem is a slightly abbreviated example) was in particular a public, courtly genre, circulating widely, expressing, in Arthur Marotti's familiar formulation, "social, political, and economic suits in the language of love";[42] furthermore, this poetic practice was often specifically gendered; Petrarchan sonnets, though often written *to* and *about* women, were circulating between men and registering *male* "suits": courtiership as courtship.[43] Poetic manuscripts, circulating in this homosocial circuit, were also sites of an elaborately collaborative poetics; the circulation of poetic manuscripts at four and five removes from the original writer, the interpolation into manuscripts of commentary and verse responses in other hands, the transcription into one manuscript of another's poems, and the circulation of multiple copies were the common practice among contemporary poets and readers.[44] Relations between writer and patron were often figured in language that disrupts a sense of singular authorship and draws the patron into the process of writing; Shakespeare writes to Wriothesley, "What I have done is yours; what I have to doe is yours; being part in all I have, devoted yours."[45] The language of poetic collaboration overlaps with that of homoeroticism; it is Ralegh who provides a reply to Marlowe's "The Passionate Shepherd to His Love."[46]

These material circumstances and the discourses that (con)figure them are foregrounded in the initial group of *Shake-speares Sonnets* (1609). What have often been called "marriage sonnets" are poems centered not on marriage but on reproduction, and a reproduction in which the participation of women is routinely elided.[47] These earliest sonnets are a man-to-man talk about making more men – maintaining the succession of homosocial generations, creating more male patrons to support more male poets: "Make thee an other selfe for loue of me, / That beauty still may liue in thine or thee" (sonnet 10, lines 13–14).[48] From its first line, the sequence emphasizes reproduction ("From fairest creatures we desire increase"), and the discourses of increase and reproduction within this male world are explicitly non-heterosexual (in the modern sense). Usury, the breeding of "increase" from barren metal, figures a veritable explosion of homosocial reproduction in the endlessly compounding interest rates of sonnet 6:

> That vse is not forbidden vsery,
> Which happies those that pay the willing lone;
> That's for thy selfe to breed an other thee,
> Or ten times happier be it ten for one,
> Ten times thy selfe were happier then thou art,
> If ten of thine ten times refigur'd thee ...[49]

In rhetoric that likewise emphasizes the reproduction of sameness, the speaker of sonnet 11 urges the addressee to "print more, not let that coppy die." The collaborative aspect of this textual reproduction is illuminated in sonnet 15, where the speaker writes to the addressee, "I ingraft you new"; punning on writing, "in/grafting" describes the larger process of replication within a sequence of identically structured poems that create growth and "increase" through their insistent imaging and rhetorical embroidery of the addressee. Like other poems that routinely construct the patron/addressee as collaborator in the poetic project, sonnet 26 both foregrounds its own circulation between men within a highly class-inflected language ("Lord of my loue . . . / To thee I send this written ambassage")[50] and asks the addressee to "put[] apparrell on my tottered louing" with "some good *conceipt* of thine" (my emphasis). The spelling *conceipt* may remind us that the addressee is both reproduced (conceived) in the sonnets and, reciprocally – or collaboratively – their "onlie begetter."[51]

If the circulation of writing – in the *The Two Gentlemen of Verona* and in the culture of circulating poetic manuscripts in which it participates – exposes the utility of Petrarchan poetics within a network of homosociality, the play's final scene is both its most extreme instance of contending Petrarchan love and male friendship *and* the succinct inscription of their ultimate relation. Protheus attempts to rape Silvia as Valentine watches; Valentine intervenes, labeling Protheus a "cōmon friend," (an oxymoronic insult in the context of gentlemanly friendship), and vows never again to trust him. But Protheus begs forgiveness – "if hearty sorrow / Be a sufficient Ransome for offence, / I tender't heere" (TLN 2197–99) – and Valentine relents: "that my loue may appeare plaine and free, / All that was mine, in *Siluia*, I giue thee" (TLN 2206–07).

This highly charged moment, in which Valentine apparently offers his beloved to the friend who has just attempted to rape her, has been a locus of discontent for many of the play's twentieth-century critics and may be the reason for the play's marked unpopularity; Arthur Quiller-Couch famously remarked that "there are, by this time, *no* gentlemen in Verona."[52] Quiller-Couch's notion of gentlemanliness is no doubt more Edwardian than Elizabethan, but he nevertheless comes unwittingly close to isolating at least one of the difficulties of this moment for twentieth-century readers when he notes that the play is part of a convention "of refining, idealising, exalting [friendship] out of all proportion, *or at any rate above the proportion it bears, in our modern minds*, either to love between man and woman or to parental love" (p. xix, my emphasis). The result for the play, he argues, is "a flaw too unnatural" (p. vii), terms that give us insight into what may be the import of an argument produced contemporaneously with early-twentieth-century crises of homo/heterosexual definition.[53] Quiller-Couch and other critics, that is, rebel against the elevation of a male–male bond over what they perceive, from a twentieth-century vantage point, as heterosexual union. (This should not in any way be confused with a critique of the representation of Silvia; both the play and Quiller-Couch's interpretation inscribe a misogyny that, in the former case, uses women as figures of transaction between men, and, in the latter, deploys women to guard against homoeroticism.)

For many critics, Shakespeare's participation in a homoerotic arrangement is incomprehensible, and numerous solutions are proposed to absolve him of responsibility. The play is said, emphatically, to fall early in Shakespeare's career (Shakespeare as well-meaning but clumsy apprentice). Or the play is Shakespeare's parodic debunking of literary absurdities, chief among them that friendship is greater than love (Shakespeare as intentionally clumsy).[54] Or the play's final scene, "so destructive of the relationships of the characters as they have been developed," is a part of the Folio text's "maze of contradictions and inconsistencies" (the text is clumsy).[55] Quiller-Couch himself argues that what Shakespeare originally wrote here was "better, because more natural, than the text allows us to know"; he proposes that this hypothetical Shakespearean original was nevertheless itself "theatrically ineffective" and revised out of the copy eventually used for the Folio by a "botcher." John Dover Wilson, among others, has similarly proposed a collaborative text.[56] These remedies to the problem of Valentine's gift of Silvia to the rapist Protheus demonstrate the extent to which interpretation of the scene has become wrapped up in, on the one hand, anachronistic notions of sexuality, and, on the other, anachronistic conceptions of collaboration ("authors" versus "botchers"). Envisioned as a negative textual practice to be deployed only *in extremis*, collaboration works as a canonic prophylactic, protecting Shakespeare from charges of insufficiently defending the primacy of (modern) heterosexuality.

I too want to suggest that collaboration is a solution to the problem the scene poses for a twentieth-century audience, but not in the restrictive and derogatory way these critics conceive of it. We have already witnessed the collaboratively homosocial circuit of writing in the play; though the play seems between its first and last scenes to put into competition male friendship and Petrarchan courtship, the last scene stages the play's ultimate collaboration of male friendship and its incorporation of the plot we would label "heterosexual." In terms that highlight the economics of this exchange/intercourse, the critical crux of

Valentine's speech forgiving Protheus brings together again the rhetorics of love and friendship:

> I am paid:
> And once againe, I doe receiue thee honest;
> ...
> And that my loue may appeare plaine and free,
> All that was mine, in *Siluia*, I giue thee.   (TLN 2201–02, 2206–07)

In its ambiguous syntax, Valentine's statement demonstrates at a climactic moment the conflation of Petrarchan love within male friendship. In this transaction, in exchange for Protheus's "Ransome" of "hearty sorrow" for the attempted rape, Valentine both gives Protheus all that he owns in Silvia (that is, he gives Silvia to Protheus), and he transfers all his love in Silvia to Protheus.

This scene of rape (significantly figured as a transgression against Valentine, not Silvia), apology, and forgiveness is central to the play's ongoing project, the (re)constitution of Valentine and Protheus as gentlemanly subjects. Valentine had earlier been banished from the court by Silvia's father for a transgression not unlike Protheus's; his interruption of the orderly traffic in women – an attempt to over-master the father/ruler in the bestowal of his daughter – had eventuated in his being labeled "base Intruder, ouer-weening Slaue" (TLN 1226–27). But Valentine's magnanimity in this final scene motivates his creation, by the Duke, as a gentleman, directly after he has successfully interrupted Protheus's similar transgression of the homosocial code. The collaborative circuit of the homosocial letter recurs at this moment, for the Duke says:

> Know then, I heere forget all former greefes,
> Cancell all grudge, repeale thee home againe,
> Plead a new state in thy un-riual'd merit,
> To which I thus subscribe: Sir *Valentine*,
> Thou art a Gentleman, and well deriu'd,
> Take thou thy *Siluia*, for thou hast deseru'd her.   (TLN 2267–72)

Literally granting Valentine a new (e)state – the status of gentleman, a position in the state of gentlemen he rules, and the inheritance of that estate/state through Silvia – the Duke's "subscription" reinscribes Valentine into the collaborative male social system. Having shown that he is capable of supervising rather than disrupting this culture's ordered distribution of women (and the significant violence it entails), Valentine is written in the character of a gentleman[57] – an act that is not unlike that performed by the title of the play itself.

The remainder of the scene and the play is a massive restoration of the play's homosocial power structure, a system no longer seen to be in competition with Petrarchan love, but underwriting it. Valentine reintegrates into courtly society the outlaws he had earlier joined; they too are "endu'd with worthy qualities ... reformed, ciuill, full of good, / And fit for great employment" (TLN 2278, 2281–82). Just as the play began with friendly "conversation," the play concludes with an all-male exchange between the Duke, Valentine, and Protheus. Furthermore, though the play ends with gestures toward marriage, this is a marriage that does not emphasize the pairing of cross-sex couples; by the last lines of the play, the women in question have disappeared from view: Silvia speaks no lines after the attempted rape, and Julia is (silently) present in boy's clothing.[58]

The play ends with Valentine and Protheus conversing about their marriage(s), but in lines that make ambiguous the play's concluding couplings: "our day of marriage," Valentine says to his friend, "shall be yours, / One Feast, one house, one mutuall happinesse" (TLN 2297–98). Friendship between men is restored through (not at the cost of) marriage to women, and the two gentlemen, in the persistent unification of the play's final line, are once again (to quote Brathwait) "no lesse selfely than sociably united." Recalling Montaigne's scene of mutual intercourse, we might remember as well, at this moment of the play's and the gentlemen's virtual consummation, Valentine's earlier pronouncement: "I knew him as my selfe."

Within a modern taxonomy of sexualities the ending of the play does not make sense, for we are in the modern scheme accustomed to polar and mutually exclusive hetero- and homosexualities, each designating the exclusive position of the individual.[59] But if we engage instead the idea of a sex/gender system in which marriage (a version of marriage that subordinates and silences women) and the homoeroticism of male friendship co-exist ("these two passions," Florio/Montaigne writes, "entred into mee in knowledge one of another"), we can begin to understand what transpires in *The Two Gentlemen of Verona*. To raise such a possible construal of homoeroticism in the play, to cut it loose from the modern sense of the "homosexual" (the "heterosexual" as well), is also, however, to allow for the possibility that eroticism between men has varying political valences in different contexts. Homoeroticism, that is, is not always and already a disruptive and unconventional deconstruction of a sex/gender system. In this play, and in the highly class-inflected context of gentlemen's conduct books and essays, homoeroticism functions as part of the network of power; it constitutes and reflects the homogeneity of the gentlemanly subject.

Enumerations

Yet but three? Come one more.
Two of both kindes makes vp fower.

A Midsommer nights dreame[60]

But to enumerate these Things were endlesse: I haue giuen the Rule,
where a Man cannot fitly play his owne Part: If he haue not a *Frend*, he
may quit the Stage.

Francis Bacon, "Of Friendship"[61]

If in its dramatization of rape and forgiveness *The Two Gentlemen of Verona* illustrates the collaborative scripting of a system in which homosocial friendship includes marriage, *The Two Noble Kinsmen* tests the limits of that conflation. Whereas *Two Gentlemen* resolves into a pair of male friends married to two different women,[62] *Two Kinsmen* refigures the homosocial calculus to put pressure on the earlier play's tidy solution. "Two of both kindes makes vp fower," according to Robin Goodfellow, and *The Two Noble Kinsmen* provides not one but *two* plots in which there are too few women for this calculated resolution: both the schoolmaster Gerrold's morris dance and the central Palamon/Arcite/Emilia plot lack a woman. Emilia's analysis of the Narcissus myth provides commentary on the larger play: "That was a faire Boy certaine, but a foole, / To love himselfe, were there not maides enough?" (p. 22). Like *The Two Gentlemen of Verona*, this play includes at its center two gentlemen, and, emphasizing even more their interchangeability and indifferentiation, the play suggests that the trajectory of their desire will likewise be identical:

> *Arc.*   . . . am not I
> Part of you blood, part of your soule? you have told me
> That I was *Palamon*, and you were *Arcite*.
> *Pal.* Yes.
> *Arc.* Am not I liable to those affections,
> Those joyes, greifes, angers, feares, my friend shall suffer?   (p. 25)

Lacking *Two Gentlemen*'s second available woman, however, this play proceeds to explore the tensions between the tropes of male friendship and the cultural imperative of monogamous marriage.[63]

In addition to the central relation of Palamon and Arcite, the play's other same-sex friendships place it squarely within the contemporary discourses of homoerotic friendship. When Theseus interrupts his marriage to go to war in the play's first scene, his friend Pirithous substitutes for him in the ceremony. Noting that "they two have Cabind / In many as dangerous, as poore a Corner," Hipolita later comments that Theseus and Pirithous's

> knot of love
> Tide, weau'd, intangled, with so true, so long,
> ⌐ And with a finger of so deepe a cunning
> May be outworne, never undone.   (p. 13)

Hipolita speaks of her husband's friendship with Pirithous in marital discourse; then as now, *knot* signified "the tie or bond of wedlock; the marriage or wedding knot" (*OED* 11b). Furthermore, the word also signified both "maidenhead" (as "virgin knot" in *Pericles* and *The Tempest* suggests) and sexual intercourse (Othello imagines "a cestern for foul toads / To knot and gender in"). In a play concerned relentlessly with the value and acquisition of "maidenhead" and accompanied here by the familiar pun on "done" and "undone," Theseus and Pirithous's "knot of love" resonates as a condition that is at once sexualized and virginal, consummated and impenetrable. In addition, this love has a mutuality that is naturalized in Emilia's description: "The one of th'other may be said to water / Their intertangled rootes of love" (p. 14).

Emilia is here privileging the maturity of Theseus and Pirithous's love over the remembered "innocence" of her own friendship with Flavina. While Theseus and Pirithous's adulthood deflects the application of a traditional critical model – in which an innocent homosexuality gives way to the developmental necessity of heterosexual maturity and marriage[64] – the play projects Emilia and Flavina's friendship in very similar terms. This is perhaps explained through the asymmetry of the system we have already witnessed, in which men simultaneously have male friends and female wives, but women have only husbands. That is, if homoerotic friendships constitute a network of male power in this culture, a similar network among adult women poses a threat to that power – as the conquering of the Amazons that opens the play amply suggests. Hipolita and Emilia's exchange precisely demonstrates the pressure on women to abandon friendship in favor of marriage; when Emilia asserts, "I am sure I shall not [love any that's calld Man]," Hipolita – the recently married former Amazon – responds, "I must no more beleeve thee in this point... / Then I will trust a sickely appetite, / That loathes even as it longs" (p. 14).

What Emilia calls the "rehearsall" of her friendship with Flavina – that is, her recounting of a relationship that Flavina's death and the larger patriarchal imperative of the play prohibits from becoming a performance[65] – recapitulates the mutuality, indifferentiation, and eroticism (here prescribed in innocence) we have noticed already in other friendship texts:

what she lik'd,
Was then of me approov'd, what not condemd
No more arraignement, the flowre that I would plucke
And put betweene my breasts, oh (then but beginning
To swell about the blossome) she would long
Till shee had such another, and commit it
To the like innocent Cradle, where *Phenix* like
They dide in perfume: on my head no toy
But was her patterne, her affections (pretty
Though happely, her careles, were, I followed
For my most serious decking, had mine eare
Stolne some new aire, or at adventure humd on
From misicall Coynadge, why it was a note
Whereon her spirits would sojourne (rather dwell on)
And sing it in her slumbers . . .   (p. 14)[66]

This description of emulous and collaborative friendship, in which one
friend's whimsical gestures are interpellated into the other ("toy"
becomes "patterne," "careles" "affections" become "serious decking"),
culminates in an ambiguous declaration: "This rehearsall / . . . has this
end, / That the true love tweene Mayde, and mayde, may be / More then
in sex individuall" (p. 14). Emilia's "individuall" is in all modern editions
emended to "dividual," a change that stabilizes the meaning of the
sentence, making it a comparison of love between women and love
between men and women – the "dividual" sexes.[67] But, as I suggested in
the discussion of Brathwait with which this chapter began, *individual*
once signified the opposite of its modern meaning, and in Emilia's speech
this prior meaning ("indivisible") suggests two historically viable readings of the line. First, Emilia may be concluding that the love between
two maids is *more* than the love between the individual ("indivisible")
sexes, a sense that recalls Cockeram's 1623 definition of *individual*: "not
to be parted as man and wife."[68] This reading is not without difficulties,
however, for at precisely the moment she seems to be privileging the love
between maids, endorsing a separatist agenda, and announcing her
refusal to love men, the Amazon Emilia speaks of the indivisibility of the
sexes. That is, to put this point less characterologically and more
discursively: at the moment a figure voices her separation from the
dominant discourse, it erupts into her speech, attempts to contain her
discursive rebellion, and works to reinterpellate her as an "individuall"
(indivisible) subject of patriarchal culture.

But understanding Emilia's "individuall" as "indivisible" also acti-
vates a second reading, one consonant with the explorations of male
friendship with which this chapter began. As I suggested above, Emilia
has noted at length her inseparability from Flavina, their lack (in modern

terms) of "individuality"; thus, the speech may conclude that the true love between two maids is indivisible *in more than simply sex*. "Decking" themselves alike, singing the same songs, Emilia and Flavina are alike in more ways than one – "two bodies individually incorporated." The play thus conjures up same-sex female love in the same discourse that here and elsewhere constitutes collaborative male friendship, but Flavina's death, and the larger plot of the play then effectively foreclose this possibility. Hipolita and Emilia's discussion of friendship concludes by reiterating doubly the central tension of the play: Hipolita admits that "If I were ripe for your perswasion, you / Have saide enough to shake me from the Arme / Of the all noble *Theseus*" – a sentence that exposes the possible primacy of female friendship over marriage. And she asserts that "we, more then his *Pirothous*, possesse / The high throne in [Theseus's] heart" – a sentence that exposes, through denial, the potential primacy of male friendship (p. 15).

Hipolita and Emilia's exchange anticipates the central scene that places male friendship and marriage in tension; Arcite and Palamon's discussion in the prison tower establishes male friendship in familiar language and then, with Emilia's entrance into the garden below, immediately disrupts it. Speaking of their "fortunes ... twyn'd together," Palamon asserts that "two soules / Put in two noble Bodies, let 'em suffer / The gaule of hazard, so they grow together, / Will never sincke" (p. 21). Arcite elaborates, arguing that the prison protects them from "corruption":

> We are young and yet desire the waies of honour,
> That liberty and common Conversation
> The poyson of pure spirits; might like women
> Wooe us to wander from.
> . . .
>   were we at liberty,
> A wife might part us lawfully . . .   (p. 21)

The speech repeatedly connects "liberty" and women; given *conversation*'s sexual valence, discourse outside of friendship is itself registered as promiscuous, made "common" (no suitable activity for noble kinsmen), and associated with the ostensible vagaries of female sexuality. Arcite had earlier lamented that, in prison, the kinsmen will be deprived of male heirs –

> No figures of our selves shall we ev'r see,
> To glad our age, and like young Eagles teach'em
> Boldy to gaze against bright armes, and say
> Remember what your fathers were   (p. 20)

– and here he juxtaposes against the vision of effeminizing liberty an ideal of homosocial reproduction:

> heere being thus together,
> We are an endles mine to one another;
> We are one anothers wife, ever begetting
> New birthes of love; we are father, friends, acquaintance,
> We are in one another, Families,
> I am your heire, and you are mine: This place
> Is our Inheritance . . .   (p. 21)

Within this totalizing schema, the friends come to occupy all social positions in the service of duplicating the homosocial network of power; they are both the only begetters and the only begotten, and "one anothers wife" in this context does not register "homosexuality" in the modern sense so much as it figures each kinsman, reciprocally, in the position of wife in order to further the continuous reproduction of male heirs. As such, the passage recalls Montaigne's scene of carefully non-hierarchized homoerotic intercourse – both the "endles mine" of Montaigne's/Boetie's "plung[ing]" "wills" and the boundary-less, endless "mine" (*meum*) of mutual self-possession.

Into this all-male arrangement, the text introduces Emilia, and, as Arcite's earlier speech had anticipated, the prospective wife eventually "parts [them] lawfully." As in *The Two Gentlemen of Verona*, female-directed male desire disrupts friendship, but this mimetic desire and the lawful imperative of monogamous marriage in which it is made to eventuate again display significant differences from a modern romanticized notion of heterosexuality and companionate marriage. Palamon and Arcite's battle for Emilia is a contention about possession; Arcite wishes to "love her as a woman, to enjoy her" (p. 24), and *enjoy* conflates in its contemporary meanings sexuality and possession of the sexual object.[69] Palamon counters:

> I . . . first saw her; I that tooke possession
> First with mine eye of all those beauties
> In her reveald to mankinde: if thou lou'st her,
> . . .
> Thou art a Traytour *Arcite* and a fellow
> False as thy Title to her.   (p. 24)

This en/titling rhetoric of acquisition and war (Arcite admits that Palamon has "First see[n] the Enemy" [p. 25]) is familiar from Theseus's earlier conflations of marriage and battle, and indeed his marriage to the defeated Amazon queen stages this rhetoric. At the beginning of the tournament that will finally settle Emilia's marriage-partner, Theseus again voices the rhetoric of possession:

> You are the victours meed, the price, and garlond
> To crowne the Questions title.
> ...
> You are the Treasure, and must needes be by
> To give the Service pay.   (pp. 80–81)

Like the Jailer's Daughter's subplot, which repeatedly emphasizes the value placed on virginity in this culture, Theseus's insistence on Emilia as "title" poses the central question of this play: of these two identical and identically desiring friends, which one shall own this maidenhead?

The text proposes several solutions to the contention of friendship and monogamous marriage. Emilia voices one quickly rejected possibility:

> Were they metamorphisd
> Both into one; oh why? there were no woman
> Worth so composd a Man: their single share,
> Their noblenes peculiar to them, gives
> The prejudice of disparity values shortnes
> To any Lady breathing . . .   (p. 82)[70]

The *ménage à deux* Emilia proposes both pushes against the limits of marital monogamy and reinscribes its misogynist hierarchy; at the same time, by uniting the friends "both into one," the solution takes seriously the rhetoric of homogeneous friendship. Theseus's more radical proposal, the death of one of the kinsmen as decided in a martial game, privileges monogamous marriage over friendship and forces a differentiation of the kinsmen that the play has obsessively resisted. The pyramid at the center of Theseus's wargame stands as an emblem of the hierarchy he wishes to instill between them and, as a monument ascending from a broad base to a point, might be said to figure the movement the play makes from multiple kinsmen to one. As Puttenham illustrates, the pyramid was also a textual figure inscribing hierarchy and singular royal or religious authority.[71]

Yet even as the play enacts this larger impetus toward marriage at the expense of friendship – one kinsman will die, the other "enjoy" Emilia – there remain ambiguities. Theseus and Pirithous's friendship, for example, remains "individual" throughout the play, even (as I suggested earlier) during the ceremony of marriage to Hipolita. Furthermore, Pirithous and a messenger's elaborate descriptions of the warriors accompanying Palamon and Arcite in the contest are a sustained, appreciative *blason* of male bodies; the messenger says of one:

his armes are brawny
Linde with strong sinewes: To the shoulder peece,
Gently they swell, like women new conceav'd,
Which speakes him *prone* to *labour*, never fainting
Vnder the waight of Armes ...   (p. 66, my emphasis)

"Are they all thus?" Theseus asks (p. 67), emphasizing the repetitiveness
of this rhetorical reproduction of and within homosociality thus gently
"conceav'd." Furthermore, though the contest is itself competitive, it
includes within it a collaborative structure, the three knights who
accompany the main contestants; Theseus says to Palamon of his
warriors, "call your Lovers from the stage of death, / Whom I adopt my
Frinds" (p. 88). The combat is both contest and, as a servant notes, a
"consummation" (p. 83).

In other words, though the play seems to privilege a competitive mode
eventuating in differentiation over a collaborative friendship in which
Palamon and Arcite are inseparable,[72] the play undercuts such a position,
exposing Theseus's solution to insistent criticism. Emilia asks, after
Arcite is declared winner, "Is this wynning?" and notes, "[the heavenly
powers] charge me live to comfort this unfriended, / This miserable
Prince, that cuts away a life more worthy from him, then all women ..."
(p. 84). This is, to be sure, no critique of her own position, but it begins
at least to suggest the cost to friendship of the marriage imperative and
recalls Arcite's victory speech: "*Emily,* / To buy you, I have lost what's
deerest to me, / Save what is bought, and yet I purchase cheaply, / As I
doe rate your value" (p. 83). Arcite's analysis in economic terms of the
relative cost of "maidenhead" and friendship is elaborated in Palamon's
speech following Arcite's death:

O Cosen,
That we should things desire, which doe *cost* us
The *losse* of our desire; That *nought* could *buy*
Deare love, but *losse* of *deare* love.   (p. 88, my emphasis)

Significantly, Palamon addresses this speech not to his bride but to his
dead kinsman in terms that reiterate that kinsman's own speech. His
words suggest both that Arcite's desire for Emilia resulted in the loss of
desire (death), and that Palamon's own desire (for Emilia) resulted in the
loss of his desire (for Arcite); these readings are indistinguishable, fused
at the collaborative, individual pronoun "we." Furthermore, the final
line suggests the paucity (from one perspective) of the exchange of
friendly for marital love. Such strenuous questioning of the play's
outcome ends only when Theseus decrees the end of discourse and the

play: "Let us be thankefull / For that which is, and with you leave dispute / That are above our question ..." (p. 88).

Reading backward: preliminaries

There may be justification for concluding, rather than beginning, this discussion of eroticism and collaboration in *The Two Noble Kinsmen* with that play's prologue, for it is not entirely clear whether the prologue was part of the play's first performances or was added later for a revival, as may be implied by its description of a play as a married woman who "after first nights stir" nevertheless "still retaines / More of the maid to sight" (lines 7–8). Whatever the occasion of its composition and performance,[73] the prologue attunes its audience to the recurrent issue of maidenhead and its costliness:

> NEW Playes, and Maydenheads, are neare a kin,
> Much follow'd both, for both much mony g'yn,
> If they stand sound, and well: And a good Play
> (Whose modest Sceanes blush on his marriage day,
> And shake to loose his honour) is like hir
> That after holy Tye, and first nights stir
> Yet still is Modestie, and still retaines
> More of the maid to sight, than Husbands paines ...   (lines 1–8)[74]

Playing on the governing trope of kinship, the prologue feminizes the play and inserts it into a masculinist economy that buys and sells women's bodies as valuable commodities. The lines furthermore establish a comparison between the new, virginal play, and the good play, a wife who continues to look virginal, despite "Husbandes paines." The prologue thus raises the issue so central to the play: who owns, who takes paines with, this particular maydenhead/play? Who is its husband?[75]

The prologue carefully establishes the play's Chaucerian patrilineage – "It has a noble Breeder, and a pure" – but it does not explicitly supply an identity for the husband. If one reads the quarto forward, beginning with its title page, the prologue seems to suggest that the collaborating playwrights Fletcher and Shakspeare contend (as husbands) against the fatherly authority of the medieval *auctor*, Chaucer:

> For to say Truth, it were an endlesse thing,
> And too ambitious to aspire to him;
> Weak as we are, and almost breathlesse swim
> In this deepe water.

Yet the prologue itself does not support such a reading (it refers, cryptically, to a singular "wrighter"), and the more consistent answer to the question of the husband is the theatrical company represented by the prologue-speaker's collaborative "we." In other words, if we read the preliminaries of the quarto *Two Noble Kinsmen* backward, we begin to see the ways in which collaboration and authorship enter the discourse of this play at different points. The names of the play's "wrighter(s)" (so prominent in modern readings intent on divining separate authors) would not have figured in a performance, and the prologue's spelling "wrighter" serves to remind us, to the extent that the prologue does acknowledge the play's composition, of the play*wright*'s status as a worker in the (co)labor of the playhouse – a craftsman and repairer (cf. ship*wright*) more than a singular originating "author" in the modern sense.[76] The prologue's major emphasis is on the theatrical company's "following" and "giving money" for new and virginal playscripts, its taking "paines" with those scripts, and its attempt to secure (within a form of representation less socially privileged than Chaucer's "fam'd workes") the "Noblenesse" of the play. The all-male theatrical company collaboratively husbands the play (*"We* pray *our* Play may be so"), which may itself retain a male gender, despite the effeminizing metaphor: "a good Play / (Whose modest Sceanes blush on *his* marriage day, / And shake to loose *his* honour) is like hir . . ." (my emphasis).[77]

But if the prologue foregrounds the all-male collaboration of the theatrical enterprise, it also suggests the extent to which theatrical production depended on a larger collaboration between acting company and audience, for the theatre audience (here also gendered male) likewise "follows" and "gives money" to see the play.[78] Furthermore, that collaboration is the cooperation of the theatre audience and acting company working together in "deepe" Chaucerian waters: "Do but you hold out / Your helping hands, and we shall take about, / And some-things doe to save us . . ." In other words, though the prologue is very careful to establish the "Noblenesse" of the play through appeals to well-bred Chaucerian authority, it significantly broadens the collaborative arena – the number of prospective husbands for the maiden it represents – resisting Theseus's decree of monogamy. The play's epilogue, more-over, initially predicates favorable reception of the play on the ubiquity of male–female desire ("He that has / Lov'd a yong hansome wench then, show his face: / Tis strange if none be heere . . ."), but it proceeds, like the prologue, to stage dramatic production in the language of collaborative affection with which we began: "ye shall have ere long / I dare say many a better [play], to prolong / Your old loves to us." "Gentlemen," it concludes, "good night."

Reading further backward in the 1634 quarto of *The Two Noble Kinsmen*, we can see that the title page that precedes the prologue adds another layer to the play's collaboration. That title page constructs "M^r. John Fletcher and M^r. William Shakspeare" as Gentlemen (Fig. 3), establishing a correspondence between its two noble kinsmen and the two gentle playwrights. This is not to say, however, that the play simply thematizes the collaboration of the title page; rather, the title page makes possible such a reading (twenty years after the play's "first nights stir") by constructing an analogy between its entitling kinsmen and its titled playwrights. The title page in fact suggests the retrospectivism of this reading, for it glosses Fletcher and Shakspeare as "the memorable Worthies of their time."

In other words, the title page only *seems* to anticipate the trajectory of *Two Noble Kinsmen* criticism (who is the singular husband of this maiden?) and to secure an allegorical reading in which playwrights contend for the ownership/husbanding of the play/maidenhead. What we might call the quarto's negotiation between its parts – a play-text resonant of its performances in the theatre between 1613 and 1634 and a title page from 1634 – is not an easy one-to-one (or rather two-to-two) correspondence.[79] Collaboration as practice (Shakspeare and Fletcher writing *The Two Noble Kinsmen*) does not necessarily result in collaboration as theme (Palamon and Arcite collaboratively desiring maidenhead). Instead, we can say that the culturally resonant values of homosocial, collaborative friendship are at play in the playscript, the prologue's description of collaborative theatrical production, and the quarto title page's construction of Fletcher and Shakspeare as gentlemen – but not in a way that relates practice and product in a straightforward relation of cause and effect. Only in 1634, reading forward, does this become a viable interpretation. As the texts at the beginning of this chapter make clear, these discourses (collaboration as "theme" or "content") were instrumental in the period, constructing and reproducing the English gentleman and those who aspired to his position. The *practice* of writing for the theatre (and the identity-formation of the wrighter) is not beyond the scope of this construction; long before he became an author in the fully modern sense of that word, Shakespeare acquired a coat of arms and became a gentleman.

The title page constitutes Fletcher and Shakspeare as bracketed "Gent."s and creates the possibility of reading them into the play as contending gentlemen; nevertheless, it does not in the end (or rather, the beginning) insist – like Theseus, or dozens of more modern observers – on wrighterly monogamy, the union of a single text and single author. Interestingly, in the play's prologue, as we have seen, the resuscitated voice of singular author/ity, Chaucer, *does* assume that the play has a singular, agonistic playwright – "O fan / From me the witles chaffe of

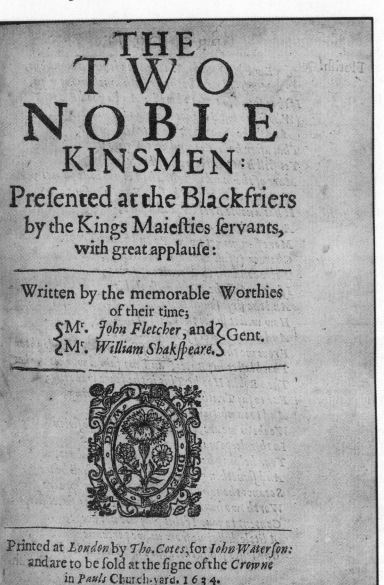

Figure 3   Title page: Mr. John Fletcher, and Mr. William Shakspeare. Gent., *THE TWO NOBLE KINSMEN* (London: Tho. Cotes for Iohn Waterson, 1634).

such *a wrighter* / That blastes my Bayes" – but Chaucer is returned to his grave without further authoritative intervention. The plural attribution he briefly contests is made only more complex, less monogamous, by the collaborative texture of the play that follows. One of the play's subplots, Gerrold's morris dance, is built around the antimasque to Francis Beaumont's *Masque of the Inner Temple and Gray's Inn*, performed at court to celebrate the marriage of James's daughter Elizabeth in 1613.[80] Tellingly named, the Jailer's Daughter may signify an escape from the very idea of constraining authorial attribution, for her discourse is a patch-work of songs and ballads – some associated with recognizable poets like Philip Sidney, others that echo and rewrite the borrowed voicings of other staged madwomen. In short, we might say that the quarto title page depicts Fletcher and Shakspeare, like Brathwait's two acquainted gentlemen, jointly speaking their Chaucerian plot; their "motto" is both a *blason* of its own noble lineage and an aphorism, a phrase with no single authorial source. "To be sure your stile may passe for currant, as the richest alloy," Henry Peacham instructs in *The Compleat Gentleman*, "imitate the best Authors as well in Oratory as History";[81] like currency, Peacham's gentlemanly style circulates, and it is an agglomeration, an alloying of genres and authors, a collaboration of what's "currant" and what's past/passed.

Playhouse

I am arguing here for a reconsideration of collaboration in dramatic writing as a mode of homoerotic textual production existing prior to and eventually alongside the more familiar mode of singular authorship, but I do not mean to suggest that collaboration, any more than the absolutist patriarchal model of authorship that (as we will see in subsequent chapters) began to supersede it, exists independent of political power and ideological construction. So often in the texts we have been considering, for example, collaboration is enabled by, or sees itself producing, a female body as textual corpus. To describe his collaboratively produced essays, "patched ... together of divers members," Montaigne quotes Horace to display a "monstrous bod[y]," part-woman, part-fish, and Florio calls his translation and reproduction of Montaigne's *Essayes* a "defective edition (since all translations are reputed femalls, delivered at second hand)."[82] More egregiously, as we have seen, the marriage that reunites *The Two Gentlemen of Verona* is produced through the violence of attempted rape and its immediate forgiveness. In looking at these texts, then, I want to disengage collaboration from an anachronistic notion of authorship, but not without also illustrating the ways in which collaboration is itself implicated in and enabled by discourses of gender, eroticism, social class, and power.

As a concluding emblem for these relations, we can consider John Aubrey's recollection of another pair of gentleman-playwrights:

> There was a wonderfull consimility of phansey between [Francis Beaumont] and Mr. John Fletcher, which caused the dearnesse of friendship between them ... They lived together on the Banke side, not far from the Play-house, both batchelors; lay together ... had one wench in the house between them, which they did so admire; the same cloathes and cloake, &c., between them.[83]

Aubrey is often discounted as an unreliable witness to the events of the seventeenth century, but, as with any reading that attempts to account for the textuality of history, I think it is important to take seriously the terms in which he frames his discussion of dramatic and domestic collaboration in the period.

As I hope is clear, it is explicitly *not* my desire here, or in this book at large, to diagnose or attribute a particular twentieth-century sexuality to Beaumont or Fletcher or any other playwright, but rather to discuss the ways in which modes of collective writing and reading are inscribed in particularly historical discourses of sex, and the ways in which the material facts of cohabitation are encoded (and reworked) in the collaborative writing of this period. Though I am aware that some will find in Aubrey's anecdote evidence that Beaumont and Fletcher were "gay" in our modern terms and that the woman "between them" functions as (in the words of one person responding to this work) "a cover," it is nevertheless important to point out this description's seeming obliviousness to the public/private distinctions we have come to see as central to a modern discourse of sexuality, the way in which there seems to be nothing to cover, no need for closet space in this shared household.

What we can see here, instead, is that the terms in which Aubrey describes the living arrangements of two dramatic collaborators resonate with the others we have seen in conduct books, essays, play-texts, and title pages: the "dearnesse of friendship"; the doubly reflexive "*con*simility of phansey"; the collaborative theatricality and intersubjective indiscernability (individuality) of two playwrights who, in a culture where clothes literally and legally made the man, share the "same cloathes and cloake, &c., between them." Co*habit*ation in multiple senses. Aubrey's "&c." may both open further erotic possibilities and gesture toward what he may take as the absolute conventionality of his statement: so obvious as not needing to be named among Christians.[84]

We may never know what happened in Beaumont and Fletcher's

shared bed – though we know, from Alan Bray's important work on male friendship in the period that men routinely shared beds in this culture, in ways that were often erotically charged.[85] Likewise, we may never know the position of the "one wench in the house between them, which they did so admire," though it is at least clear in Aubrey's locution that she is more "which" than "whom" – not clearly differentiated as a servant or a sexual partner.[86]

That Aubrey's anecdote situated "on the Banke side, not far from the Play-house" reproduces terms and structures circulating in genres and cultural locations as seemingly distant as gentlemen's conduct books and the channel-crossing and elite dedications of Florio's translated essays is, I think, important – and my justification for leading you, in work focused on the theatre, to these other locales. For, at the same time that we want to be clear about the material conditions of collaboration in the theatres, we cannot ignore that those conditions were inseparable from, and often understood within, the discourses that structured and enabled life, reading, and writing elsewhere in early modern England.

The knowledge that *is* available in this anecdote, in other words, is a knowledge that forces us to distance ourselves from a modern paradigm of artistic creation – in which writing transcends living, in which textual production and the enculturated forms of eroticism are held to be strictly separate, dividual. Living arrangements and writing arrangements share a common vocabulary, and Aubrey's brief life of Beaumont (which is also, inseparably, a brief life of Fletcher) obliterates our sense of separate living, working, sleeping, and writing space. Living near the Play-house; playing house. Writing together; lying together. "No lesse selfely than sociably united." "Gentlemen, good night."

3   Representing authority: patriarchalism, absolutism, and the author on stage

> And now at last, by the Mercy of God, and the continuance of our Labours, it being brought vnto such a conclusion, as that we haue great hope that the Church of *England* shall reape good fruit thereby; we hold it our duety to offer it to your MAIESTIE, not onely as to our King and Soueraigne, but as to the principall moouer and Author of the Worke.
>
> Translators' dedication of the 1611 Holy Bible, "the Authorized Version"[1]

> I will reade politicke Authours.   *Twelfe Night, Or what you will*[2]

In the previous chapter we saw the brief resurrection of Chaucer, as narrated by the prologue to *The Two Noble Kinsmen*. There the prologue's speaker imagines that a bad production of the play would

> shake the bones of that good man,
> And make him cry from underground, O fan
> From me the witles chaffe of such a wrighter
> That blastes my Bayes, and my fam'd workes makes lighter
> Then Robin Hood ...

This chapter is an extended amplification of Chaucer's brief interjection ("O fan from me the witles chaffe ... "), for his intrusion into the text here as a figuration of the author is by no means isolated. Chaucer does not in a strict sense *appear* here; no actor embodies him on stage, and his words are merely imagined by the prologue as a hypothetical "cry from underground." Other author figures in this period do, however, appear on stage to speak. This chapter, then, traces the tentative emergence of figurations of authorship in plays of the early seventeenth century, within a theatrical and textual practice that until this time had reserved no place for authorship as we know it.

The Two Noble Kinsmen names Chaucer its story's "noble Breeder," and, as we will see, authorship is during the era of its emergence inseparable from discourses of paternity and political authority, within a culture that normatively privileges fatherhood and nobility. The 1598 edition of Chaucer's collected works, for example, advertised on its title page that it contained not only "Arguments to euery Booke gathered," but also "His Portraiture and Progenie shewed"; the volume included an engraving entitled "THE PROGENIE OF GEFFREY CHAUCER" (Fig. 4), an elaborate display of the author's paternity.[3] As I will show in this analysis, paternity is not in this period merely a metaphor or analogy for authorship, as has often been suggested or assumed.[4] The mutual implication and constant conjunction of these terms in Renaissance discourse is complex, and I want to suggest that a recurrent evocation of paternity as (simply) a "metaphor" for authorship both suggests that it is a trope to be engaged or disengaged by writers at will and vastly underestimates its power and instrumentality in certain sex/gender systems.

What was an author?

> ... the Kinges were the authors & makers of the lawes, and not the lawes of the Kings.   James I, *The Trve Lawe of free Monarchies* (1598).[5]

The word *author* now means "the writer of a book or books";[6] our customary modern usage greatly simplifies (even obscures) the complex network of meanings the word inhabited in the sixteenth and seventeenth centuries, a network we can only begin to glimpse in words like *authorize*, *authority*, and *authoritarian*.[7] One cluster of significations of *author* in this period was a "person who originates or gives existence to anything," including what the *OED* calls "things material" – that is, "An inventor, constructor, or founder," "The Creator," "He who gives rise to or causes an action, event, circumstance, state, or condition of things," "He who authorizes or instigates; the prompter or mover." *Author* also meant "One who begets; a father, an ancestor." In addition to the familiar modern meaning ("One who sets forth written statements; the composer or writer of a treatise or book"), *author* could also refer to "The person on whose authority a statement is made; an authority, an informant." In the not so distant past, the word had also suggested "One who has authority over others; a director, ruler, commander."[8]

There are a number of things to remark upon in the *OED*'s list of almost entirely obsolete definitions for the word *author*. Not only are these seemingly disparate meanings contemporaneous in the sixteenth and seventeenth centuries, but they also all enter the English language at approximately the same time (that is, according to the *OED*, the 1370s–80s). In other words, there was a time when it was not possible to say that, for example, paternity was a metaphor for authorship – that one thing was being described in the language of the other. In many of *OED*'s

Figure 4   "THE PROGENIE OF GEFFREY CHAUCER," in THE Workes of
our Antient and Learned English Poet, GEFFREY CHAVCER, newly
Printed (London: by Adam Islip at the charges of Bonham Norton,
1598).

early historical examples of *author*, it is virtually impossible to separate out (as the *OED* nevertheless attempts to do) what we would now consider the distinct meanings of the word. Here, for example, is *OED*'s first recorded citation for the recognizably modern definition, "One who sets forth written statements ... ": "c1380 WYCLIF *Wks.* (1880) 267 If holy writt be fals, certis god autor ther-of is fals."[9] *Author* here obviously carries with it meanings beyond "writer," including "The Creator" (and thus, "a father"), "he who authorizes or instigates," "an authority," and "one who has authority over others." Likewise, as the first epigraph to this chapter suggests, one regularly finds occurrences of the word in now-unexpected places; in a context of "Labour" and fruitfulness about which we will have much to say, the writers of what is arguably the period's largest collaborative project – the translation of the "Authorized Version" of the Bible in 1611 – cite James I both as "King and Soueraigne," and as "the principall moouer and Author of the Worke." We should also note the relentless gendering of the *OED*'s list – the marking of this entire constellation of meanings as male, and the attendant difficulty of female authorship in such a context, a topic to which we will return in chapters 4 and 5.

Terminology is central to an understanding of these issues, and I will use the term *author/ity* to signal the discursive situation I have outlined above, an era in English culture, extending well into the seventeenth century, when *author* carried with it several strands of meaning only beginning to separate – or rather, only beginning to form *as strands*. The slash in the term *author/ity* will help us to keep in mind a word signalling both the *author* (the writer) that is within it and the authority that so often accompanies the use of the term in this period. We can take as an influential (that is, culturally privileged and widely circulated) example of this conjunction a set of texts by and about James I. As the 1611 Bible's dedication suggests, he is a figure situated at the intersection of contemporaneous meanings of *author*: authority, father, instigator, ruler, writer.

Authorized versions

> Remember thee?
> Yea, from the Table of my Memory
> Ile wipe away all triuiall fond Records,
> All sawes of Bookes, all formes, all presures past
> That youth and obseruation coppied there;
> And thy Commandment all alone shall liue
> Within the Booke and Volume of my Braine ...
>
> *The Tragedie of Hamlet, Prince of Denmarke* (TLN 782–88)

First published in 1616, *The Workes of the Most High and Mightie Prince, Iames, By the grace of God Kinge of Great Brittaine France & Ireland Defendor of ye Faith &c.* is a locus of author/ity in all its senses. This folio volume's engraved title page displays, in a way that can best be described as overdetermined, the symbols of royal authority (Fig. 5); an elaborate edifice containing the allegorical figures of Religion and Peace, it is topped with royal arms and crowns representing James's four kingdoms, and two angels descend to bestow a larger, heavenly crown and the motto "SVPER: EST."[10] The facing frontispiece portrait of James (Fig. 6) also deploys the signs of political and religious authority; the portrait depicts James crowned, enthroned, and in full regal dress, holding the orb and scepter. On a table to his right are the staff of Justice and, significantly, a book entitled *Verbum Dei.* The portrait is itself both under- and over-written by divine words; above James is the motto "BEATI PACIFICI" and below a poem noting that, more than crowns and triumphs, "knowledge makes the KING most like his maker."[11] Both of these texts emphasize the author-as-"maker." James's *Workes* thus emulate and derive authority from the *verbum dei* suffusing the emblematic engravings; they imitate and are "SVPER"-vised by the divine author.

The preliminary materials of the *Workes* further emphasize that the authority James emulates and himself displays is patriarchal, in the restricted sense.[12] The *Workes* are dedicated to James's heir, in language that imitates the divine father–author and bespeaks James's position as both *pater familias* and *pater patriae*: "TO THE THRICE ILLVSTRIOVS AND Most Excellent Prince CHARLES, THE ONELY SONNE OF OVR SOVERAIGNE LORD The King" (a3). Like the earlier *Basilikon Doron*, dedicated to the now-dead Prince Henry, this book demands the son's emulation; James Montagu, Bishop of Winton, the collector of the *Workes*, writes in his dedication: "these *Workes* come not to you, as vsually Bookes doe to men of great *Dignitie*, for *Patronage* and *Protection*; for Protection is properly from iniurie; and that the Royall *Author* of them is best able to right: But to you they come partly for preseruation ... and more principally for a Patterne" (a3ᵛ-a4). The authority to protect the works is already vested in "the Royall *Author*," a use of the term that clearly brings with it the sense of "writer" but also of "right-er" – in the *OED*'s phrase, "one who has authority over others; a director, ruler, commander."[13] The duty of the son, however, is "preservation" and "pattern" – two objectives that are hardly mutually exclusive, as Winton makes clear.[14] The son is to imitate the father, a relationship mediated by the *Workes*, and in taking the *Workes* as his pattern he himself becomes their embodied preservation. The objective is the similitude of a purely

Figure 5   Title page: James I, *THE WORKES OF THE MOST HIGH AND MIGHTY PRINCE, IAMES, By the grace of God Kinge of Great Brittaine France & Ireland Defendor of ye Faith &c.* (London: Iames, Bishop of Winton, 1616)

Figure 6   Frontispiece portrait: *THE WORKES OF THE MOST HIGH AND MIGHTY PRINCE, IAMES, By the grace of God Kinge of Great Brittaine France & Ireland Defendor of ye Faith &c.* (London: Iames, Bishop of Winton, 1616).

patriarchal reproduction, as Winton suggests later in his "Preface to the Reader": "*GOD* hath left his *Maiestie* a *Sonne*; a *Prince*, as in outward *Liniaments*, so in inward *Abiliments*, (I need say no more) an *Alter-Idem*, a second-selfe" (e2ᵛ). Just as Charles reproduces the body ("outward Liniaments") of James, the book seeks to imprint itself as a "pattern" on his inward person. The word *Abiliments* suggests the scope of the intended authorial, fatherly control; in a sense strange to modern readers used to the idea of inwardly generated capabilities, *abiliments* yokes the prince's "abilities" and what we might call (remembering the senses of the French *habiller*, to dress, to prepare) the interpellated clothing of the royal self.[15]

If the Bishop of Winton seeks to extend patriarchal control in the direction of James's son, he is no less interested in tracing James's author/ity as a writer back to combined political and ecclesiastical authority. In a way that perhaps indicates how *author* and its related terms are beginning to separate into discrete meanings, Winton works in his "Preface to the Reader" to keep these strands together. He defends the king against the charge that kings should not write books: "since that Booke-writing is growen into a Trade; it is dishonorable for a *King* to write bookes; as it is for him to be a Practitioner in a *Profession*" (b2ᵛ). That is, he defends James against the space that threatens to open up between the author/writer and the author/authority. His lengthy defense is instructive, for it cites as the beginning of royal authorship no less an authority than God, the first of numerous biblical precedents:

First to beginne with the *King of Kings* God himselfe, who as he doth all things for our good; doeth he many things for our Imitation. It pleased his Diuine wisedome to bee the first in this Rancke [i.e. of kings], that we reade of, that did euer write. Hee wrote, and the writing was the writing, saith *Moses*, of God ... the matter was in Stone cut into two Tables, and the Tables were the worke of God written on both sides. *Diuines* hold, that the Heart is the principall Seate of the Soule; which Soule of ours is the immediate worke of God, as these Tables were the immediate worke of his owne fingers ... And certainly from this little *Library*, that God hath erected within vs, is the foundation of all our Learning layd; So that people Ciuillized doe account themselues depriued of one of the best abilities of nature, if they be not somewhat inabled by writing ... (b3)[16]

Winton's example carefully aligns the meanings of *author*; father, king, authority, originator, and writer are fused in the first writing of the divine author. Furthermore, the example of the ten commandments reiterates at another level the patriarchal inscription of Charles we noticed in the dedication. James writes the *Workes*, which serve as a pattern for Charles's "inward Abiliments"; likewise, God writes the

Decalogue with "his owne fingers," and inscribes the law in "us" as a "little Library." The patriarchal movement of this analogy (from God to "us," from James to Charles) is reiterated in the trajectory of Winton's argument: "From these tables of God, wee may come to the writing of our Blessed Sauiour ... " (b3) – like Charles, an "Onely Sonne." The argument proceeds through a number of biblical precedents, the "Greeke *Fathers*" and "Latine *Fathers*," and the British monarchs.

That James's *Workes* should encode patriarchal absolutism – a theory and practice of government in which the king's authority over the kingdom is said to be analogous to that of the father over the household and derived from God – is not surprising. Citing its widespread appearance, Susan Dwyer Amussen writes that "[w]hatever their vision of the origin or nature of government, the analogy between family and state remained a basic tool for most writers of political theory in the seventeenth century";[17] influential work by Gordon Schochet and more recently Jonathan Goldberg has detailed James's prominent position in the formulation and circulation of this discourse and its mutually reinforcing functions at both the national and the familial levels.[18]

As Schochet points out, however, patriarchal absolutism was often derived from the imperative of the fifth commandment – a more specific example of God's writing than Winton provides, patriarchal in both its mode of production and its content (at least as interpreted by Renaissance writers). *God and the King* (a 1615 pamphlet published, purchased, and studied at James's command) cites this moment of divine writing as the basis of its argument: "the fift commandement, *honour thy Father and thy Mother*: where as wee are required to honour the *Father* of priuat families, so much more the *Father* of our Country and the whole kingdome."[19] I want to assert that, in tracing the continuities and ruptures of the king/father/authority equation in texts from this period, we cannot simply bracket or separate out authorship. James does not merely write (and thus become an author of) texts that encode a theory of patriarchal absolutism. The construction of his (and, as I will suggest, others') authorship in this period is bound up with the very terms he is writing about.[20]

The Trve Lawe of free Monarchies – James's treatise on government first published in 1598, widely circulated in the early years of his reign in England, and included in the 1616 *Workes* – articulates the familiar, foundational comparisons of patriarchal absolutism: "The King towardes his people is rightly compared to a father of children, and to a head of a bodie composed of diuers members."[21] Both of these comparisons crucially recirculate in the Bishop of Winton's formulation of the king's authorship in the 1616 preface:

yet hath it been euer esteemed a matter commendable to collect [workes] together, and incorporate them into one Body, that we may behold at once, what diuers Off-springs haue proceeded from one braine ... to labour much in the recouering those that haue bene lost; to giue euery childe the owne Father; to euery Booke the trew Author. (b1ᵛ–b2ᵛ)

Authorship, and the re-membering of a dismembered authorial canon, cannot here be separated from questions of political authority and patriarchal lineage. "[T]he discourse and the direction flows from the head," James writes in *Trve Lawe* (D3ᵛ), and Winton in a sense compresses the reproductive and corporeal analogies when he desires to "behold at once, what diuers Off-springs haue proceeded from one braine." We might also remark on the compression performed in the seemingly interchangeable phrases that end this passage. "To giue euery childe the owne Father" is apparently the same as "to [giue] euery Booke the trew Author," but it is important to note here not only the equation of children and books we saw earlier in the inscription of "the onely sonne" Charles, but also, given that *owne* and *one* are often homonyms in this period,[22] how almost imperceptibly the possession of legitimacy ("the owne Father") slides into the singularity of fatherhood (the "one" Father) and the "trew" attribution of singular, possessive authorship.

The collection of dismembered textual and familial "parts" into a singular corpus – the urgency of Winton's determination "to preserue in one body, what might easily haue bin lost in parts" (a3ᵛ) – was of course a prime political consideration in 1616. With the death of Prince Henry in 1612, Charles became the only remaining male heir ("the onely sonne") of a regime that had invested much discursive energy in government by patriarchal absolutism, promising and naturalizing the smooth succession from father to son in a realm that had only recently emerged from decades of heirless anxiety under Elizabeth.[23] Winton, whose motto as both royal pastor and textual gatherer is "*Dispersa colligere*," works to shepherd in the threatening diversity of James's scattered corpus: "of these *Workes*, some were out before; some other of them neuer saw light before; and others were almost lost and gone; or at least abused by false copies, to their owne disgrace and his *Maiesties* great dishonour" (a3ᵛ). In a paradigm that aligns father, king, and writer, this textual situation (framed in language familiar to students of the later Shakespeare folio) is politically volatile. The gathering of the *Workes*, the re-membering of a dispersed authorial corpus, thus works to authorize Charles's succession. (Hamlet's textualizing promise – "Remember thee?" – takes on an added resonance in this context.) Conversely, Charles, "preserue[s James] in one body"; writing to Charles of his dead brother, Winton declares, "His part ... is falne to your Lot" (a3), and Charles's succession (his gathering to himself of "lost and gone" "parts") thus authorizes the collected *Workes*.

By citing at length the discourses of author/ity working in the *Workes* of James, I do not mean to suggest that James's book was the originating, controlling, or sole site of these author/itative discourses. As the *OED* suggests, the conjunction of writer, father, and authority was assumed long before 1616; James's reign, however, brought these terms to a place of prominence in English culture. The *Workes*, we might say, are merely an influential volume on a shelf that also includes the 1598 treatise *The Trve Lawe*, the 1611 Authorized Version of the Bible, and the 1615 pamphlet *God and the King*. Nor was the figure of the king the only locus of these discourses; as Jonathan Goldberg and Catherine Belsey have shown, for example, patriarchal authority was an organizing trope of familial portraiture throughout the Stuart period.[24] It is important furthermore to stress that even so culturally privileged a text as the king's collected works did not eliminate or circumscribe competing contemporary discourses. In the very process of gathering the *Workes* together, Winton raises the prospect of a dismembered, scattered royal corpus. And in his review of the succession of royal writers, he cannot entirely ignore two figures troubling James's insistent patriarchalism: his predecessor, Elizabeth, and his mother, Mary Queen of Scots – though he emphasizes their translations (a genre often associated with women in this period) and needlework.

I want to take the king's book as a marker for a conjunction of discourses we would now separate into the fields of sexuality, textuality, and political authority, and to shift our focus in the direction of texts written for and performed in the theatre in the early decades of the seventeenth century. The idea of the author, I will suggest – insofar as it takes a tentative place within a genre and material practice that had been traditionally resistant to its articulation – emerges in conjunction with a language of patriarchal absolutism. As the remainder of this chapter demonstrates, that emergence is articulated and contested by contemporary play-texts in a number of ways.

Resurrecting the author

The theatre of this period usually reserved no space in its play-texts for their writers; all the evidence we have from the period suggests that the production of plays in the theatre tended to distance the performance of a play from, rather than connect it to, those who wrote it. Writers only occasionally profited directly from the performance of their work, and, as is well known, they held no proprietary rights in the scripts they sold to the acting companies. Unless a playwright was also a member of the acting company, he would not have appeared on stage, and, if he did act, his participation would not have been restricted only to those plays he wrote or assisted in writing.[25] Furthermore, there is no easy (that is, conventional) fit between the "I" of a script and its writer(s); plays did not include the ostensibly transparent authorial "I" cultivated in some other period genres, and the actor presented the words of his part as his own, speaking as if on his own authority. Indeed, the idea of attribution was treated as irrelevant or was resisted in the theatres; as Timothy Murray notes, the "identification and glorification of sources was not a convention cherished by the players, who preferred disguised sources, collaboration, alterable texts."[26]

In this general context, then, it is noteworthy that, in the first two decades of the seventeenth century, London theatres performed at least ten plays that *did* elaborately attribute sources, tracing their writing back to an origin. In each of these cases, the source is literally embodied on stage; the author of a source-text – for example, Guicciardini in *The Divils Charter* (1607), Gower in *Pericles, Prince of Tyre* (1609), Homer in *The Golden Age*, *The Siluer Age*, and *The Brazen Age* (1609–13), and Bardh in *The Valiant Welshman* (1610–15?) – is resurrected in order to present, to re-present, the tale he had ostensibly written.[27]

These representations of authors function in several ways that reiterate what we have noticed about the word *author* above. First, Homer, Gower, et al. work to authorize (give authority to) the plays they present by appealing to "antient and learned" pre-texts – to use the 1598 Chaucer folio's terms. In *The Golden Age*, Homer, "the man / That flourish'd in the worlds first infancy," claims to be the very origin of language in the world: "When it was yong, and knew not how to speake, / I taught it speech, and vnderstanding both / Euen in the Cradle" (pp. 5–6).[28] Homer's assertions of priority carry a parental (if not clearly patriarchal) resonance, as the evocation of infancy, speech-instruction, and cradle may suggest. Gower, often speaking in a stylized Middle English, authorizes the play he presents by citing the Latin formula "Et bonum quo Antiquius eo melius" – the older a good thing is, the better it is.[29] As we will see, his relation to a patriarchal model is more complex.

Second, these figures also author-ize (give an author to) their plays. As presenters of the play's action, they clearly draw upon the conventions that constitute figures like the chorus, prologue, and others that seem to speak with the authoritative "we" of the acting company; however, with the appearance of Homer or Gower or Guicciardini, the play makes particular the figure presenting and supervising the action. It invests specific agency in his presentation in a way that these other figures do not replicate. A useful comparison is the relatively amorphous figure that narrates *The Life of Henry the Fift*. Presenting himself as one who "prompt[s]" "those that haue not read the Story," this speaker is variably identified as "Prologue," then "Prologue-like," and thereafter "Chorus." His play-ending gesture toward author/ity is likewise nonspecific: "Thus farre, with rough, and all-vnable Pen, / Our bending Author hath pursu'd the Story" (TLN 3368–69). "Our bending Author" (and it is not entirely clear whether this term refers to a playwright or an earlier writer of "the Story") is unidentified and subject to the authority of the theatrical company – a description that parallels Bentley's findings on the relation of writers to the companies.[30]

In a way that draws upon but diverges significantly from normative theatrical practice in the period, then, the authorial presenters in a significant group of plays that includes *The Golden Age*, *Pericles*, and *The Divil's Charter* establish a space for an identified author-figure on the stage. This is not, however, to say either that this authorial space is uncontested or that the author as we know it simply arises on the stage in the first decade of the seventeenth century. The emergence of the author is, as we will see, a tentative process that draws upon already-extant discourses (here, classicism, author/ity, paternity – what Bishop Winton calls "Greeke and Latine Fathers") at the same time that it seems to formulate something new.[31]

Enter Gower

... we must locate the space left empty by the author's disappearance, follow the distribution of gaps and breaches, and watch for the openings that this disappearance uncovers.

"What Is an Author?"[32]

I doe beseech you
To learne of me who stand with gappes
To teach you.
The stages of our storie ...

Gower, in *Pericles* (G2^v)

The appearance of Gower in *Pericles* is a particularly fitting illustration of the complex process Foucault labels "the author-function." The story Gower re-presents on stage as his own draws upon a number of other texts, some of which were probably more familiar in 1608–09 (and certainly more recently in circulation) than Gower's *Confessio Amantis*, which had last been printed in 1554. As is well known, the play also draws heavily upon Lawrence Twine's *The Patterne of Painefull Aduentures*, entered in the Stationers' Register in 1576, and published in at least two editions, one only a year before the play's earliest performances and registration for printing in 1608.[33] That the name "Pericles" appears in neither Gower's nor Twine's versions of the story further suggests that other stories are collated in this play, perhaps including that of the similarly shipwrecked Pyrocles of Sidney's *Arcadia*.[34] Gower, in other words, is by no means simply (or solely) the prior writer of the text he represents on stage, and this disjunction between the play's apparent pre-texts and its representation of its source emphasizes that Gower instead *functions* as an author, stands in as the ostensibly singular locus of the play's plural origin and generation.[35] Indeed, the play begins by illustrating the idea of the author *as function*, for, in describing the resurrection of Gower from the grave, the actor playing his part also describes the taking on of the authorial role:[36]

> TO sing a Song that old was sung,
> From ashes, auntient Gower is come,
> Assuming mans infirmities,
> To glad your eare, and please your eyes ...   (A2)

"Assuming mans infirmities," the speaker literally takes on the body of this author – in/corporates him, in/habits him. George Wilkins's contemporaneous prose version of the play similarly registers the functionality – as opposed to the instrumentality or agency – of the author, when it "intreat[s] the Reader to receive this Historie in the same maner as it was *under the habite* of ancient Gower the famous English Poet, by the Kings Majesties Players excellently presented."[37] In Wilkins's revealing locution, the players are the agents of the play's presentation, while "the famous English Poet" provides the "habite" of the play – the "clothes, garments, habiliments," but also the "demeanor, deportment, behaviour" and "customary way of acting" (*OED*).

If the figure of Gower works to embody the play's numerous pre-texts under one authorial "habite," his speeches also attempt to define or constrain the meaning of the spectacle he stages. He is thus, in another way, a "principle of thrift in the proliferation of meaning," to use Foucault's familiar formulation. This is especially apparent in the play's several dumb shows, each of which Gower extensively introduces and glosses; as he says in introducing one: "What's dumbe in shew, I'le plaine with speach" (E1), or later, "Your eares vnto your eyes Ile reconcile" (G2ᵛ). Gower's most sustained attempt to define the action is the final speech of the play, an eighteen-line commentary (sometimes labeled "Epilogue" in modern editions) that reduces the play's incidents to moral abstractions: "monstrous lust," "learned charitie," "vertue preferd" (I3ᵛ).

As my repeated use of terms like "tentative" and "attempt" begins to suggest, however, the play exhibits some resistance to such authorial control, and Gower is by no means rendered as the free-standing author of later Anglo-American history. His own attribution of "his" tale oscillates between singular ownership ("my rimes" [A2], "my cause" [A2ᵛ]), collaborative production ("our sceanes," "our storie" [G2ᵛ]), and received sources ("I tell you what mine Authors saye" [A2]). Gower's speeches, furthermore, frequently dwell on the necessity of audience collaboration in the spectacle he ostensibly supervises:

> the vnborne euent,
> I doe commend to your content,
>
> . . .
> Which neuer could I so conuey,
> Vnlesse your thoughts went on my way . . .   (F2)

In other ways the play seems to proliferate beyond his control; the *précis* he provides in the prologue – "The purchase" of the play, he says, "is to make men glorious" (A2) – has only a slight relevance to the action that follows. Gower's final speech, too, is an incomplete summary; it elides major characters (Lysimachus, for example), and devotes more lines to a narration of Cleon and Dionyza's deaths than it does to Pericles and his family (I3ᵛ). These attempts at summary and control illustrate what Gower in one speech calls "gappes": "I doe beseech you / To learne of me who stand with gappes / To teach you." Unlike modernized texts of the play, which typically emend these lines to place Gower "i'th' gaps" of the play, supervising and "filling out" (in the words of the Arden edition) the play's "action proper" (p. 121), the speech as printed in the quarto acknowledges the gaping *incompleteness* of Gower's author/ity.

Another significant erosion of Gower's authoritative position is the fact that the play frequently does not separate him from the representation he ostensibly creates and presents. Modern editions carefully distinguish Gower's narrating discourse from the rest of the play – following Malone, both the Arden and the Riverside editions, for example, cordon off Gower's speeches from the scenes into which those editions divide their texts' five acts.[38] The 1609 *Pericles* quarto, however, neither divides the text into acts and scenes nor consistently separates Gower's discourse from the remainder of the play,[39] and the earliest text to provide act divisions, the third Shakespeare folio, does not separate out Gower's part. The speeches themselves indicate the extent to which Gower is situated within, rather than outside, the sphere of theatrical representation. His first speech ends, for example, with an acknowledgment of "yon grimme lookes" – a reference to Antiochus's Daughter's dead suitors that brings him into the first scene he depicts. The conclusion of a later speech further demystifies the distinction between representing author and represented action:

> In your imagination hold:
> This Stage, the Ship, vpon whose Decke
> The seas tost *Pericles* appeares to speake.
> *Enter Pericles a Shipboard.*

The speech not only places Gower and Pericles in the same position ("This Stage, the Ship"), but it also alludes to the speaking position as itself a representation: Pericles and Gower alike "appear" (enter) on stage in order "to speak" and, at the same time, only appear (seem) to speak. Later, as we will see, Gower shows Pericles viewing the monument of his putatively dead daughter and then intrudes into the show he has ostensibly created by approaching and reading the monument's epitaph (G3). Gower is insistently a part of the play he represents.

Dumb shows

Gower's implication in his representation leads in another direction, however, for it makes clearer the connections in *Pericles* between representations of authorial control and other senses of author/ity we noted earlier in patriarchal–absolutist texts by and about James I. Gower's authoritative intrusions are frequently structured as dumb shows; he typically introduces a dumb show, displays the silent action, then provides a detailed gloss. Significantly, Gower's first two dumb shows (his second and third speeches of the play) center on the exchange of written texts:

> *Dombe shew.*
> *Enter at one dore* Pericles *talking with* Cleon, *all the trains with them: Enter at an other dore, a Gentleman with a Letter to* Pericles, Pericles *shewes the Letter to* Cleon; Pericles *giues the Messenger a reward, and Knights him: Exit* Pericles *at one dore, and* Cleon *at an other.* (C1ᵛ)

> *Enter* Pericles *and* Symonides *at one dore with attendantes, a Messenger meetes them, kneeles and giues* Pericles *a letter,* Pericles *shewes it* Symonides, *the Lords kneele to him; then enter* Thaysa *with child, with* Lichorida *a nurse, the King shewes her the letter, she reioyces: she and* Pericles *take leaue of her father, and depart.* (E1)

In each case, Gower explicates the show ("Your eares vnto your eyes Ile reconcile") and provides a reading of the text that has changed hands. These shows stand in significant juxtaposition to Gower's next speech;

though it is not labeled a dumb show, it provides a lengthy description of
the heroine Marina, who until this point in the play has appeared only as
a silent new-born child:

> Now to *Marina* bend your mind,
> Whom our fast growing scene must finde
> At *Tharsus*, and by *Cleon* traind
> In Musicks letters, who hath gaind
> Of education all the grace,
> Which makes hie both the art and place
> Of general wonder ...   (F1ᵛ)

Gower's speeches, in other words, move from the revelation of texts
exchanged in silence to the description of "absolute Marina," herself a
silent show thus far in the play.

Gower's fifth speech, which also includes a dumb show, is a collation
and culmination of this process, for in it Gower shows Pericles viewing
the tomb of his ostensibly dead daughter, then Gower himself reads
aloud the text Pericles views in the show – a text that is itself (again) a
depiction of Marina (now, at least to Pericles, permanently dumb):

> *The fairest, sweetest, and best lyes heere,*
> *Who withered in her spring of yeare:*
> *She was of Tyrus the Kings daughter,*
> *On whom fowle death hath made this slaughter.*
> *Marina was she call'd ...*   (G3)

The progression of Gower's presentation is thus from his introduction of
the story, to dumb shows depicting the exchange of dynastically important texts, to representations of a "dumb" heir and daughter as text. The
play, in other words, is structured around, and instructs its audience in,
modes of patriarchal representation.

Compare, now, the first incident of the play, the entrance of Antiochus's Daughter as described first by her father and then by Pericles,
her suitor:

> *Ant.* Musicke bring in our daughter, clothed like a bride,
> For embracements euen of *Ioue* himselfe;
> At whose conception, till *Lucina* rained,
> Nature this dowry gaue; to glad her presence,
> The Senate house of Planets all did sit,
> To knit in her, their best perfections.
> > *Enter Antiochus daughter.*
> *Per.* See where she comes, appareled like the Spring,
> Graces her subiects, and her thoughts the King,
> Of euery Vertue giues renowne to men:
> Her face the booke of prayses, where is read,

> Nothing but curious pleasures, as from thence,
> Sorrow were euer racte ...   (A2ᵛ)

"Clothed like a bride" and "appareled like the Spring," Antiochus's Daughter is given a parallel dumb-show description as she enters. As in Gower's speeches, she becomes explicitly a text that Pericles reads – "her face the booke of prayses" where pleasure is "read" and from which sorrow has been "racte" (erased). Yet the most prominent textualization of this nameless, almost completely silent woman (she has a single two-line speech) comes in the form of her father's riddle, which her successful suitor must either answer correctly or die:

> The Riddle.
> *I am no Viper, yet I feed*
> *On mothers flesh which did me breed:*
> *I sought a Husband, in which labour,*
> *I found that kindness in a Father;*
> *Hee's Father, Sonne, and Husband milde;*
> *I, Mother, Wife, and yet his Child:*
> *How they may be, and yet in two,*
> *As you will liue resolue it you.*   (A3ᵛ)

The answer to the Riddle, as Phyllis Gorfain has observed, is Antiochus's nameless daughter's name[40] – she is the "I" of the riddle – and thus, though here the text is provided to the audience (unlike Gower's practice in the initial dumb shows), Antiochus, the father/author of this text, exerts virtually absolute control over its interpretation, just as he attempts to retain absolute sexual control over his daughter. The absolutism with which Antiochus prohibits the circulation of daughter and text is evident in his pursuit of the knowing Pericles: "He hath found the meaning / For which we meane to haue his head" (A4ᵛ).

The first incident of the play thus gives a sexual (and endogamous) valence to the issues of authorial control we have noticed in the construction of Gower; seen in this context, the incest that structures the Antiochus scene (and that echoes in the series of father–daughter relations throughout the play) figures a particularly totalizing version of the (dangerous) control the author-function is said to exert. Though he flees Antioch and its patriarchal–absolutist monarch, however, Pericles is no enemy of fatherly author/ity, as his explanation of his travels to his counsellor Helicanus makes clear: "I sought the purchase of a glorious beautie, / From whence an issue I might propogate" (B2). The structure of what is often regarded as an unstructured play lies in this dynastic trajectory, and a new adventure finds Pericles washed up on the shore of Pentapolis, ruled by "the good *Symonides*," known for "his peaceable

raigne, and good gouernment" (C3). This king too, Pericles learns from
some local fishermen, has "a faire Daughter," and like Antiochus's
Daughter she is the object of a contest: "to morrow is her birth-day, /
And there are Princes and Knights come from all partes of / the World,
to Iust and Turney for her loue" (C3). Pericles goes to participate in the
contest for the King's daughter Thaisa, but he is notably first armed with
(made to in/habit, we might say) his own patriarchal inheritance, which
the fishermen drag from the sea: "[this] Armour ... was mine owne part
of my heritage, / Which my dead Father did bequeath to me" (C3^v).

Though Thaisa, like Antiochus's Daughter, is an object of display
("our daughter ... / Sits heere like Beauties child, whom Nature gat, /
For men to see, and seeing, woonder at" [C4]), she at least has a name
and participates in the presentation of the script her father benevolently
controls. At the beginning of the tournament, Thaisa reads aloud the
motto on each of the competing knights' shields; for three of the six
knights, Simonides interprets the Latin motto:

> *The first Knight passes by.*
> *King.* Who is the first, that doth preferre himselfe?
> *Thai.* A Knight of *Sparta* (my renowned father)
> And the deuice he beares vpon his Shield,
> Is a blacke Ethyope reaching at the Sunne:
> The word: *Lux tua vita mihi.*
> *King.* He loues you well, that holdes his life of you.
> . . .
> . . . *Kin.*   What is the fourth.
> *Thai.* A burning Torch that's turned vpside downe;
> The word: *Qui me alit me extinguit.*
> *Kin.* Which shewes that Beautie hath his power & will,
> Which can as well enflame as it can kill.
> . . .
> . . . *Kin.*   And what's the sixt, and last; the which,
> The knight himself with such a graceful courtesie deliuered?
> *Thai.*   Hee seemes to be a Stranger: but his Present is
> A withered Branch, that's onely greene at top,
> The motto: *In hac spe viuo.*
> *Kin.* A pretty morrall frō the deiected state wherein he is,
> He hopes by you, his fortunes yet may flourish.   (C4–C4^v)

In this scene of patriarchally supervised reading, the daughter continually
stresses the hierarchy of the relation ("my royall Father ... my renowned
father ... my royall father"). She describes the knights' shields and texts
but does not interpret them; inscribed in the privileged, masculinist
discourse of Latin, they are interpreted by the kingly father, who
(re)constructs each as a text about the daughter. The motto of the sixth

knight, Pericles, is exemplary of this process; *In hac spe viuo* ("I live in this hope") becomes "He hopes *by you*, his fortunes yet may flourish." That Pericles's dynastic agenda coincides with Simonides's also becomes clear in this speech: the "withered Branch" of the Periclean dynasty – the "deiected state" of heirless Tyre – hopes to "flourish" (to thrive, but also to flower, to reproduce) through Thaisa. Throughout these early episodes, the play intrudes into Pericles's travels the problem of succession in Tyre; thinking Pericles dead and the kingdom without a legitimate heir, the country's lords, in what is termed a "mutanie" (E1), almost convince Hellicanus to ascend the throne.

In contrast to this scene of passive reading, Thaisa later writes her own text to her father, but Simonides again carefully deploys that text to his own ends, first using it to be rid of Thaisa's other suitors:

> *Enter the King reading of a letter at one doore,*
> *the Knights meete him ...*
> *King.* Knights, from my daughter this I let you know,
> That for this twelue-month, shee'le not vndertake
> A maried life ...   (D3–D3ᵛ)

Simonides then presents another version of the letter:

> Now to my daughters Letter; she tells me heere,
> Shee'le wedde the stranger Knight;
> Or neuer more to view nor day nor light.
> T'is well Mistris, your choyce agrees with mine:
> I like that: nay how absolute she's in't,
> Not minding whether I dislike or no.
> Well, I do commend her choyce, and will no longer
> Haue it be delayed ...   (D3ᵛ)

Thaisa's letter seems to usurp the power of her monarch-father – "nay how *absolute* she's in't" – but her wish notably replicates his own. Earlier, at the post-tourney banquet, Thaisa had just as carefully reproduced her father's script in asking the central question of patriarchal author/ity:

> *king.* And furthermore tell him, we desire to know of him
> *Of whence he is, his name, and Parentage?*
> *Tha.* The King my father (sir) has drunke to you.
> *Peri.* I thanke him
> ...
> *Tha.* And further, he desires to know of you,
> *Of whence you are, your name and parentage?*   (D2, my emphasis)

Later, Simonides again uses Thaisa's letter to test Pericles's courage, and Pericles reads it (correctly, in a sense) as a strategem of royal power that closely resembles Antiochus's earlier use of the daughter/text: "*Per.* What's here, a letter that [Thaisa] loues the knight of *Tyre*? / T'is the Kings subtiltie to haue my life ... " (D4). The scene resolves with the marriage that both Pericles and Thaisa desire, in a theatrical speech of Simonides:

> *King.* Yea Mistris, are you so peremptorie?
> I am glad on't with all my heart,
> Ile tame you; Ile bring you in subiection.   *Aside.*
> Will you not, hauing my consent,
> Bestow your loue and your affections
> Vpon a Stranger? who for ought I know,
> May be (nor can I thinke the contrary)   *Aside.*
> As great in blood as I my selfe:
> Therefore, heare you Mistris, either frame
> Your will to mine: and you sir, heare you;
> Either be rul'd by mee, or Ile make you,
> Man and wife ...   (D4^v)

Simonides here oscillates between the patriarchal–absolutist monarch and (in slightly misplaced asides) the benevolent father, but the mystification this oscillation enacts is enormous and instructive. As the speech reaches its end, it is no longer possible to distinguish between the absolutist king ("Ile tame you; Ile bring you in subiection") and the match-maker, and the speech concludes in a sentence that begins as a threat ("Either be rul'd by mee, or Ile make you ... ") but ends in the couple's marriage as "Man and wife." Thaisa is permitted a "peremptorie" desire, but it is one that pre-empts only the identical wish of her father; patriarchy seems to allow, benevolently, what it in fact demands. ("Be rul'd by mee, [and] Ile make you man and wife," we might emend.)

Concluding this scene, Simonides notes that the marriage "pleaseth me so well, that I will see you wed, / And then with haste you can, get you to bed" (D4^v). The intersecting agendas of Simonides's patriarchal authority (managing the representation and timely reproduction of his daughter), Pericles's propagation, and the play's presenting author are made clear in Gower's speech that directly follows: "*Hymen* hath brought the Bride to bed, / Whereby the losse of maydenhead, / A Babe is moulded" (D4^v). Contemporary uses of *mould* included "To produce or create (a material object) in a certain form; to shape as a sculptor or modeller" (v.^{2}, 3.),[41] and Gower's verb fuses the sexual and authorial modes of (pro)creativity. Thaisa becomes the "matrix" (*OED*'s term, closely related to *mater*) for the "issue" Pericles has vowed to "propogate."[42] In Gower's ensuing dumb show (quoted above), Thaisa appears "with child" at the same moment that a letter reveals Pericles himself to be of royal issue; in Gower's speech he both conceives and becomes a royal heir: "Our heyre apparant is a King" (E1).

We might at this point pause to acknowledge some differences between the model of patriarchal textual and sexual reproduction with which we began and the version I have been analyzing in the play of *Pericles*. James's *Workes* provided an idealized model, in which patriarchal–absolutist authority is reproduced unproblematically in the male heir Charles, who is (in the world of this fantasy, at least) to take the father's book "for preseruation" and "for a Patterne." The book is to be the sole mediation between the endless regress of the father–son dynastic chain. *Pericles* registers, I have been arguing, a similar attention to patriarchal–absolutist propagation; however, in its attempts to detail the accomplishment of Pericles's dynastic intention, the play also raises two issues that are problematic for its patriarchal paradigm: female children and maternal chastity. Both Marina and Thaisa, that is, mediate the succession of kings presumed in Pericles's paradigm. The play poses, and proposes an answer for, the question: How do you solve a problem like Marina?

Fathers testament

We have already noticed the play's repeated representation – by Gower, Antiochus, and Simonides – of daughters, episodes that explicitly detail the traffic in women that characterized the sex/gender system of this period. As an example of the unmystified exchange of women, Marina's appearance and subsequent career in the brothel at Mytelin is therefore of crucial importance to the issue of author/itative representation. In the first brothel scene, the Bawd instructs her accomplice, Boult, to advertise Marina (newly purchased from a group of pirates) in the Mytelin marketplace:

> *Bawd. Boult*, take you the markes of her, the colour of her haire, complexion, height, her age, with warrant of her virginitie, and crie, He that will giue most shall haue her first, such a maydenhead were no cheape thing, if men were as they haue beene: get this done as I command you.
> *Boult*. Performance shall follow.   *Exit*. (F4^v)

Steven Mullaney has argued that *Pericles*, and the brothel scenes in particular, register an "unwillingness to represent the highly theatrical transaction between an actor and an audience ... an evasion of the economic and cultural roots of the popular stage itself,"[43] yet this exchange between Boult and the Bawd connects advertising with the "performance" of theatrical representation, reminding us of, rather than obscuring, Mullaney's foundational insight: the geographical proximity in Jacobean London of the market, the theatre, and the brothel.[44] Bawd's instructions further associate the selling of Marina with the representations we have already seen in the play – including Gower's own description of Marina's "fingers long, small, white as milke," in comparison to her friend Philoten's "gracefull markes" (F1^v). These connections are further emphasized on Boult's return from the market-place:

Baud ... Now sir, hast thou cride her through the Market?
Boult. I haue cryde her almost to the number of her haires, I haue drawne her picture with my voice.
Baud. And prethee tell me, how dost thou find the inclination of the people, especially of the yonger sort?
Boult. Faith they listened to mee, as they would haue harkened to their fathers testament, there was a Spaniards mouth watred, and he went to bed to her verie description. (G1)

There are significant resonances here with Antiochus' presentation of his daughter and Gower's representation of Marina. Gower too has "take[n] the markes of her," has "drawne [Marina's] picture with [his] voice," and the play has sent him forward/foreword as an authoritative advertiser, his representation a canonical "fathers testament" within the profitable institution of the theatre. Mullaney argues that *Pericles* effaces the mercantile theatricality of Marina in its source, but as we might expect from a predominantly male-owned and -operated theatre, that mercantilism is not so much effaced as transferred, from Marina to the male figures who are constantly re-presenting her. "Under the habite of ancient Gower," "the Kings Majesties Players" present their wares for sale.

This is not to say that author/itative representation – Antiochus's Daughter, Simonides's Thaisa, Gower's Marina – is in some way simply *equal to* prostitution, as Marina's subsequent career in the brothel makes clear. Marina refuses to submit to prostitution and intervenes in the sexual dumb show prepared for her by speaking "holie words" to the brothel's customers and converting them to chastity. When Boult attempts to ravish her into submission, she convinces him that she can be sold in another way:

here, heers gold for thee, if that thy master would gaine by me, proclaime that I can sing, weaue, sow, & dance, with other vertues, which Ile keep from boast, and will vndertake all these to teache. I doubt not but this populous Cittie will yeelde manie schollers. (H1^v)

In other words, Marina's objection is not to her sale, *per se*, but to her sale as an unchaste sexual object; she asks, in fact, that her chaste virtues be similarly "proclaimed" throughout the city. Significantly, at the conclusion of this negotiation, Gower enters immediately and proclaims exactly what Marina had asked *of Boult*:

> *Enter Gower.*
> *Marina* thus the Brothell scapes, and chaunces
> Into an *Honest-house* our Storie sayes:
> Shee sings like one immortall, and shee daunces
> As Goddesse-like to her admired layes.
> Deepe clearks she dumb's, and with her neele composes
> Natures owne shape, of budde, bird, branche, or berry,
> That euen her art sisters the naturall Roses
>   ... and her gaine
> She giues the cursed Bawd, here wee her place,
> And to hir Father turne our thoughts againe ...   (H2)

Advertising Marina again, Gower's intrusion demonstrates the difference between sanctioned and condemned forms of the traffic in women. The difference is chastity, the discourse that ensures the legitimate reproduction of the patriarchal line and that Marina is herself made to speak. If, in other words, we look to Marina for a feminist critique of the systems that advertise, represent, textualize, and circulate women in this culture, we find her critical only of prostitution, and only through the larger patriarchal discourse of female chastity. Marina's most notorious convert at the brothel is Lysimachus, the governor of Mytelin: "had I brought hither a corrupted minde," he says, "thy speeche had altered it" (G4^v). His conversion to chaste government allows her to marry this prince, who had previously solicited her as a prostitute.

Report thy parentage

It is in fact Marina's conversion of Lysimachus, and her fame as a speaker of the rhetoric of chastity, that causes her to meet her father in what the criticism labels "the recognition scene." We might better call it the scene of author/ity, for in it Pericles asks again and again the question Thaisa had earlier asked him, according to her father's example: "your name and parentage?" Indeed, it is the very word "parentage" in Marina's speech that revives Pericles from his long silence. Pericles quotes, in some disarray, Marina's words back to her:

Per. My fortunes, parentage, good parentage, to equall mine, was it not thus, what say you?

Mari. I sed my Lord, if you did know my parentage, you would not do me violence. (H3^v)

Thus begins the lengthy scene in which, invoking Foucault's Beckett, we might say that it is made to matter insistently "who is speaking." "Report thy parentage," Pericles orders Marina; "Tell thy storie" (H4). Marina does so in stages, first relating her name and its patriarchal–absolutist derivation: "The name was giuen mee by one that had some power, my father, and a king" (H4^v). Pericles demands more parental detail ("what mother?"), and Marina notes, similarly, "My mother was the daughter of a King." "I am," she admits after further interrogation, "the daughter to King *Pericles*, if good king *Pericles* be." This final revelation, the name of the father, is at first sufficient, and the daughter seems, in an unusual reversal, to reconstitute Pericles's fatherhood:

> Oh come hither,
> *thou that begetst him that did thee beget,*
> Thou that wast borne at sea, buried at *Tharsus*,
> And found at sea agen, O *Hellicanus*,
> Downe on thy knees, thanke the holie Gods as loud
> As thunder threatens vs, this is *Marina*.   (I1, second-line emphasis mine)

These revelations are not sufficient, however, and, still harping on legitimacy, Pericles demands further evidence:

> What was thy mothers name? tell me, but that
> for truth can neuer be confirm'd inough,
> Though doubts did euer sleepe.
> *Mar*. Frist sir, I pray what is your title?
> *Per*. I am *Pericles of Tyre*, but tell mee now my
> Drownd Queenes name, as in the rest you sayd,
> Thou hast beene God-like perfit, the heir of kingdomes,
> And an other like to *Pericles* thy father.

The efficiency of Pericles's self-identification serves to point up the complexity of Marina's (it has required a scene, not half a line), and the mother's name is the final piece in a network of interlocking questions. The syntax of Marina's reply is significant: "Is it no more to be *your* daughter, then to say, my mothers name was *Thaisa*, *Thaisa* was my mother ... " (I1, first emphasis mine). Marina becomes, in her own phrasing, Pericles's daughter through her mother, who has herself already been guaranteed as the "daughter of a King." In its insistence on the mother's name, this scene elaborately demonstrates the problem women represent for this system of patriarchal reproduction: unlike both Antiochus's Daughter and Thaisa herself, Marina has a mother; that that mother was also Pericles's wife must be carefully ascertained.

And yet the play continues to dwell on what Marjorie Garber, in a discussion of Shakespearean authorship, has called "the undecidability of paternity";[45] even the mother's name is insufficient guarantee of

Marina's derivation, as the remainder of the play demonstrates. The recognition scene of Pericles's author/ity and Marina's authorship is interrupted by the appearance of the goddess Diana, who instructs Pericles to make a sacrifice at her temple in Ephesus. Thaisa, whom Pericles thinks dead, is a votaress of Diana, and thus this theophany of divine chastity eventuates in a second "recognition scene," one that supports and seemingly completes the first. At Diana's temple, Pericles recovers his wife, and her appearance there in "vastall [*vestal*, but perhaps also *vassal*] liuerie" as a "Votarisse" of Diana serves as a marker of her chastity and a guarantee, *ex post facto*, of Marina's legitimacy. Pericles again, however, requires proof of Thaisa's identity. Before she has recovered from fainting at his sight, Pericles demands to see the jewels he had placed in her coffin. When Thaisa recovers, he questions her on the name of his counsellor Helicanus, the correct answer to which he greets with the exclamation, "Still confirmation." Yet, the "truth can neuer be confirm'd inough," and Pericles asks Cerimon, "will you deliuer how this dead Queene reliues?" (I3). Cerimon attempts to anchor this chain of contingencies with assurances that exist offstage, outside the realm of the play's representation: "I will my Lord, beseech you first, goe with mee to my house, where shall be showne you all was found with her. How shee came plac'ste heere in the Temple, no needfulll thing omitted." (I3). That speech alludes back to the text Pericles had written and enclosed in Thaisa's coffin:

> *Heere I giue to vnderstand,*
> *If ere this Coffin driues aland;*
> *I King* Pericles *haue lost*
> *This Queene ...*
> *She was the Daughter of a King ...*   (E4)

This text (with an insistence on patriarchal relations we have witnessed elsewhere in the play) demonstrates the tenuousness of the proofs on which Pericles rests his dynasty. Along with Cerimon's other "letters of good credit" announcing Simonides's death (I3), this text allows Pericles to announce the continuance of his rule in a peculiarly patriarchal form. Pericles and Thaisa will rule in Simonides's kingdom, Pentapolis, an inheritance that enacts Pericles's earlier description of Simonides: "Yon Kings to mee, like to my fathers picture" (D1^v).[46] Lysimachus will marry Marina and, in Pericles's words, "our sonne and daughter shall in *Tyrus* raigne" (I3^v). The ending thus attempts to solve the problem of female children in the patriarchal line (both Thaisa and Marina) by displacing them; over the lineally closer claims of their wives, Pericles and Lysimachus each inherit a "father's" kingdom.

But as I suggested above these relations are tenuous, resting on a chain (a genealogy) of proofs and confirmations that culminates in the text Pericles enclosed in Thaisa's coffin. In other words, though the play gestures toward confirmation outside the sphere of its representation, it ends by appealing and alluding to itself. "Know you the Charecter?" Cerimon had earlier asked Thaisa; "It is my Lords" was her reply (F1), and Pericles's character – his position as patriarchal father, his position of authority – is thus guaranteed only by a text in his own character, of his own author/ity. "Thou that begetst him that did thee beget," Pericles had addressed Marina, and his paradoxical utterance applies to the questions of derivation and author/ity that have constituted this play. The daughter here begets the father; the text begets its author. Gower provides further illustration, in an early speech:

> Fortune tir'd with doing bad,
> Threw [Pericles] a shore, to giue him glad:
> And heere he comes: what shall be next,
> Pardon old *Gower*, this long's the text.
> > *Enter Pericles wette.*   (C1ᵛ)

The Arden edition tellingly emends the final line of Gower's speech to "Pardon old Gower, – this 'longs the text" (p. 41) and provides the gloss "belongs to." Gower in this reading is made to establish himself outside, beyond, the text of the play he presents, what the Riverside edition calls, glossing this same line, "the text of the play proper"; "this" – Pericles's entrance – "belongs to" the text of the play. And yet, as the Riverside suggests, a less contorted possibility is that "the text" in question here is not "the play proper" but rather Gower's speech; "the text of my speech is this long and no longer."[47] In this supposed editorial crux, we witness again the tenuousness of the begetting author; the author becomes here a function of the text itself – not prior to, outside, or beyond it. Old Gower is produced by – and only as long as – his text.

Problem child

> About one matter there can at any rate be no doubt: Shakespeare wrote most or all of Acts iii–v. His hand is most obvious in iii.i, the scene of the storm and the casting overboard of Thaisa's body, and in v.i, the first recognition scene ... These observations will be shared by every sensitive reader. They require no defence.
> > F. D. Hoeniger, in the Arden *Pericles* (p. liv)

The Arden's emendation of the line we have just analyzed, with its attempt to construct Gower as an author prior to and outside the text that produces him, suggests at a local level the extent to which the larger text of *Pericles* has itself been asked relentlessly the question of its paternity – "we desire to know of him / Of whence he is, his name, and Parentage." Criticism has in large part focused on what Arden editor F. D. Hoeniger calls "the problem of its authorship" (p. lxii).[48] *Pericles* has provoked a series of influential articles that speak of it in similar terms: for example, Kenneth Muir's article "The Problem of *Pericles*" (one of many attempts to construct a genealogical relation of Twine, Wilkins, and the play-text) and Philip Edwards's "An Approach to the Problem of *Pericles*" (the widely accepted account of the text's two memorially reconstructing reporters and three compositors).[49] Indeed, the conclusion to Edwards's article makes clear that the real quarry in the treatment of textual "problems" is the author/father of this play:

The problem that has to be solved is whether the different aptitudes of the two reporters are the *sole* cause of the difference in literary value between the two halves of the play; whether, in fact, the original play of *Pericles* was all of one standard, all by one author, and that the first reporter, in his crude attempts to rebuild a verse structure and in his reliance on a palpably defective memory, has perverted language such as is found in the later acts. (p. 45, his emphasis)

Here and elsewhere, Edwards employs a language of perversion; from its very inception, the New Bibliography assigned the quarto the moral tag "Bad," but Edwards goes further in describing Wilkins as a "slippery customer" (p. 39) and remarks that "compositor y" has "an immoral habit of adding the last word of a line to the beginning of the next rather than widen the measure of his composing stick" (p. 31). With the attempt to discern *Pericles*'s "one author," the derogation of Wilkins and an immoral compositor who disrupts both the play's lines and its lineage (intruding his "composing stick" where it doesn't belong), and the Arden edition's catalogue of "The Causes of Corruption" (Arden, p. xxxi), we are, I would assert, back in the rhetoric of paternity and chastity so central to the play itself. New Bibliographic treatment of the play, yearning for a lost original and its ostensible proof of Shakespearean paternity, has constructed a narrative in which Shakespeare's offspring (like Marina) is kidnapped and ravished, perverted and corrupted:

> *Pira*.2. A prize, a prize.
> *Pirat*.3. Halfe part mates, halfe part. Come lets haue
> her aboord sodainly.
>   *Exit*. (F3–F3ᵛ)[50]

Pericles figured centrally in the initial New Bibliographic pirate narrative, A. W. Pollard's *Shakespeare's Fight with the Pirates*,[51] and it is interesting to note that Hoeniger finds Shakespeare indisputably in this text at two dynastically central moments: the scene in which Marina is born, and the scene in which she is finally reunited with her father.

These points of resemblance between the approach of the criticism and the discourses of the play represent the extent to which incipient seventeenth-century concerns over authorship and paternity have emerged in the succeeding centuries as a dominant ideology. But, at the same time that we can identify such correspondences, we must be aware of the ways in which this play-text, like many others in the period, does not conform to our modern notions of authorship and decidable paternity. Despite its evident popularity in the early seventeenth century – there were six quarto editions of the play by 1635 and it apparently triggered the publication of the Wilkins "novel" – and despite the attribution of the play to William Shakespeare on its 1609 title page, the play was not included in the first folio collection of Shakespeare's plays. Denied the author/ity of that volume, it was eventually included in the second issue of the third folio (1664); it appears on the title page as one of "seven Playes, never before Printed in Folio" but is not included in the volume's catalogue, and it begins at the end of the volume, after *Cymbeline*, along with six plays that are no longer considered Shakespearean.[52] Indeed, these plays were apparently an "afterthought" in the third folio (as Pollard noted), for *Pericles* begins this section with new pagination and signatures. And yet *Pericles* is differentiated from its now-"spurious" colleagues because they begin the signatures and pagination anew after *Pericles*, as a *second* afterthought.[53] There is no point in this textual history, in other words, where the attribution of authorship is simple or unconflicted.

The possible exception to this statement is, of course, Shakespeare's name on the title page of the 1609 text (Fig. 7). With that attribution, the title page registers an emergent concern over linear paternity familiar from the play itself and also advertises

> the whole Historie,
> aduentures, and fortunes of the said Prince:
> As also,
> The no lesse strange, and worthy accidents,
> in the Birth and Life, of his Daughter
> *MARIANA.*

And yet, if we accept tentatively the findings of Edwards and Hoeniger without their moral aspersions,[54] if, that is, they are correct about the complexity of the quarto's production – its numerous compositors, reporters, and, perhaps, collaborators, its insistent disruption of linear genealogy – the quarto's attribution is at the very least reticent. What does it mean for this play-text – derived from Twine, Gower, maybe Sidney if not Wilkins, acted in the theatre and elsewhere,[55] perhaps

THE LATE,

And much admired Play,

Called

Pericles, Prince

of Tyre.

With the true Relation of the whole Hiſtorie,
aduentures, and fortunes of the ſaid Prince:

As alſo,

The no-leſſe ſtrange, and worthy accidents,
in the Birth and Life, of his Daughter
MARIANA.

As it hath been diuers and ſundry times acted by
his Maieſties Seruants, at the Globe on
the Banck-ſide.

By VVilliam  Shakeſpeare.

George Steevens

Imprinted at London for *Henry Goſſon,* and are
to be ſold at the ſigne of the Sunne in
Pater-noſter row, &c.
1 6 0 9.

Figure 7   Title page: William Shakespeare, *Pericles, Prince of Tyre*
(London: for Henry Gosson, 1609).

reconstituted as a text for printing by actors or other witnesses to its theatrical production, "composed" by at least three relineating workers in a printing house – to be "By William Shakespeare"?

We can return to the maligned, slippery Wilkins for another way to read this attribution, recalling that he "intreat[s] the Reader to receive [his] Historie in the same maner as it was *under the habite* of ancient Gower the famous English Poet, by the Kings Majesties Players excellently presented." Like Wilkins, the quarto emphasizes that the play "hath been diuers and sundry times acted by his Maiesties Seruants, at the Globe on the Banck-side," and, in this context, the attribution of the quarto to Shakespeare becomes legible as a similar attempt to situate the play under an authorial "habit." At the same time that it may register an incipient concern over author/ity in theatrical texts, the title page of *Pericles* suggests that we break the post-Enlightenment habit of reading authorial names as statements of the facts of textual production with meaning independent of the culture in which they appear, and should instead regard them as functions of production, as the costume or "habit" of a printed text.[56] For to say that the title page of *Pericles, Prince of Tyre* reads "By William Shakespeare" is an incomplete and inadequate description. "William" and "Shakespeare" are separated on this page by a device of two leaves growing in opposite directions. The leaves and the names, furthermore, anticipate the symmetrical design of the printer's ornament that appears directly below this attribution. The words "William Shakespeare" become part of, and function as, an ornament. Shakespeare: print's attire.

Speciall delivery

It has been recognized for some time that *A King and no King*, the contemporaneous play to which I now turn, draws a number of its character names, relationships, and incidents from Xenophon's *Cyropedia*, a text that presents a portrait of an ideal king, Cyrus.[57] Translated by Philemon Holland for the education of Prince Henry at King James's request, the book was apparently circulated at court and eventually published in 1632, after the deaths of both Henry and James and under the supervision of Philemon's son, also named Henry. What is of interest here is not only that the book seems to inform the play in ways related to the proper conduct of kingship (as Philip J. Finkelpearl argues), but that from the outset this book is conceived (I use the term deliberately) within a network of patriarchal–absolutist relations. Its translation, circulation, dedication, and publication are implicated in the terms we have analyzed in James's *Workes* and *Pericles*, as Henry Holland's letter dedicating the published text to Charles I demonstrates:

And now, most deare *Soveraigne*, unto this present version of *Xenophons Cyrupediam* out of Greek, which is, as I may say, the Authour his Master-Peece, and my fathers worke likewise, your Majestie hath the sole right; in regard that he enterprized it long since, and that by speciall order and direction from your Royall Father [James I], delivered unto him by one of his neere servants in Court; (even when your selfe were in your tender yeeres) for the contemplation and use of your most Generous and Magnanimous Brother, *Prince Henry*, now in Heaven.[58]

Henry Holland writes of the book that is the "Master-Peece" both of the "Authour" Xenophon and of his own father – a book commissioned for another, royal Henry by his father, James I, and in this sense not unlike James's own *Basilikon Doron* and the later *Workes*. With Prince Henry dead, Charles inherits "the sole right" to the book, a statement that in itself does much to suggest an earlier idea of textual property, before authors possessed "sole" rights to their texts or translations. And, in the elaboration of this network of patriarchal inheritances and master/ pieces, the separate persons involved become less important than the insistent repetition of filial relations, with Author, translator, and king collapsing into each other at the ambiguous male pronouns: "unto this present version ... which is, as I may say, the Authour his Master-Peece, and my fathers worke likewise, your Majestie hath the sole right; in regard that *he* [Xenophon? Holland? James?] enterprized it long since, and that by speciall order and direction from your Royall Father, delivered [the speciall order? the text?] unto him [Holland? James?] by one of his [Holland's? James's?] neere servants in Court."

It is perhaps easy enough to reduce this process to a simple narrative: James gave Philemon Holland special order and direction to translate this text, which Holland then delivered to James through one of James's courtiers. And yet, the mode of presentation here – the delivery of this text – both emphasizes patriarchal relations and problematizes paternity; given James's "speciall order," can Holland be said to have "enterprized it"? Who is (to recall the Authorized Version) "the principall moouer and Author of the Worke"? Is the text delivered to or from the "Royall Father"? Even as it works within a patriarchal mode of authorship that attempts to assign texts singular father–authors, its application of the patriarchal analogy obscures that certainty. Henry Holland's explanation of the text's inception and circulation ends with a pun that again emphasizes filiation, but likewise unmoors the notion of "sole right": "of late my father ... destined [the book] to me his sonne, that in regard both of the Author and Argument, it might lie no longer in obscurity, but at length (and as I hope in good time) see the light of the Sunne." Again stressing filial inheritance ("destined it to me"), Holland presents the book to Charles, who, he suggested above, had also inherited its "sole right." The passage's final word again collapses Henry Holland and the surrogate Henry (Charles), for this letter records the transaction through which this text has seen the light of both these "sons."

This passage may seem (and indeed is, in a number of senses) far removed from plays in the Jacobean theatres and printing houses: it is merely a paragraph from some prefatory material to the translation of a text often cited as a "source" for the play to which we now turn. But I analyze it here in some detail because it demonstrates the extent to which the idea of author/ity in these plays is informed by and implicated in a mode of textual reproduction – "delivery," we can call it, appropriating Holland's language – represented in patriarchal–absolutist terms. The relation of *A King and no King* to *Cyropedia* is not limited to the citation of names and incidents and the exhibition of a king who is the diametric opposite of the idealized Cyrus; the play reproduces a concern with the very modes of textual production, inheritance, and genealogy figured in the seemingly marginal dedicatory letter.[59]

"Draw neere thou guiltie man, / That art the author of the loathedst crime / Fiue ages haue brought forth," Arbaces, king of Iberia, says to Gobrius, the Lord Protector, in the final scene of *A King and no King* (p. 80).[60] Citing "all those witching letters" that Gobrius had written him during his absence at war in Armenia – letters that praised his "beloued Sister," "extolst her beautie," and caused him to fall in love with her – Arbaces accuses Gobrius of authorship in a number of senses, and Gobrius admits he is both the cause of Arbaces's incestuous desire and the writer of the letters:

> *Gob.* This I grant, I thinke I was the cause.
> *Arb.* VVert thou? Nay more, I thinke thou meantst it.
> *Gob.* Sir I hate a lie
> As I loue God and honestie, I did:
> It was my meaning.   (p. 81)

With this admission of intentionality, Arbaces threatens the imminent death of the author, only to find himself in a recognition scene of *Pericle*an proportions:

> *Gob.* Know you kill your Father. *Arb.* How?
> *Gob.* You kill your Father.
> *Arb.* My Father? though I know it for a lie
> Made out of feare to saue thy stained life:
> The verie reuerence of the word comes crosse me,

> And ties mine arme downe.
>   *Gob.* I will tell you that shall heighten you againe, I am thy
> Father, I charge thee heare me.   (pp. 81–82)

In the theatrical context we have already identified – the widespread appearance of authorial presenters in contemporaneous plays – it is crucial to notice that this moment of patriarchal identification simultaneously marks Gobrius as the authorial presenter of this play, for he is shown to have inscribed its plot thus far, and he determines its eventual outcome. Gobrius's climactic narrative makes Arbaces the son neither of the previous king (whom he had thought his father), nor of the dowager queen Arane (whom he had thought his mother), but of Gobrius himself. Gobrius's authorship is thus both presentational (like Gower's) and patriarchal; he begets a story *and* a son, as the repetition of the word *bring* at the beginning of his narrative illustrates:

> *Arb.* Bring it out good Father,
> Ile lie, and listen here as reuerentlie
> As to an Angell ...
>   *Gob.* Our King I say was old, and this our Queene
> Desired to bring an heire ...   (p. 84)

Bring out meant both "to express, utter" and "to produce"; "Enseare thy Fertile and Conceptious wombe, Let it no more *bring out* ingratefull man," the *OED* cites from the roughly contemporaneous *Timon of Athens*. *Bring* itself (as well as *bring forth*, as we will see in *The Tempest*) could mean simply "to give birth," which Arane desires to do in this passage. Gobrius performs both functions, as Arbaces's later exclamation to Mardonius suggests: "There are a thousand things deliuerd to me / You little dreame of" (p. 86). Indeed, Gobrius's story, his explanation of Arane's false pregnancy and childbirth, itself depends upon his powers of patriarchal delivery:

> *Gob.* Now when the time was full,
> Shee should be brought abed; I had a sonne
> Borne, which was you: This the Queene hearing of,
> Mou'd me to let her haue you, and such reasons
> Shee shewed me as shee knew would tie
> My secresie: shee sware you should be King;
> And to be short, I did deliuer you
> Vnto her, and pretende you were dead ...
>   ... [the Queene] made the world belieue
> Shee was deliuer'd of you ...   (p. 85)

This usage is crucial for, as Gobrius's syntax above (with what we might call a pregnant line break) makes clear, it situates all reproductive power

in the father: "And to be short, I did deliuer you / Vnto her." Delivered
by his father, Arbaces has no mother (here or elsewhere in this text);
female participation in reproduction, when it does occur, either is
inauthentic –

> That night the Queene fain'd hastilie to labour,
> And by a paire of women of her owne,
> VVhich shee had charm'd, shee made the world belieue
> She was deliuer'd of you   (p. 85)

– or eventuates in female offspring (in this case, fathered by an old, feeble
man who is thought impotent or sterile and dies before the birth).[61]

These developments, late in the action, are situated within the play's
larger preoccupation with patriarchal absolutism. After the lengthy war
with Armenia, Arbaces brags in familiar absolutist rhetoric that he has
"laid [Armenia's] Kingdome desolate / With this sole arme, propt by
Diuinity" (p. 4) and upon his return announces to his people, "I will be a
Father to you" (p. 30). Given the association of patriarchal–absolutism
and authorship we have witnessed in other texts, it is perhaps not
surprising that at several points in the play, Arbaces also attempts the
sort of authorial fiat Gobrius enacts at play's end; however, his attempts
at creation through discourse are far less successful. Returning from the
war, for example, he brings back to his people as "payment" for their
sacrifices "a little word ... peace" (p. 28), which the citizens immediately
misconstrue as a vegetable: "did not his Maiestie say, he had brought vs
home Peaes for our money? ... Yes, and so we shall anon I warrant you,
haue euery one a pecke brought home to our houses" (p. 30). His
attempt to rewrite his relation to his sister Panthea ("Shee is no kinne to
me, nor shall shee be; / If she were any, I create her none" [p. 35]) is
immediately reversed. This example locates an important difference from
the ideology of author/ity as we have read it in James and in *Pericles*:
Arbaces the patriarchal–absolutist monarch and Gobrius attempt the
same rewriting (for the chief effect of Gobrius's narrative too is that
Arbaces and Panthea are no relation), but Gobrius alone is successful.

In this regard, it is also important to note that the play seems
throughout to be a contest of two "plots" (the play's own term,
pp. 18–19). The queen mother Arane struggles to restore her daughter
Panthea to her rightful place as queen, and Gobrius attempts to solidify
his son's place on the throne. Arane's description of her script sets up a
familiar juxtaposition:

> *Ara.* Accursed be this ouercurious braine,
> That gaue that plot a birth; accurst this wombe,
> That after did conceiue to my disgrace.   (p. 19)

Like Gobrius's later tale, Arane here aligns in parallel construction theatrical and reproductive plots. Gobrius repeatedly intervenes in her plots, however; he stops her from killing Arbaces to make Panthea queen, substitutes his own "delivery," and thus disrupts her attempt at what seems to be matriarchal reproduction and control. "Seems," because, as Gobrius's narration at play's end exposes, Arane has only seemed (in part through Gobrius's efforts) an advocate of female rule and an "unnaturally" powerful matriarchal presence – "so little grace / Doth gouerne her," Gobrius had argued, "that shee should stretch her arme / Against her King, / so little womanhood / And naturall good-nesse, as to thinke the death / Of her owne Sonne" (p. 17). In fact, however, the play does not allow the alternative of a matriarchal escape from patriarchal genealogy: Arane is actually the promoter not of female rule *per se* but of a return to the true patriarchal line, which Panthea represents as the sole heir of the old king. Speaking to Arane, Gobrius's reading of Panthea's lineage is significant: "There is a Ladie takes not after you, / Her Father is within her" (p. 17).

Gobrius's plot – and, we must notice, the plot that ends the play – thus has it both (patriarchal) ways. He both restores the original patriarchal line (Panthea inherits from the old king) and establishes his own son (apparently conceived and "delivered" through solely patriarchal genera-tion) as king by marriage – a marriage itself written into being by Gobrius's "witching letters." In other words, though the play routinely discredits the intemperate "tyrant" Arbaces (as several critics have noted),[62] it in the end (re)places this "Father" "propt by Diuinity" on the throne and gestures toward the impending marriage of representa-tives of the true patriarchal line and the patriarchal author. It is not altogether certain that "prop" and "propagate" have a common ety-mology, but we might notice that Arbaces is "propt" not only by divinity but also by his father's narrative. *A King and no King*'s title-page engraving suggests just such an equation; there a divine hand reaches down from a cloud to place/remove a crown on a king (Fig. 8). By taking away his patriarchal claim but restoring him through marriage, Gobrius similarly intervenes in a way that simultaneously uncrowns and crowns a king.[63]

Gobrius out-plots Arane, but there are other ways the play throws his author/ity into question. By elaborately relating how Arbaces and Panthea are not related, Gobrius's narrative implicitly acknowledges and restores the incest taboo the play has seemed continually on the verge of transgressing; as Gayle Rubin has convincingly argued, the incest taboo is the rule of the sex/gender system that perpetuates the circulation of women and patriarchy (in the narrow sense of that term).[64] The play has

A King and no King.

Acted at the *Globe*, by his Maieſties Seruants.

Written by *Francis Beamount*, and *Iohn Flecher*.

AT LONDON

Printed for *Thomas Walkley*, and are to bee ſold
at his ſhoppe at the Eagle and Childe in
Brittans-Burſſe. 1619.

Figure 8   Title page: Francis Beamount, and Iohn Flecher, *A King and no King* (London: for Thomas Walkley, 1619).

nevertheless already voiced a radical critique of that taboo and thus the very basis of patriarchy and Gobrius's claims within it. In the scene in which Arbaces and Panthea struggle with their desire and the knowledge of its prohibited status, Arbaces bemoans "Accursed man," who, he says, "hast all thy actions bounded in / With curious rules, when euerie Beast is free: / What is there that acknowledges a kindred / But wretched Man?" (p. 67). Proceeding further into his denaturalizing critique, he asks,

> Is there no steppe
> To our full happinesse, but these meere sounds
> Brother and Sister
> ...
> I haue liu'd
> To conquer men, and now am ouerthrowne
> Onely by words, Brother and Sister: where
> Haue those words dwelling? I will find vm out
> And vtterly destroy them, but they are
> Not to be grasp't: let vm be men or beasts,
> And I will cut vm from the earth, or townes,
> And I will rase vm, and then blow vm up:
> Let vm be Seas, and I will drinke them off,
> And yet haue vnquencht fire left in my breast:
> Let vm be any thing but meerely voice.   (p. 67)

These lines undercut Gobrius's author/ity on several grounds. First, they explicitly raise the possibility that the incest taboo is "a curious rule" and the terms of familial relationships "words" and "meere sounds." As the play, like Rubin's argument, suggests from the outset, this taboo is inextricably linked to what she has called "the traffic in women" and the expansion of male networks of power; before he decides to save his sister for himself, Arbaces assigns her in marriage to the Armenian king Tigranes in order to establish an alliance between their kingdoms. Second, the terms of Arbaces's argument enable a critique of the solution that ends the play, for those terms point up the extent to which Gobrius's play-concluding narrative is itself "meerely voice" – a narration of "meere sounds" that determines the network of familial (and thus extrafamilial) relations. That network includes "Brother and Sister," but also the term *father*, which, even as he acknowledges its authority in this culture, Arbaces cites in the terms of his earlier argument: "The verie reuerence of *the word* comes crosse me, / And ties mine arme downe" (my emphasis).

A final erosion of Gobrius's presentation is its authorization by Bessus, the play's *miles gloriosus*:

Arb ... I am Arbaces, we all fellow subiects,
Nor is the Queene *Panthæa* now my Sister.
  Bes. Why if you remember fellow subiect *Arbaces*,
I tolde you once she was not your sister, I say she
look't nothing like you.   (p. 87)

That Bessus – who has himself undergone the transformation from
"*Bessus* the coward" to "*Bessus* the valiant" (p. 44) and has spent the
play manipulating the terms and rules of soldierly honor – concurs with
and supports Gobrius's narrative further deconstructs its ostensible
authenticity. Gobrius's tale of familial, dynastic relations may be no
more authoritative than Bessus's own manipulations designed to delay
and avoid fighting with any of his many challengers.

Like *Pericles* and a number of other plays of this same period, then, *A
King and no King* includes an authorial presenter implicated in a rhetoric
of patriarchal absolutism, but it does so in tentative terms. Though the
play manages to maintain its patriarchal lineage and restore the country's
"father," the father–author–monarch equation is here splintered into a
number of figures. A self-styled patriarchal–absolutist, Arbaces's attempts at authorship are unsuccessful; Gobrius, who functions within the
play as an authorial presenter, is a father but no king. Just as the play
ends with a king and no king, it registers an author and no author.

It is perhaps only appropriate, then, that in the letter dedicating the
1619 quarto to Sir Henry Nevill, its publisher Thomas Walkley says that
the play has Nevill's "approbation and patronage, to the commendation
of the Authors, and incouragement of their further labours." It is a
reasonably sure thing that "Francis Beamount," listed along with "Iohn
Flecher" as a collaborator on the title page of this same quarto, laboured
no further after his death three years prior to the first appearance of
Walkley's letter. (We shall see in the next chapter, however, that
Beaumont continued to accumulate/generate work after his death by
what we might call a process of special delivery). In one very literal sense,
A King and no King has by 1619 an author (Fletcher, alive and productive
until 1625) and no author.

The juxtaposition of the title-page attribution to Beaumont and
Fletcher, the dedicatory letter encouraging "their further labours," and a
play that enthrones and deposes varying forms of author/ity speaks to
the complexity of authorial emergence in the plays of this period. As we
saw in the previous chapter's analysis of discourses of collaboration,
there is no easy fit between the apparent mode of a play's production and
its *representations* of textual reproduction; in this case a play advertised
as collaborative produces figurations of singular author/ity.[65] We are
analyzing – as Chaucer's brief appearance as "Noble Breeder" in the

collaborative *The Two Noble Kinsmen* demonstrates – an era of complicated transition in theatrical texts, from a paradigm of collaboration to
one of singular authorship.

So rare a wondred father

It is clear from Miranda's first line that author/ity in *The Tempest* is
deeply implicated in the structures of patriarchalism we have already
analyzed in detail: "If by your Art (my deerest father)," Miranda begins,
and this intersection of the patriarchal relation and "art" is elaborated in
the art-full puns of Prospero's speech a few lines later:

> I haue done nothing, but in care of thee
> (Of thee my deere one; thee my daughter) who
> Art ignorant of what thou art, naught knowing
> Of whence I am ...   (TLN100–03)[66]

This scene enacts Miranda's inscription as the artistic creation of her
father Prospero; as has often been noted, she is in this scene written by
him, given a history, interpellated as a subject of his extended and
insistent discourse.[67] To put this in the terms of this speech, her very
essence ("thou art ... ") is inscribed in a repeated verb of being that is
the homonym of Prospero's "art." Furthermore, these lines initiate the
play's island scenes both by emphasizing Miranda's relation to Prospero
("my deerest father ... thee my daughter") and by noting her derivation
from Prospero (alone); Miranda is "ignorant of what [she is]" because
she does not know what her father is. As in *Pericles*, this patriarchal
derivation is mediated uneasily by maternal chastity: "Thy Mother was a
peece of vertue, and / She said thou wast *my* daughter" (TLN 148–49). In
this play, the straightforward projection of a patriarchal lineage ("my
daughter ... onely heire, / And Princesse; no worse Issued") is facilitated
by the mother's absence – that is, an enabling invocation and immediate
erasure of her mediation.[68]

To read Miranda as Prospero's "art" is not sufficient, however, for
Prospero's larger "project" (a word he himself uses: "Now do's my
Proiect gather to a head" [TLN 1946]) is the staging of a dynastic
marriage between Miranda and Ferdinand, a union that establishes his
descendants in a place of even greater authority as Kings of Naples. The
culmination of Prospero's spectacular project is his staging of Ferdinand
and Miranda playing chess, a moment he introduces with a patriarchal
locution familiar from Gobrius's authorial presentation in *A King and no
King*. "I will requite you with as good a thing," Prospero tells his
audience,

At least *bring forth* a wonder, to content ye
As much as me my Dukedome.
Here Prospero discouers Ferdinand and Miranda, playing at Chesse.

(TLN 2138–42, initial emphasis mine)

Engaging the reproductive sense of *bring forth* (cf. *Macbeth*'s "Bring forth Men-Children onely"), Prospero, like Gobrius, both arrogates to himself the power of patriarchal reproduction and demonstrates his position as an authorial presenter. Punning on Miranda's name ("wonder"), he gives birth not only to his wondrous daughter, but also to the spectacle of the dynastic marriage he has carefully plotted, at the moment that he also regains political authority. The folio text's description of this moment ("Here Prospero *discouers* ..."), perhaps the work of the scribe Ralph Crane, includes the verb of so many period stage directions; signaling the uncovering or displaying of a spectacle, the drawing back of a curtain or arras, the word allies Prospero with the mechanics of theatrical presentation.[69] Significantly, *discover* also had a particular meaning in the game Prospero displays Miranda and Ferdinand playing: "to remove a piece or pawn which stands between a checking piece and the king, and so to put the latter in check" (*OED*). Prospero stages his discovery for a king (Alonso), and the spectacle of a man and woman playing chess (signifying, Frank Kermode notes, "highborn and romantic love"[70]) places that king "in check" by allying Prospero's lineage with his. *Discover* was also widely used in colonialist discourse of this period, where dis-covering, or seeing, ostensibly marks possession.[71] We will return shortly to the colonialist resonances of this play; at this point it is sufficient to say that, bringing forth a wonder, Prospero "discovers" his author/ity in a number of senses.

Though they focus on another of Prospero's spectacles, Francis Barker and Peter Hulme have similarly argued the importance of Prospero's representational control in the play. They see Prospero as "a playwright" (p. 201) who presents a particular version of history and achieves (not without momentary difficulties) a desired outcome through his manipulation of theatrical spectacle.[72] Barker and Hulme have convincingly demonstrated the importance of "distinguishing between Prospero's play and *The Tempest* itself" (p. 203); nevertheless, they conclude that "in the end [Prospero's] version of history remains *authoritative*, the larger play acceding as it were to the containment of the conspirators in the safely comic mode ... " (p. 203, their emphasis). Barker and Hulme are by no means the only critics to posit a playwright Prospero (and the play's continuing biographical fascination has resulted either from or in many such interpretations),[73] but in the context of a historicizing analysis of dramatic authorship, it is important to question the ease with which the term "playwright" can be applied to this play. As my attention to Prospero's bringing-forth may suggest, I want to examine more carefully the terms of such a metadramatic argument. What are the contingencies of a "playwright's" appearance on the stage at this particular moment in English history? What are (in Barker and Hulme's useful phrase) the "discursive con-texts" of the playwright's emergence onstage in this play?

As we have already noted, one of those con-texts is Prospero's spectacle of patriarchalism and dynastic alliance, and the second scene of the play is its presentation to and inculcation in Miranda. As Miranda and Prospero's exchange at the first entrance of Ferdinand illustrates, this is Renaissance sex/gender education in the patriarchal mode:

> *Pro.* The fringed Curtaines of thine eye aduance,
> And say what thou see'st yond.
> *Mira.* What is't a Spirit?
> . . .
> *Pro.* No wench, it eats, and sleeps, & hath such senses
> As we haue . . .
> *Mir.* I might call him
> A thing diuine, for nothing naturall
> I euer saw so Noble.
> *Pro.* It goes on I see
> As my soule prompts it . . .   (TLN 551–66)

But the sight Prospero arranges with Ariel's compliance is also, precisely, a theatrical scene, discovered by the advancing "Curtaines" of Miranda's eyes, "prompted" by Prospero. This emphatically theatrical "discovery" serves to make strange the "naturalness" of what we would call [hetero-sexual] love at first sight; the category of the "naturall" (as Miranda's speech points out) is exhibited here to be carefully stage-managed.

Prospero's most elaborate production is the celebratory betrothal masque he presents for Ferdinand and Miranda, a spectacle that attempts, with its images of abundance and "increase" (TLN 1767ff.), to establish a naturalness to their relation that its ornate production belies. Concerned as it is with the abundant production of legitimate issue, the masque returns obsessively to chastity; that this legitimacy is theatrically produced and non-natural is exposed in what Barker and Hulme have called "the only real moment of drama" in the play, the interruption of Prospero's authoritatively controlled spectacle:

Prospero *starts sodainely and speakes, after which to a strange hollow and confused noyse,* [the Reapers and Nimphes of the masque] *heauily vanish.* (TLN 1805–8)

With this extensive stage direction marking the deterioration of artifice, Prospero momentarily loses control of the play:

> *Pro.* I had forgot that foule conspiracy
> Of the beast *Calliban*, and his confederates
> Against my life: the minute of their plot
> Is almost come ...   (TLN 1809–12)

Significantly, the interruption of Prospero's presentation celebrating abundant, legitimate issue, is figured as an attempt against *Prospero's* life; the masque registers the extent to which, in the words of Stephen Orgel, "fears for Miranda's chastity are implicated in [Prospero's] sense of his own power, how critical an element she is in his plans for the future."[74] Here, as in *Pericles*, the text notes the daughter's centrality in "begetting" the authority of the father.

It is important to notice, furthermore, that the insurrection interrupting Prospero's dramatic presentation is itself a "plot," represented in a similarly metadramatic vocabulary. Glancing at the appearance here in derogatory mode of the prefix I earlier associated with collaboration ("*con*spiracy," "*con*federates"), we can say that the play stages, in this one dramatic moment, a clash of author/ity – Prospero's ability to control both the masque, "Some vanity of mine Art" (TLN 1695), and his daughter's production of legitimate "Issue" – and a collaborative plot with political aspirations of its own. That is, the play encodes at this moment the intersection of an author-figure who presents himself as both "bringing forth" and controlling representation ("Spirits, which by mine Art / I haue from their confines call'd to enact / My present fancies" [TLN 1782–84]), and a collaborative and improvisatory band of "Fellowes" (TLN 2269), a term used widely in the period to denote members of a theatrical company.[75]

Caliban's subjection and insurrection have their origin in his earlier attempt to rape Miranda and divert Prospero's legitimate lineage ("Thou didst preuent me, I had peopel'd else / This Isle with *Calibans*" [TLN 490–91]), an event that his interruption of the betrothal masque recapitulates with increased and polygamous force. (We should harbor no illusions, that is, that the clash of patriarchal authority and collaborative subversion has a liberating potential for Miranda.) This collaborative insurrection is no less easily prevented, but once again we must notice the terms in which that prevention is enacted. On Prospero's orders, Ariel diverts the collaborators from their "plot" with "glistering apparell, &c.," and these costumes are later called (in a stage direction) "their stolne Apparell" (TLN 2248). Prospero's containment of the rebellion, in other words, might be said to stage a typical period critique of the theatre; actors were constantly being accused of shape-shifting, breaking sumptuary laws, dressing in "glistering apparell" inappropriate to their class-status, apparel "stolne" from other locations in this culture.[76]

Caliban, Trinculo, and Stephano are punished with an act that audiences in the theatres witnessed on a daily basis; if this incident figures "the containment of the conspirators in the safely comic mode" (Barker and Hulme, "Nymphs and Reapers," p. 203), it also marks them as the "fellows" of a theatrical company.

The strategy by which Prospero combats the insurrection and re-establishes his authority eventually undercuts it, for in the interim he has himself appeared "in his Magicke robes" and then in the "fine" costume of the Duke of Milan:

> *Ariell,*
> Fetch me the Hat, and Rapier in my Cell,
> I will discase me, and my selfe present
> As I was sometime Millaine . . .
> *Ariell sings, and helps to attire him.*   (TLN 2039–42)

The text dwells on this moment, announcing the change of costume and then marking it with a song. Prospero's "discasing" as magician and theatrical presenter and his reattiring in more politic form suggests that he is not outside the realm of representation he ostensibly supervises ("I will . . . my selfe present"), and second, that his authority is constructed and legitimated by the very mode he has used to subvert the rebels. The play articulates this possibility in its final scene, with Alonso doubting at several points the legitimacy of Prospero's self-presentation and de-manding authoritative proof:

> Where thou bee'st he or no,
> Or some inchanted trifle to abuse me,
> (As late I haue beene) I not know . . .   (TLN 2070–72)

> If thou beest *Prospero*
> Giue vs particulars of thy preseruation,
> How thou hast met vs heere, whom three howres since
> Were wrackt vpon this shore?   (TLN 2099–2102)

> some Oracle
> Must rectifie our knowledge.   (TLN 2234–35)

Voiced by a king, these speeches register the possibility that Prospero's author/ity is a representation, a costuming of "glistering apparell," "some inchanted trifle." Alonso questions whether, after so much exaggerated theatricality, it is possible to trust this last spectacle, presented as The Real. As in *Pericles* (where "truth can neuer be confirm'd inough"), proof, the authorization of Prospero, is deferred, here by the authority himself; the guarantees Prospero offers are heavily qualified:

Doe not infest your minde, with beating on
The strangenesse of this businesse, at pickt leisure
                            ... I'le resolue you,
(*Which to you shall seeme probable*) of euery
These happend accidents   (TLN 2237–41, my emphasis)

Importantly, even as he has renounced his magic and dressed himself in
political authority, Prospero retains throughout this scene his powers of
presentation; answering Alonso's plea for proof in the last speech before
the epilogue, Prospero's totalizing promise resonates with his earlier
patriarchal generation, the "bringing forth" of dynastic wonders: "I'le
deliuer all" (TLN 2313).

Discovering the globe

... the *Author* hath writ it iust to his *Meridian* ...
                the Booke-holder, about the Stage-keeper, "The Indvction on the Stage,"
                                                                Bartholmew Fayre[77]

He invades Authours like a Monarch, and what would be theft in other
Poets, is onely victory in him.
                Neander, speaking of Ben Jonson in John Dryden's *Of Dramatick Poesie*[78]

It is customary to end with *The Tempest*. That is, it has been customary
to end discussions of the authorship of one particular Renaissance writer
with *The Tempest*, because the play has been taken to encode an
autobiographical commentary on authorship at the close of an authorial
career: Shakespeare's farewell to his theatre, his art. This critical paradigm is by no means extinct; in a recent book on "the collective
production of literary pleasure and interest," for example, Stephen
Greenblatt moves from considering *Measure for Measure* to *The Tempest*
by remarking that "near the close of his career Shakespeare reflected
upon his own art with still greater intensity and self-consciousness ..."[79]
This interpretation has often made for an orderly biographical trajectory,
but it is complicated by what is usually recorded in the available
chronology; Shakespeare's career seems instead to take up (or, as the
previous chapter suggests, to resume or continue) collaboration, in *The
Two Noble Kinsmen*, the lost *Cardenio*, and (perhaps) *Henry VIII*.[80]
    If my interpretation shares with Greenblatt's an interest in what he
calls "the playwright as princely creator," I differ in taking *The Tempest*
not as an end but as a beginning. Indeed, the play provides a beginning
as the first play in *Mr. William Shakespeares Comedies, Histories &
Tragedies*, a volume that is both the first successful collection of plays
attributed to Shakespeare and the first to attempt his construction as an
author.[81] Though we customarily think of *The Tempest* as valedictory

(and it appears at the back of modern collected editions like the Oxford and Riverside), I want in this context to think of its possibilities as introductory, an inscription of the *beginnings* of authorship on the English stage. Such an analysis, at the same time, moves the play out of one local context to which it is usually said to refer (the arc of Shakespeare's career, the romance of Shakespeare's family),[82] and reads it instead in the larger context of the theatre and printed theatrical texts. We will never prove that this play is Shakespeare's valediction, the final expression of his "self-conscious" and previously extant feelings about his "art." But we can find evidence that, like the contemporaneous plays introducing the figure of the authorial presenter, *The Tempest* is an inscription and performance of authorship's intrusion into a theatre that had not customarily welcomed or even noted its presence.

The Tempest speaks resonantly within the "con-texts" of burgeoning English colonialism; in Barker and Hulme's convincing reading the playwright Prospero presents a particular version of colonial beginnings on the island and achieves mastery over his colonial subjects through his manipulation of theatrical spectacle.[83] Keeping in mind Barker and Hulme's useful notion of "con-texts," as well as Prospero's kinship with the other authorial presenters we have examined, I want in a sense to read the colonial reading back onto the history of the theatre and the author – to argue that the colonial meanings the play circulates participate in an array of texts that also inform and reform the play and the institution that produced it. Put simply, if *The Tempest* registers the colonization of the Americas, Ireland, and (internally) of England itself,[84] the play also stages the author colonizing the theatre. Part of Prospero's "insubstantiall Pageant" – insubstantial, but politically effective in a local way nonetheless – is "the great Globe it selfe," a phrase that (it is both obvious and necessary to say) names both a theatre and a planet.[85]

The Tempest is contemporaneous not only with a range of colonialist literature (including, for example, the first publication of *Purchas his Pilgrimage* in 1613), but also with *Bartholmew Fayre*, a play that explicitly stages the intrusion of an author into the theatre in its unusual "Indvction on the Stage." "Gentlemen; not for want of a *Prologue*, but by way of a new one," the Booke-holder says, "I am sent out to you here, with a *Scriuener*, and certaine Articles drawne out in hast betweene our *Author*, and you" (A5). The novelty of this appearance is marked in this line by the "new" prologue "drawne out in hast," and, as has been argued by several critics, it is perhaps the earliest explicit appearance of the *playwright*-author on the English stage.[86] This Induction, in its sustained mock-contract between author and audience, makes explicit

the contestation of the author's relation to theatrical space we have
analyzed in other texts. Alongside *Pericles*, and other plays that bring
authorial figures onto the stage, *The Tempest* participates in that
contestation through the discourse of colonization. Like Prospero, the
Booke-holder of Jonson's induction wrests control of the theatre from
the Stage-keeper, spokesman for the improvisatory and collaborative
mode of theatrical production of an ostensibly prior era: "Master
Tarletons time." As Peter Stallybrass and Allon White observe, Jonson's
"authorship" is "an act performed on and against the theatrical script"
(p. 75). The "Master *Poet*," the Stage-keeper says, has "kick'd me three,
or foure times about the tyring-house ... for but offering to put in, with
my experience" (A4ᵛ), and we might usefully compare to this the abuse
of Caliban, the notably prior resident of the island Prospero colonizes, at
the hands of his book-holding master: "I shall be pincht to death"
(TLN 2272). It is perhaps no surprise in such a context that Caliban has
usually been taken as the "*Seruant-monster*" derided in *Bartholmew
Fayre*'s induction (A6). Further – like Prospero teaching Caliban speech,
like Homer teaching "speech, and vnderstanding both / Euen in the
Cradle" – this induction instructs the theatre in a new authorial discourse
that crucially renegotiates the relations of power between actors and
playwrights; the magnitude of this usurpation is illustrated by comparison with the relatively powerless situation of Jonson's protégé, the
playwright Richard Brome, as it is represented in the only surviving
contract between an acting company and a playwright from this period.
The playwright of the time, this contract makes clear, is a disempowered
employee of the theatrical company.[87]

In this context, we can return to the terms in which *The Tempest*
figures authorial colonization. I have already alluded to Prospero as a
Booke-holder. He repeatedly associates political authority with textual
possession ("my Librarie / Was dukedome large enoughe"), and, if in
Milan overattention to study had allowed his usurpation, books enable
authority on the island Prospero takes from Caliban; a crucial part of
any insurrection, Caliban insistently reminds his collaborators, is "First
to possesse his Bookes" (TLN 1446). Political authority, and indeed the
very idea of hierarchy on the island has a textual basis: "without [his
Bookes] / Hee's but a Sot as I am; nor hath not / One Spirit to
command" (TLN 1447–48). Caliban stands resolutely outside the
domain of the script (even after he is trained to speak), as his threat to
Prospero's masque illustrates.

Crucially, *The Tempest* figures the intrusion of author/ity in the theatre
as a masque-writer, not as a "playwright" (the term used by Greenblatt,
Barker and Hulme). Author/ity, Prospero's artistry, is not depicted in

what we now know to be the terms of a playwright collaborating in the business of the theatre. Though like Gobrius and Gower he is associated with political author/ity and patriarchal representation and reproduction, Prospero's embodiment of these features is instead shifted onto the genre of the masque; from a generic perspective, the perspective of the public theatre, his appearance becomes a kind of foreign occupation, a non-indigenous intrusion. A number of court masques presented in the decade prior to *The Tempest*, in fact, have a striking relevance to Prospero's presentation in the play as we have analyzed it; here is Orgel's annotated list:

The light of royal presence turns the Ethiops of *The Masque of Blackness* white; the union of bride and groom in *Hymenaei* mirrors the uniting of the two kingdoms of England and Scotland through the new sovereign; the militant virtue exemplified in the heroines of *The Masque of Queens* is guided and controlled by the pacific virtue of the royal scholar; *Oberon* declares that the heir to the throne owes his power and his place to his father the king. (p. 45)

To the extent that Prospero's representations register closely related issues, then, *The Tempest* may be said to present author/ity not as something emerging from *within* the theatre, but imported into it from another cultural location – *outside*.

As I have already argued, the play does not leave Prospero altogether in control, and it is significant that at play's end he leaves the space he has colonized to wield his spectacular author/ity elsewhere, offstage. In the play's epilogue, which Prospero speaks, he is re-subjected to the demands of the collaborative theatre we identified in *The Knight of the Burning Pestle*; the language of the epilogue reverses earlier power relations between Prospero and his audience: "Let me not / ... dwell / In this bare Island, by your Spell, / But release me from my bands / With the helpe of your good hands" (TLN 2326–31).[88] If the speech posits a sanguine revision of Prospero's purpose in the play (here he says his "proiect ... was to please"), the final couplet demands further audience scrutiny of that project: "As you from crimes would pardon'd be," he says, "Let your Indulgence set me free." The epilogue stages at this moment a dialectic of absolutism and accountability; it both recalls that Prospero had only a few lines earlier occupied a position of absolute authority (able to offer Ariel the freedom he must himself now beg from the audience) and at the same time implicitly attributes to Prospero's project a criminality that requires pardon.[89]

Prospero's relinquishing of authority and his re-placement within the jurisdiction of the theatre audience has a striking analogue in the Bardh's final speech as the authorial presenter of *The Valiant Welshman*:

> now of you old Bardh intreates to tell,
> In good or ill, our Story doth excell.
> If ill, then goe I to my silent Tombe,
> And in my shrowde sleepe in the quiet earth,
> That did intend to giue a second birth.
> But if it please, then Bardh shall tune his strayne,
> To sing this Welshmans prayses once againe.
> Bells are the dead mans musicke: ere I goe,
> Your Clappers sound will tell me I, or no.   *Exit.*[90]

The Bardh both associates himself with the acting company ("our Story") and, like Prospero, subjects himself to the capital authority of the audience, allowing them to prevent a literal revival of the author and the play – to abort a production that Bardh describes as "a second birth." Unlike the Induction to *Bartholmew Fayre*, which exiles the stage's representative of theatricality and carefully circumscribes the audience's rights and participation in its Author's play, both *The Tempest* and *The Valiant Welshman* in the end submit their authorial figures to the "indulgence" of the audience. In an era before lexical standardization, it is, finally, tempting to hear in Bardh's last line an acknowledgment of the audience's power to constitute through the affirmation of applause ("aye or no") the very existence of authorial subjectivity: "tell me I, or no."[91]

A local habitation, and a name

> Prospero, who controls this comprehensive Shakespearean world, auto-matically reflects Shakespeare himself.
> G. Wilson Knight, *The Crown of Life*[92]

> ... the play belongs to Prospero in a way that seems downright un-Shakespearean.
> David Sundelson, " 'So Rare a Wonder'd Father': Prospero's *Tempest*"[93]

Given the traditional biographical interpretation of *The Tempest* (let Knight be its spokesperson), the reading outlined above may suggest another possibility. In *The Tempest*, Shakespeare describes (so the story might run) the colonization of the previously improvisatory and colla-borative theatre by a figure who (masque-creator and book-holder that he is) represents not Shakespeare himself, but rather Ben Jonson. Shakespeare subtly undercuts this Jonsonian figure's authority – by disrupting the masque, refusing to provide the rectifying "oracle" Alonso demands, and making Prospero, in the end, beg the theatre audience for freedom from confinement and pardon for his author-itarian "crimes."

Such a reading is biographically alluring, but its allure is of course that of the anachronistic author-question. An allegorization of a Shake-speare/Jonson rivalry puts us squarely back into an author-centered, agonistic paradigm that is only beginning to emerge in this and other plays of the period.[94] (In other words, if Shakespeare is the representative of a pre-authorial collaborative theatre, why is he concerned with a Jonsonian rival?) The more convincing argument, I think, is to read the play as registering – in a way that is neither coherent allegory nor decipherable intention – a number of the tensions and places of fracture in the new discourse of author/ity only beginning to emerge within the theatre. To the extent that authorship is emergent in the "authorial presenters" of this and other plays, *The Tempest* displays the range of authorship's intersection with and implication in other discourses of the period: the rhetoric of patriarchal reproduction, the language of political authority and absolutism, the discourse of a global imperialism and colonization.

Unavailable in print for more than a decade after its earliest perfor-mances, *The Tempest* can be read as a crowning authorial statement, the "issue" of Shakespeare, only when it takes a place at the beginning of the first folio collection, a volume that participates (as we shall have a chance to see more fully in the next chapter) in a patriarchal–absolutist forma-tion of author/ity. By that point, in 1623, the contestation of colonized theatrical space might be said to be settled (so to speak), at least as the folio text momentarily has it. For on the last page of *The Tempest* in that volume – after the text of the play and alongside its epilogue – the play's location is announced in a way that erases the earlier collaborative mode of the theatre (call it Caliban, or "Master *Tarletons* time"). "The Scene," the folio says, is "an vn-inhabited Island." This simple setting registers a central myth of colonialism (Columbus "discovering" America, the erasure of indigenous populations and cultures), and once again it is instructive to read colonialist discourse back onto the theatre. In 1609, as we have seen, George Wilkins's version of *Pericles* had shown an acting company presenting plays "vnder the habite" of the author and had thus registered in nascent form a contestation of author/ity between actors and authors. In contrast, the last page of the folio *Tempest*, in a way that the play itself belies, represents the author as moving into a theatre figured simply as uncontested, uninhabited space.

4   Reproducing works: dramatic quartos and folios in the seventeenth century

I must confesse *I* have *Gravidum Cor, fetum Caput*, a kind of *Impostume* in my head, which I would be delivered of, and know no other way of *Evacuation*, that can please me like this.

Mercurius Elencticus, 23 February–1 March 1648[1]

In the previous chapter, I argued that a notion of authorship emerged tentatively in theatrical texts of the early seventeenth century, and that this emergence was articulated in terms of a patriarchal–absolutist model of authority. I emphasized the performative theatrical quality of that emergence, but as that chapter's opening glance at James's *Workes* indicates, and as I indicated by drawing attention to the printed apparatus of the play-texts, these developments were not independent of authorial emergence in printed texts. It is largely that printed apparatus that will concern us in this chapter. We will take as an illustrative example of the emergence of authorship in printed theatrical texts the plays associated with the names Beaumont and Fletcher, beginning with those plays as printed in quarto, and proceeding to an analysis of the volume that first began to collect them (or rather, to construct them *as* collectable, and to structure the terms of that collection), the first Beaumont and Fletcher folio of 1647. At the same time, we will necessarily be concerned with the conditions and conventions of production in the plays associated with, and collected under the names of, other authorial figures, including Ben Jonson, William Shakespeare, and, in a brief final chapter, Margaret Cavendish.

Print's attire

As I suggested in chapter 1's consideration of *The Knight of the Burning Pestle*, play-text quartos printed early in the late sixteenth and early seventeenth centuries generally did not record the presence of an author or authors, but were instead "authorized" by their advertised connection with theatrical production, the presence of actors (and their patrons), theatres, and audiences. A prominent statement that appears in some form on virtually every quarto from this period (despite the wide variety of acting companies and printers) is formulaic, advertising the text "as it was sundrie times acted by" (for example) "the Right Honourable the Earle of Pembroke his seruants."[2] Although the name of the acting company of course varies widely, the emphasis on the text's theatricality remains in most versions. It advertises the text of this play "as" it was performed on the stage, and that important and under-scrutinized *as* registers the quartos' insistence on their theatrical genesis, introducing the acting companies into the texts. Other variations on this statement – what we might call the texts' guarantee of theatricality – emphasize specific theatrical locations ("at the Globe on the Banck-side," or "in the two Vniversities ... and elsewhere").[3] Furthermore, this theatrical guarantee also often includes a reception history, a suggestion that the play in its original format was received "with general approbation" or "great applause."

Importantly, however, the theatrical is not the only presence on the quarto title pages. Elizabeth Eisenstein has shown that printers began to foreground their manufacture of texts (and thus differentiate them from manuscripts) by bringing the traditional colophon to the front of their products, on the title page,[4] and printers likewise make a prominent appearance on play-text quartos. A colophon not only attributes the play's printing (thus injecting it into the realm of reward, responsibility, and accountability administered by the Stationers' Company), but also tells, it must be remembered, *where* the play-text might actually be purchased; as Peter Blayney's provocative research has suggested by mapping the geography of London print culture, locations are significant.[5] The emphatic situating of these title pages – their placement of the play-text "at the Globe on the Banck-side" *and* "at the signe of the Sunne in Pater-noster row,"[6] for example – should remind us that these texts functioned foremost in their own time as marketable commodities: first, as theatrical commodities much like props and costumes,[7] valued for their ability to draw paying crowds into the often highly successful business places of the theatres; second, as print commodities, marketed by publishers who attempted to capitalize on the popularity generated by theatrical performances. The quarto title page (in a sense muted or at least reconfigured by dramatic folios, as we shall see) stands at the intersection of two interconnected media markets. It bears the marks of the text's transition from one medium ("as it hath beene publiquely acted ...") to another ("Imprinted at London and are to be sold ..."). The value of this mobile commodity, as the title pages emphatically demonstrate, derives from its close connection with a performance history and a theatrical venue.

But though the quarto title pages inscribe the transition between media, they attempt to smooth or erase this transition from performance to print. Genre designations signaling theatricality, sensational bits of the plot ("the obtayning of *Portia* by the choyse of three chests"), the names of memorable characters ("with *Auntient Pistoll*") and particular actors ("*VVith* KEMPS *applauded Merrimentes*"), the guarantee of theatrical performance, the names of acting companies, the locations and reception of performances – all of these staples of quarto title pages foreground performance as the marketable attribute of these texts.[8] Writing "to the friendly peruser" of a play quarto, actor/playwright Robert Armin tries to finesse the transition from stage to page, hoping that, in lieu of a subsequent performance, the reader will "accept this dumbe show."[9]

Armin's words suggest what we can observe on the title pages of the many play quartos from the early seventeenth century: quartos are working in this culture as the silent surrogates for the ostensible thing itself, theatrical performance. The emphasis in these publications is not on a "reading" text (that is, a work authorized by its putative status as dramatic literature) but rather on a text that functions as a record of – a *reconstitution* of – a particular theatrical performance a reader/consumer may have heard of or attended. Thomas Bodley famously barred play-text quartos from his newly founded university library, and we might read his statement,[10] along with these observations about the quartos themselves, as an indication that in this period play-text quartos did not function as books in the conventional sense. Often lacking the bookish apparatus of most other period volumes (dedicatory letters, commendatory poems, addresses to readers) and emphasizing instead their connection with theatrical performance, they had no clear place in the libraries of the period. What counts as a book is culturally variable. That the Bodleian was the first recorded purchaser of the 1623 Shakespeare folio, which included many of the "same" texts disparaged by Bodley's earlier remarks, suggests that play-texts *per se* were not the issue, but rather the format in which those plays came packaged.[11]

I glance at these features of quarto title pages because it is especially important to emphasize what loomed large for the early seventeenth-century reader/consumer of these texts. Focused intently on one piece of information – a playwright's name, only occasionally present – bibliography in the current century has largely ignored the constellation of other figures present on quarto title pages and has read them as peripheral bits of information useful only insofar as they substantiate, call into question, or lead back to an authorial identity.[12] When playwrights' names do begin to appear on quarto title pages, however, they remain only one of the many features recorded there. Often typographically smaller than the other items on these pages, writers' names appear as another marketing strategy among the several already mentioned. As Peter Stallybrass has suggested, for example, "M. William Shak-speare" may appear on the 1608 quarto of the *True Chronicle Historie of the life and death of King Lear* as a way of differentiating this *Lear* from *The True Chronicle History of King Leir*, published three years before.[13] In *Pericles*, as we saw in the previous chapter, the playwright's name literally functions as an ornament.

The increasing frequency of title-page attributions to playwrights in the first three decades of the seventeenth century is clearly related to the discourses of authority we have examined in the previous chapter, but not necessarily in the sense that authors took control of their texts and insisted upon attribution of properties rightfully theirs in a language of patriarchal–absolutism. Furthermore, the more frequent presence of writers' names on play quartos is also related to the publication of texts of the same genre in folios, beginning with Jonson's *Workes* in 1616 and the 1623 Shakespeare folio; to the extent that plays were now also said to be books, they increasingly developed *in quarto* the apparatus of the book, including authorial ascription, and preliminary materials.

The plays of the so-called "Beaumont and Fletcher canon" can serve to specify the process I am describing, since we will return to this group of plays when we consider the Beaumont and Fletcher folios published later in the century.[14] Prior to the first collection of Beaumont and Fletcher plays in the 1647 folio, forty-six editions of plays eventually associated with their names had appeared in quarto.[15] Of these forty-six, all of the editions that were published *without* a title-page attribution of authorship (eight in all) appeared *before* 1623, the date of the first Shakespeare folio. (One of these early editions, the undated *Masque of the Inner Temple* [probably 1613], also circulated in a form that included a title page ascribing it to Beaumont.[16]) Although three other attributed editions appeared before the 1616 Jonson folio – *The Faithfvll Shephear-desse* and *Cupids revenge* (attributed to Fletcher) and *The Scornefvl Ladie* (attributed to both) – editions with writers' names began to appear rapidly in 1619–20, and after 1622 *no* edition of a play eventually included in the Beaumont and Fletcher canon was published without ascribing authorship, whether to Fletcher (nine editions), Beaumont and Fletcher (nineteen), Fletcher and Shakespeare (*The Two Noble Kinsmen*), or the anomalous "B.J.F." (*The Bloody Brother*).[17] Of the five plays (in eight editions) that appeared without dramatists' names before 1623, the two republished after that date both include an attribution to Beaumont and Fletcher.

By the late 1620s and 1630s, when most of these editions were published, the quartos had begun to develop the elaborate apparatus of other literary texts. Where earlier quartos attempted (as I have argued) to pass themselves off as representations of a theatrical event, these editions include character lists, dedicatory letters, and addresses to the reader. Unlike previous editions of the play, the 1631 *A King and no King* (Fig. 9), for example, draws attention to itself as a printed replacement for a play in its title-page inscription "The STATIONER to DRAMATO-PHILVS," punning on the play's title: "A Play and no Play, who this Booke shall read, / Will iudge, and weepe, as if 'twere done indeed."[18] Where earlier quartos had attempted to efface the transition from the theatrical performance "done indeed" to the printed "Booke," this text emphasizes the distinction: it is no longer a surrogate, but a deliberate *substitute* for the theatrical experience. Unlike its predecessors, this edition also includes a list of "The Personated Persons," a further indication of its constitution as a readerly text.

Although these quartos continue to include a statement guaranteeing their theatricality ("Acted at the *Blacke-Fryars*, by his MAIESTIES Seruants"), another figure begins increasingly to authorize these texts, appearing not only on title pages (as we have noted) but also in the preliminary apparatus of the quartos. Where quartos earlier in the century had simply preceded playwrights' names with "By," "Written by," or "Made by," later quartos occasionally use the word "Author." The history of *Phylaster. Or Loue lyes a Bleeding* records this shift: while the first two quartos (1620 and 1622) record that they are "Written by" Beaumont and Fletcher, the 1628 third quarto revises this attribution to "The Authors being Francis Beaumont and Iohn Fletcher."[19] The 1639 quarto *Monsievr Thomas*, attributed to "The Author, IOHN FLETCHER, Gent.," also includes a dedication "To the Noble Honovrer of The dead Authors works and memory, Master Charles Cotton," and a commenda-tory poem signed by the playwright Richard Brome "In prayse of the Authour, and his following Poeme."[20] Both these preliminary pieces shift the play away from a construction as theatrical event and toward consideration as a more emphatically legible "work" and "poeme." Brome's poem urges readerly acceptance of the play because " 'tis authoriz'd by the Authors name." At its earliest performances, the play was not praised ("it did participate / At first presenting but of common fate"), but, Brome argues, that was a time "When ignorance was judge, and but a few / What was legitimate, what bastard, knew" (A2). What may begin as a note on the historicity of aesthetic judgment – at the time the play was first acted, few could discern what was a "legitimate" play – quickly reveals itself as an interpretation based on the identification of an author: "The world's growne wiser now: each man can say / If *Fletcher*

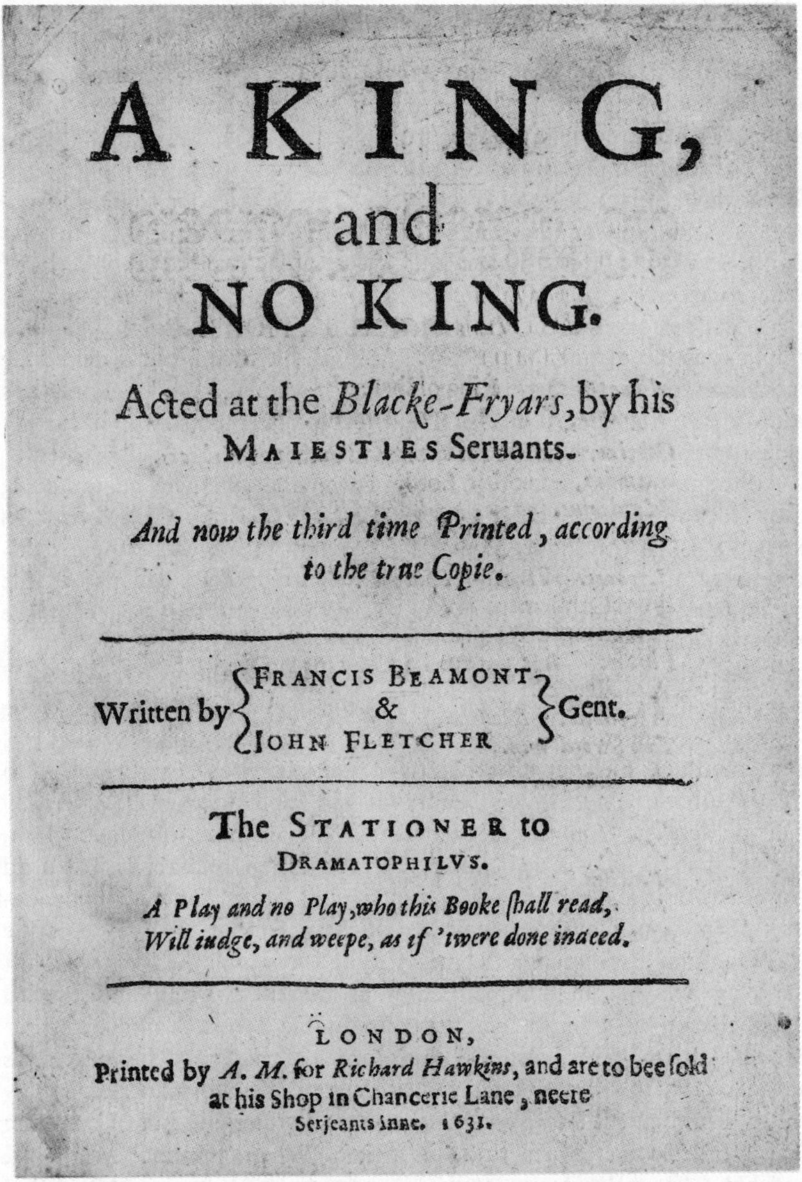

A KING,

and

NO KING.

Acted at the *Blacke-Fryars*, by his
MAIESTIES Seruants.

*And now the third time Printed, according
to the true Copie.*

Written by $\left\{\begin{array}{c}\text{FRANCIS BEAMONT}\\ \& \\ \text{IOHN FLETCHER}\end{array}\right\}$ Gent.

The STATIONER to
DRAMATOPHILVS.

*A Play and no Play, who this Booke shall read,
Will iudge, and weepe, as if 'twere done indeed.*

LONDON,
Printed by *A. M.* for *Richard Hawkins*, and are to bee sold
at his Shop in Chancerie Lane, neere
Serjeants inne. 1631.

Figure 9   Title page: Francis Beamont & Iohn Fletcher Gent., *A KING,
and NO KING* (London: by A. M. for Richard Hawkins, 1631).

made it 'tis an exc'lent play" (A2). With this statement, the preceding lines, with their concern over legitimacy and bastardy, clearly figure authorship in the patriarchal–absolutist mode we identified in chapter 3. The "Prologue" to the 1637 *The Elder Brother*, also stressing an authorial identification, likewise asks, "may it raise in you content and mirth, / And be receiv'd for a legitimate birth."[21]

If the more frequent appearance of playwrights' names on quarto title pages and the publication of dramatic folios organized around author-figures signals in some sense "the birth of the author," we must never-theless notice that such terminology is misleading; at the outset, at least, the author, to the extent that he is born, is often already dead. With the exception of a canceled title page to *The Masque*, and the possible exception of the first edition of *Scornefvl Ladie* (published in 1616, the year he died), Beaumont never appeared as an author prior to his death. Fletcher's name appeared alone on two quartos during his life, but began to appear with increasing frequency as a member of the amalgamated Beaumont and Fletcher name after Beaumont's death, and still more frequently (both alone and with Beaumont) after his own death in 1625. As authors, Beaumont and Fletcher are stillborn.

Generations

Farewell, thou child of my right hand, and joy;
My sin was too much hope of thee, lov'd boy ...
Rest in soft peace, and, ask'd say here doth lie
Ben. Jonson his best piece of poetry.
            "On My First Son," *Epigrammes* XLV, *Workes* (1616)

Quarto play-texts, in general, highlight a network of figures associated with play-making – actors, audiences, printers, sometimes (and increas-ingly) writers – a situation that began to change, as I have suggested, contemporaneously with the publication of dramatic folios, particularly *The Workes of Beniamin Jonson* in 1616 and *Mr. William Shakespeares Comedies, Histories, & Tragedies* in 1623. As a number of recent studies have shown, those volumes rearranged and reconstituted this network of figures, and began to organize the plays around a central authorial figure. Studies by Peter Stallybrass and Allon White, Joseph Loewen-stein, Timothy Murray, and others on the Jonson folio, and by Peter Blayney, Margreta de Grazia, and Leah Marcus on the Shakespeare folio, have suggested the immense amount of cultural work involved in converting at these two sites texts written for the theatre (in which the author was at the very least decentered) into volumes that could organize texts under a single patronymic.[22] I want to emphasize here what has been implicit in at least some of the productive critical treatment of these two important volumes; while it is crucial to recognize the new mode in which these folio volumes work, it is important not to see the construction of dramatic authorship in the early seventeenth century as anything resembling a *fait accompli*. Many of these studies have emphasized the tentativeness of this new mode of organization – its reliance on earlier models of classicism and patronage, and its continued dependence on the network of figures associated with the theatre and the publishing house – and I want at the same time to stress that the folio continued to be a site of contestation, a busy and often discursively chaotic authorial construction site, well into the 1660s, as we will see.

I resist the notion that dramatic authorship becomes an accomplished fact with the publication of the Shakespeare folio in 1623 because such a construal often assumes that authorship is a desire in the minds of authors that pre-exists its articulation; the appearance of authorship in the Ben Jonson and Shakespeare folios of 1616 and 1623 respectively is said to give voice to that which is always–already present, the presumptive human desire to possess what one has written. Authorship, in this paradigm, does not come into being so much as it is at long last given articulation; *emergence*, the word I have generally used in this book, is no doubt an imperfect term as well, especially if it is taken to imply that authorship comes out from within some interior, anterior space. This I take to be the assumption of Loewenstein's description of Jonson's "bibliographic ego"; likewise, a careful sentence in Marcus's recent reading of the Shakespeare folio – "the construction of a transcendent, independent place for art was a project that empowered seventeenth-century authors and opened up a whole range of new possibilities for their lives and work" – holds within it her assumption that "Authors wanted to be recognized as individuals with their own identifying attributes." The emergence of authorship, in such a scheme, becomes another step in the ongoing march of human freedom; the category of the "individual" (with its corollary identifications and attributes) is severed from history and from its implication in the very modes of writing we are analyzing.[23]

Throughout this project, it has been my assumption, first, that "seventeenth-century authors" did not exist independently of their construction in the textual materials we read, and that, to the extent that there appears to have been a desire for authorship, that desire is itself related to the textual articulation of authorship elsewhere.[24] Second (and following from this), since the dramatic folios early in the century did not simply voice already-present desires, they also did not simply bring forth authorship in the apparently immutable and timeless form familiar to us today. As this chapter will demonstrate, through an analysis of the first Beaumont and Fletcher folio, the viability of the author as the paradigm of textual production in drama was still very much open to question in 1647. Far from being an accomplished event ("the birth of the author") authorship continued to be negotiated in relation to collaboration. As we will see in this volume's retrospective view of collaborative texts written earlier in the century, collaboration is also rewritten in relation to the emerging regime of the author.

The Beaumont and Fletcher volume will also suggest the extent to which notions of textual production remain inseparable from discursive realms now usually viewed as distinct: sexual, reproductive, political, dynastic. De Grazia's important rereading of the Shakespeare folio preliminaries has stressed the tropes of affiliation, filiation, and consanguinity in the Shakespeare first folio; "the 1623 preliminaries," she writes, "work to assign the plays a common lineage: a common origin in a single parent and a shared history of production."[25] We have had occasion to notice that, in gathering its plays under a single patronymic, Heminge and Condell's address "To the great Variety of Readers" takes its cue from Winton's dedication of James's 1616 *Workes* and its central place in the rhetoric of patriarchal succession; we can add to this list of patriarchally inflected folios the 1598 Chaucer works and the *Cyropedia*, among many others. While the apparatus of the Jonson folio has not been as open to such an interpretation, the epigram that serves as epigraph above suggests that Jonson's book was not unacquainted with the rhetoric of patriarchal reproduction, and, as we noted earlier in connection with the phrase "Greeke and Latin Fathers" in James's *Workes*, the classical authorship out of which Jonson is often said to have fashioned his own[26] cannot be cordoned off from a rhetoric of patriarchalism – not least at the nexus represented by the word *author*. The consideration of the Beaumont and Fletcher folio that follows will suggest both how influential the patriarchal model (new to dramatic collections in 1623) had become by mid-century as a way of organizing dramatic texts and, at the same time, how open to contestation it remained.

Double-take

Immediately upon opening the 1647 Beaumont and Fletcher first folio, one is faced with the co-existing figurations of authorship and collaboration as modes of textual production. Entitled *Comedies and Tragedies Written by Francis Beavmont and Iohn Fletcher Gentlemen*, the volume

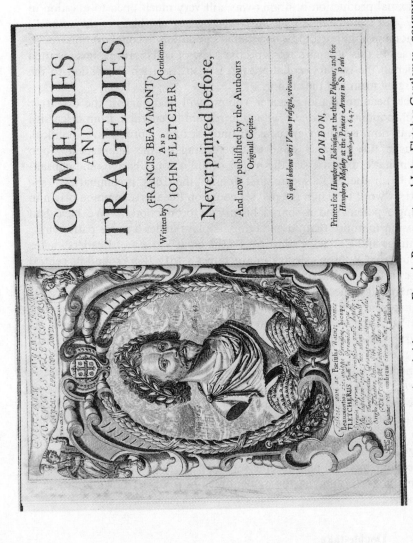

Figure 10 Frontispiece portrait and title page: Francis Beavmont and Iohn Fletcher Gentlemen, *COMEDIES AND TRAGEDIES* (London: for Humphrey Robinson and Humphrey Moseley, 1647).

juxtaposes this dual attribution with a portrait of Fletcher alone on the facing page (Fig. 10).[27] Rising as a classically sculpted bust out of a natural scene,[28] Fletcher is both accoutred in and surrounded by the conventions of authorship in the recognizably classical mode utilized by Jonson; he wears a toga and crown of laurels, the figures of Tragœdia and Comœdia recline above him on the margins of the engraving, and his portrait is both under- and over-written with Latin inscriptions denoting his position as poet. The volume both stresses the plurality of its attribution by bracketing its writers as "Gentlemen" in a fashion familiar from earlier collaborative title pages, *and* it visualizes its attribution as a singular author in classical garb. Though the title page itself would suggest that its term "Authours" is dual in this context ("now published by the Authours Originall Copies"), the juxtaposition of frontispiece and title page opens the possibility that (as in the early quarto of *The Knight of the Burning Pestle*) "Authours" may function here as either singular or plural possessive.[29] (The scope of this plural possession may open out even further when we consider, as we will at the end of this chapter, Aston Cokain's later argument that Massinger had collaborated extensively in the folio's plays without published recognition.[30]) The volume's seeming vacillation between singular authorship and dual collaboration is by no means stabilized by the extensive preliminary materials that lie between the title page and the plays themselves. Of the folio's thirty-seven commendatory poems, only seven are addressed to both Beaumont and Fletcher together; twenty-three are addressed to Fletcher alone, without (or with merely momentary) reference to Beaumont. Beaumont is the subject of three poems. And a number of the commendatory poems are addressed to one man but speak at length of the authors' collaboration.

There is what might be called a traditional bibliographical explanation for this ambiguity; that is, on the basis of some statements in the volume, one might propose a narrative explaining the conflicting claims of the title page and engraving. In his preface "The Stationer to the Reader," Humphrey Moseley (one of the volume's two publishers) says, "It was once in my thoughts to have Printed Mr. *Fletcher's* workes by themselves, because single & alone he would make a *Just Volume*: But since never parted while they lived, I conceived it not equitable to seperate their ashes" (A4ᵛ). One might argue that Moseley had intended to print the Fletcher-only volume and indeed had solicited commendatory poems for that purpose, but for some reason unknown to us decided instead to print the plays of both men together. But, in such a case, one would also have to posit a Moseley so oblivious in his function as collector and collator that he did not notice the apparent contradiction between engraved portrait and title page, or the fact that the majority of the commendatory poems in the volume are addressed to Fletcher alone.

In his prefatory discussion of the frontispiece, Moseley devotes some attention to the apparent conflict: "I was very ambitious to have got Mr. *Beaumonts* picture; but could not possibly, though I spared no enquirie in those *Noble Families* whence he was descended, as also among those Gentlemen that were his acquaintance when he was of the *Inner Temple*: the best Pictures and those most like him you'l finde in this *Volume*" (A4^v). Like Moseley's aborted attempt to separate Fletcher's plays into a "Just Volume," "single & alone," his effort here to differentiate the two writers (the attempt to supply two portraits, to provide separate genealogies of family and "acquaintance") eventuates not in distinction but in inseparability: Beaumont's "best Pictures and those most like him" are to be found in this volume of (undifferentiated) Beaumont and Fletcher plays. The impetus of this statement toward differentiation ("read Beaumont's texts as his best likeness") is itself a convention, as readers of the Shakespeare first folio preliminaries will immediately recognize; the lack of Beaumont's portrait in Moseley's collection resonates with the concluding lines of the poem accompanying the engraved portrait in the Shakespeare volume: "Reader, looke / Not on his Picture, but his Booke."[31] Literally unable to look on Beaumont's picture, the reader of Moseley's volume is sent in a direction that both fails to differentiate Beaumont from Fletcher and alludes to the conventionality of such attempts. Apparently compensating further for this lack, Moseley attests that Fletcher's portrait accurately depicts him (it was "cut by severall Originall Pieces"), or at least "As much as could be, you have here, and the *Graver* hath done his part" (A4^v). In what is only apparently a *non sequitur*, Moseley then proceeds without interruption to retrace the trajectory he had mapped for desirers of Beaumont's image; where earlier he had sent readers from the (lacking) portrait to the book, here he describes Fletcher's manuscript practice:

What ever I have seene of Mr. *Fletchers* owne hand, is free from interlining; and his friends affirme he never writ any one thing twice: it seemes he had that rare felicity to prepare and perfect all first in his owne braine; to shape and attire his *Notions*, to adde or loppe off, before he committed one word to writing, and never touched pen till all was to stand as firme and immutable as if ingraven in Brasse or Marble.

As de Grazia has noted, this too is a conventional statement, drawing on "a long history extending back to the pre-print era of classical rhetoric"[32] and alluding to its more recent inscription in the Shakespeare folio where, in a familiar claim, Heminge and Condell attest that Shakespeare's "mind and hand went together: And what he thought, he vttered with that easinesse, that we haue scarse receiued from him a blot in his papers" (A3). Fletcher's portrait cannot fully secure "his unimitable Soule" (the "Painters confessed it, was not easie to expresse him"), and the evidence evinced to supply that lack ("Mr. *Fletchers* owne hand") itself alludes heavily to a prominent precursor-volume – other hands describing another hand. The very demonstration of Fletcher's "*rare felicity*" is its conventionality.

Both narratives – the narrative of the oblivious publisher and the story of the careful stationer who attempts but is unable to secure the individuality (in the modern sense) of his two writers – seem untenable.[33] There is, instead, another possibility beyond the confines of a binary opposition that depends upon the publisher's reliability or unreliability as a witness. Moseley's preface isolates for us a moment in which the attempt to differentiate writers of collaborative texts written earlier in the century, to identify singular authors and organize volumes accordingly, is nascent in English culture, but that urge is neither universally prescriptive nor internally consistent. Moseley's preface begins by discussing Beaumont and Fletcher as a corporate entity, attests that it is "not equitable to seperate their ashes," and proceeds to attempt precisely that.[34] Abruptly ending his ruminations on Fletcher's manuscript practice and introducing the commendatory verse-writers, Moseley concludes his preface in the singular: "But I keepe you too long from those friends *of his* whom 'tis fitter for you to read . . ." (my emphasis).

Just as the urge to identify authorial origins is not consistently applied, it also does not exclude other claims. In his preface Moseley argues: (1) That he received his copy for the texts from the acting company. (2) That the actors "omitted some Scenes and Passages . . . as occasion led them," but that he has restored the complete text: "now you have both All that was *Acted*, and all that was not; even the perfect full Originalls without the least mutilation; So that were the *Authours* living, (and sure they can never dye) they themselves would challenge neither more nor lesse then what is here published" (A4). And (3) (in a postscript to the commendatory verses) that "some *Prologues* and *Epilogues* (here inserted) were not written by the *Authours* of this *Volume*; but made by others on the *Revivall* of severall *Playes*" (g1). From the standpoint of authorial authenticity (a standard Moseley himself invokes at points in this argument), these are three baldly conflicting claims. He argues that he has received copies in which there is nothing "*Spurious* or *impos'd*," since the copy derives from "such as received them from the *Authours* themselves" (A4). At the same time, he makes clear that those from whom he received the manuscripts routinely altered the texts and circulated copies that reflected those alterations, according to established theatrical practice.[35] Furthermore, he later writes that he has included pieces of plays "not written by the *Authours* of this *Volume*." Though these statements do not stand up to a modern standard of authorial authenticity, we can see that there are other principles at work. It is clear from this phrasing in Moseley's postscript, for example, that the term "Authour" is working not in the sense of those who have written (and take credit for) every word in the volume, but rather those who *authorize* it with their prominent names, those who give it its primary author/ity; they are "the *Authours* of this Volume," but not entirely its writers. Further, it is clear from Moseley's preface that, much more important than a consistent approach to the question of plural or singular, inseparable or discernible authorship, is the standard of a vendible volume. Moseley advertises his book as complete and completely new; unlike its Jonsonian and Shakespearean precursors, the Beaumont and Fletcher volume contains none of the plays that had been previously printed in quarto,[36] and with one announced exception, it claims to print every Beaumont and Fletcher play thus remaining out of print in 1647. It avers that it prints "All that was *Acted*, and all that was not," and, contradicting its own assertions of fidelity to authentic Beaumont and Fletcher text ("published by the Authours Originall Copies"), it also prints prologues and epilogues to revivals. The comprehensiveness thus embodied will last indefinitely: "the Reader must expect no future Alterations" (A4).

We can read the excesses and contradictions of Moseley's claims (and those, as we will see, of the larger volume) as inscriptions of a particularly pivotal moment in English cultural history – a moment when collaboration (and the attendant lack of concern, in certain discourses, over authorial attribution) has not yet been fully supplanted by the regime of the singular, proprietary author within which we now write. The liminality of this moment is illustrated by the articulation of what now appear to us as conflicting positions, and the Beaumont and Fletcher first folio is particularly interesting in the way that it attempts to work out conflictual discourses of writing. Within an increasingly authorial climate, the book is a retrospective glance at texts written in the more collaborative past.

Head-counts

We have already noted in passing how John Fletcher's portrait in the frontispiece to this folio calls forth some conventions of singular dramatic authorship, and I want to note here in more detail the ways in which this folio draws upon the conventions of the earlier dramatic folios of Jonson and Shakespeare to engage the idea of singular author/ity. We might say that the folio form itself, at least as it was beginning to be used to collect dramatic texts, carries with it the notion of singular authorship – that is to say, the famous precursors of the Beaumont and Fletcher folio used a singular figure, as de Grazia has argued, as an organizing trope for their texts. (Although from our perspective such an organization seems self-evidently natural, there are a number of other ways in which one might categorize and collect texts.) To the extent that such an organization had been worked out by the first and second Shakespeare and Jonson folios, the Beaumont and Fletcher volume does not so much work to construct such an organization as it works to appeal to this emergent tradition, in a number of ways. Like the Shakespeare first folio, the Beaumont and Fletcher folio includes a dedicatory epistle from the King's Men, and that letter is directed to the surviving dedicatee of the Shakespeare collection, as the letter itself prominently notes. The 1623 volume had been addressed

TO THE MOST NOBLE
AND
INCOMPARABLE PAIRE
OF BRETHREN.

1623.   *Ed. 1623.*

WILLIAM
Earle of Pembroke, &c. Lord Chamberlaine to the
Kings moſt Excellent Maieſty.

AND

PHILIP
Earle of Montgomery, &c. Gentleman of his Maieſties
Bed-Chamber. Both Knights of the moſt Noble Order
of the Garter, and our ſingular good
LORDS.

Noting the death of William, Philip's "(now glorified) Brother," the dedication to the Beaumont and Fletcher folio plays upon the earlier dedication, combining the "incomparable paire" into one figure whose titles serve as a collation of the previous dedicatees:

TO

THE RIGHT HONOVRABLE

PHILIP

Earle of Pembroke and Mountgomery:
Baron Herbert of Cardiffe and Sherland,

Lord Parr and Rofs of Kendall; Lord Fitz-Hugh,
Marmyon, and Saint Quintin; Knight of the moft noble Order of
the Garter; and one of His Majefties moft Honourable Privie Councell :
And our Singular Good Lord.

Likewise signed by members of the acting company (and invoking that tradition), this dedication draws upon the Shakespeare dedication, and, in a way that is perhaps compensatory in this doubly authored volume, draws attention to its consolidation of authority in a "Singular Good Lord" – a patron who is both exceptionally good and singly present.

A number of recent considerations of dramatic folios have emphasized the construction of the Jonson folio in particular over and against the category of the theatrical,[37] and, again playing on a historical contingency (like the death of brother William), the Beaumont and Fletcher volume connects itself to the tradition of authorial folios. As James Shirley (himself a playwright) argues in the next of the volume's prefaces, "To the Reader":

And now Reader in this *Tragicall Age* where the *Theater* hath been so much out-acted, congratulate thy owne happinesse that in this silence of the Stage, thou hast a liberty to reade these inimitable Playes, to dwell and converse in these immortall Groves, which were only shewd our Fathers in a conjuring glasse, as suddenly removed as represented, the Landscrap [i.e. landscape] is now brought home by this optick ... (A3)

Shirley here deploys the closing of the theatres five years earlier to authorize the volume he introduces, ostensibly constructing a new and less fleeting space of "liberty."[38] At once capitalizing on a nostalgia for, and writing against the ephemerality of the theatre ("as suddenly removed as represented"), he draws upon the trope of permanency so memorably constructed in the edifice that serves as title page to Jonson's volume. At the same time, however, writing in a print culture rapidly expanding in the initial absence of state censorship (and then with increasing regulation under Parliamentary control),[39] Shirley works to distinguish this volume from the flood of pamphlets and news-sheets coincident with the closing of the theatres:

the Landscrap is now brought home by this optick, and the Presse thought too pregnant before shall be now look'd upon as greatest Benefactor to Englishmen, that must *acknowledge* all the felicity of *witt* and *words* to this Derivation (A3–A3^v)

This "optick," quite literally a new way of seeing drama, brings the dramatic text "home" (again, literally), and the press's formerly excessive reproduction is restyled in the language of patronage as the "greatest Benefactor to Englishmen." The gendering of this metaphor of textual reproduction is significant; Shirley's sentence rewrites the press from a dangerous female fecundity toward apparently male benefaction, in the context of an argument that seeks to reproduce in more permanent form for its gentlemanly audience the representations fleetingly experienced by their "Fathers." Like Moseley's description of Fletcher's "rare felicity" in preparing and perfecting his texts "in his owne braine," Shirley traces "all the felicity of witt and words" back to the "Derivation" of a now-male press. This complex of reproductive and optickal allusion may rewrite – and for us, serve to reanimate the familiar rhetoric of – the Shakespeare folio, whose address to the readers offers its texts to "your view ... as he *conceiued* the[m]" (A3, my emphasis).

The form of the Beaumont and Fletcher volume and its allusions to a tradition of dramatic folios organized around a singular figure are not the only way in which the volume speaks to the emergent concerns of singular authorship: several of the commendatory verses speak within and rework the discourses we have already associated with the emergence of authorial figures in the theatre. A number of the poems play upon the notion of the resurrected authorial presenter, in the mode of Gower, Homer, or Guicciardini; Richard Lovelace writes "To FLETCHER Reviv'd," and I.M. opines that "The Poet lives; wonder not how or why / *Fletcher* revives, but that he er'e could dye" (c4ᵛ). In the most extended use of this trope, Robert Gardiner writes:

> Wonder! who's here? *Fletcher*, long buried
> Reviv'd? Tis he! hee's risen from the Dead,
> His winding sheet put off, walks above ground,
> Shakes off his Fetters, and is better bound.   (c2)

Gardiner concludes his poem with what may be an allusion both to contemporary politics and to Heywood's *Ages* plays, originally presented by the revived figure of Homer;[40] the folio, he argues, "at last unseque-sters the Stage, / Brings backe the Silver, and the Golden Age." Likewise punning on the "bound" and printed edition of the plays, Robert Stapylton invokes the notion of the authorial presenter, telling Fletcher that "we ... may th'*Impression* call / The *Pretor* that presents thy Playes to all" (a4ᵛ). Given Jonson's attempt to assert an authorial place within a canon of, and via the conventions of, classical authorship, H. Howard's imagining of Fletcher revived in "Elyzium" is a particularly interesting rewriting of the deceased author. Howard inserts Fletcher into the competition of "those Ancient Laureates"; Homer and Virgil both confess that Fletcher exceeds them in both epic and pastoral modes, and suggest that when next they write *they* will borrow from *him*. This is a particularly startling refiguration of the playwright, since, as we have already noted, the figures who routinely functioned as dramatic presen-ters earlier in the century never appeared as contemporary playwrights but as dead classical or medieval authors. In a way that is intricately implicated in the events of the revolution, the versifiers also invoke an absolutist conception of authority familiar from our discussion of *A King and no King*, *Pericles*, James's *Workes*, and other texts. G. Hills labels Fletcher "the King of Poets" and "Monarch of Wit" (f1ᵛ), and in a final, politically charged couplet, John Harris describes how Fletcher "came to be sole Monarch, and did raign / In Wits great Empire, abs'lute Soveraign" (f4ᵛ).

For all of their other resonances (and we will return to some of these), such descriptions of Fletcher are also attempts at inscribing his distinc-tiveness – the evaluative vocabulary that places him above Homer and Virgil, the discourse of absolutism that makes him "sole Monarch."

Many of the poems in the volume addressed to Fletcher or Beaumont singly emphasize their singularity and (as Moseley does) the self-sufficiency of their creations. Joh. Earle for example writes that Beaumont's writing is "all so borne within thy selfe, thine owne, / So new, so fresh, so nothing trod upon" (c3ᵛ), and Jos. Howe writes that "FLETCHER now presents to fame / His alone selfe and unpropt name" (f2) – a proposition that is at the very least arguable, following as it does the volume's title page and several poems that discuss in detail the pair's collaborative practice. Other commendatory verses display more locally this larger tension of the volume. Listing the ways in which one can praise and distinguish Fletcher, T. Palmer concludes: "What shall I doe? all Commendations end, / In saying only thou wert BEAUMONTS Friend?" (f2ᵛ). The discourse of male friendship enters the poem at this climactic point, and the highest imaginable proof or compliment of Fletcher's singularity comes in saying that he is Beaumont's friend. Fletcher's singularity is thus paradoxically anchored in the doubleness and constitutive reflexivity we saw in other formulations of friendship discourse in chapter 2.

We have remarked upon patriarchal reproduction in a number of folio volumes that invest much textual energy in the consolidation of singular author/ity (James's *Workes*, *Cyropedia*, the Shakespeare folio), and though it advertises itself as a collection of collaboratively written plays, the Beaumont and Fletcher folio is nevertheless published within this regime of textuality increasingly focused on the fathering singular author. A moment like the end of Palmer's poem thus illustrates the sheer suggestive anomalousness of the volume – how quickly its claims within the emerging patriarchal–absolutist paradigm of singular authorship break down, how close those formulations remain to the discourses of collaboration and male–male friendship, how collaboration is nevertheless increasingly inexplicable (here "all Commendations end"). While several of the volume's preliminaries attempt to proceed with the project of patriarchal authorship (we have already witnessed both Fletcher and Beaumont giving singular birth within their own brains), a significant number of the commendatory verses wrestle suggestively with the problem we might describe as follows: how to explain collaborative textual production within the emerging consensus of patriarchal–absolutist authorship? The act of writing collaboratively before and after the emergence of the author signifies as two very different acts; the folio (and *this* book) negotiates that transition, and the contested discourses of seventeenth-century sexualities figure centrally in this question.

Strange unimitable intercourse

The force of the 1647 volume's anomaly may be seen clearly in a poem falling early in the preliminaries, Jo. Pettus's "Upon the Works of BEAUMONT, and FLETCHER" (a4ᵛ). Pettus speaks of an entity "Beaumount–Fletcher," "[w]hose strange unimitable Intercourse / Transcends all Rules." He argues that Beaumount–Fletcher alone have reached the "*Mysteries* of Wit," that they speak "The *Intellectuall Language*" unknown in his troubled era, and that "from *Wit, Sweetnesse, Mirth*, and *Sence*, / This Volume springs a new true *Quintessence*." Pettus's vocabulary of transcendence is one way of marking the exceptional nature of collaboration – it is mysterious (in a quasi-religious sense), speaks a higher language, and gives birth to elevated substance that is both "new" and "true." Pettus's figuring of this collaboration's textual offspring as "new" is striking (given its lengthy history), and his term "strange" emphasizes this. *Strange* of course originally meant "foreign," but it subsequently accrued the meanings "diverse," "different," "unusual," and (relevant here) "unknown, unfamiliar; not known, met with, or experienced before" (*OED*). The word's appearance in this poem, that is, denotes the extent to which collaboration (at the very least, this particular collaboration) is being marked as a new and different phenomenon within the regime of singular authorship, *even though it has historically preceded it*. The text thus produced is introduced in the reproductive terms of patriarchal authorship ("This Volume springs ...") but is new and anomalous. Another period meaning of *strange* is relevant here as well: "Unfamiliar, abnormal, or exceptional to a degree that excites wonder or astonishment; difficult to take in or account for; queer, surprising, unaccountable" (*OED, strange* 10). "Strange unimitable intercourse" in this sense might be considered a redundancy: exceptional and unimitable.

Pettus's word "intercourse" is central to his description of collaboration, and it is difficult for us as modern readers to separate out the apparently obvious sexual valence. The *OED* does not record the word *intercourse* as referring to sexual activity (at least between differently gendered persons) until late in the eighteenth century. There is the possibility that *intercourse* could refer to same-sex transactions;[41] nevertheless, it is in the word *strange* that we will, strangely enough, find the stronger suggestion of sexual discourse. Michael Warner has recently explored the geographical particularity of the seventeenth-century term *sodomy* – its reference to an act originating in a specific geographical location that is pointedly *elsewhere* (Sodom) – and, as Alan Bray's work has suggested, there is ample documentation of the period's tendency to identify sodomitical activity as outside English culture, or imported by alien figures within it.[42] In Warner's investigation, too, the word *strange* has recurred in the sodomitical context of at least one seventeenth-century treatise.[43] I want to suggest here that Pettus's use of *strange* and the word's recurrence in several verse-writers' discussions of the Beaumont and Fletcher collaboration signals both the apparent newly "strange" (odd, unusual, queer) status of collaboration within a nascent authorial paradigm *and* the rumblings of dissonance between a sexually valenced discourse of male friendship and an (again, nascent) articulation of companionate marriage that tended to use friendship's vocabulary.[44] Here Beaumont and Fletcher begin to register as "queer," in the more recent sense of that term.

A number of the volume's commendatory verses attempt simply to refigure this strangeness within a patriarchal–absolutist model of singular authorship. John Web, for example, applies the familiar discourse of male friendship ("two wits in growth / So just, as had one Soule informed both"), but he also resorts to a modified patriarchal model, imagining the "rich Conceptions of your twin-like Braines." The conveniently early death of Beaumont allows him, furthermore, to consolidate the twins in one: "Thence (Learned *Fletcher*) sung the muse alone, / As both had done before, thy *Beaumont* gone" (c2^v). The pronoun ("thy Beaumont") may cast a glance in both directions: it signals a sort of monogamous coupling (Fletcher's Beaumont, and no one else's), and a hierarchy of possession, in which Fletcher as surviving author *mono*polizes dramatic creation. Jasper Maine emphasizes the indiscernibility of the collaborative texts – "we, / In all things which you did[,] but one thred see; / So evenly drawne out, so gently spunne" (d1) – and yet his statement registers the increasing urgency of the author question and his distance from the process of undifferentiated collaboration earlier in the century. Concluding his poem, Maine performs a consolidation similar to Web's in his description of the volume's publication:

> what thus joyned you wrote, might have come forth
> As good from each, and stored with the same worth
> . . .
> In you 'twas League, in others impotence;
> And the Presse which both thus amongst us sends,
> Sends us one Poet in a paire of friends.   (d1^v)

Depicting collaboration (from his authorial perspective) as usually "impotent," Maine implicitly figures singular authorship as "potent" – a word that resonates not as sexual discourse (until the late nineteenth century) but as a term of absolute power (cf. *potentate*, or, more resonantly, the phrase from the Latin credo, *patrem omnipotentem*). Maine concludes by making this doubly authored volume the product of a singular poet, in a sense mystifying collaboration into the author-function. He thus attempts to make sense of the volume's opening contradiction; as its frontispiece suggests, this book might be read as "one Poet in a paire of friends."

Roger L'Estrange's poem "On the Edition of Mr *Francis Beaumonts*, and Mr *John Fletchers* PLAYES never printed before" attempts simply to interpolate collaboration into a poem apparently written about Fletcher alone. With its separately possessive forms of the playwrights' names, the title suggests the uneasy conjunction of doubleness and singularity, and in the poem itself, the name "Beaumont" appears suddenly and extra-lineally, bracketed with "Fletcher":

> For (in *Me*) nothing *leſſe* then *Fletchers Name*
> Could have *begot*, or *juſtify'd* this *flame*.
> *Beaumont*⎱
> *Fletcher* ⎰ *Return'd?* methinks it ſhould not be.
> *No*, not in's *Works*: *Playes* are as *dead as He*.

The poem uses the familiar convention of the collaborative title page, the bracket (cf. Figures 3, 9, and 10), but the interjection of Beaumont's name disrupts the meter, without concern for the ensuing disparity in pronouns, which remain singular: "his" works, "as dead as He." Furthermore, like the plays in the previous chapter and like other verses in this volume, the poem uses the convention of the resurrected authorial presenter ("Fletcher Return'd?"), merely attempting to interpose colla-boration within this newer paradigm, in a way that the text itself exhibits as afterthought and contradiction.

A more complex version of this interpolation, and one we will now examine in detail, is suggested by Berkenhead's poem "On the happy Collection of Master *FLETCHER'S* Works, never before PRINTED" (E1ᵛ). The historically early appearance of an apostrophe marking Fletcher's possession of his works in the title may serve to introduce us to the poem's ostensible emphasis; it begins by commanding Fletcher to "arise" and defend his sovereign textual property against the pilfering of

"Usurpers." Fletcher does not arrive from the afterworld unaccompanied, however ("Nor comes he private, here's great BEAUMONT too"), and the poem proceeds to comment at length on the process of their collaboration. In a way that prefigures the work of twentieth-century critics of Beaumont and Fletcher,[45] Berkenhead writes, "Some thinke Your Witts of two Complexions fram'd, / That One the Sock, th'Other the Buskin claim'd" (a mode of criticism that would divide the plays by genre), but he rejects this description of collaboration in the familiarly reflexive discourse of male friendship:

> But you were Both for Both; not Semi-witts,
> Each Piece is wholly Two, yet never splits:
> Y'are not Two *Faculties* (and one *Soule* still)
> He th'*Understanding*, Thou the quick free *Will* . . .

Refusing to divide up plays into scenes and the playwrights into attributes (though at the same time registering the urge to do so), Berkenhead instead identifies them, in a phrase that resonates with the "consenting Consort" we read in Richard Brathwait's frontispiece, as "Two, full Congeniall Soules."

The long middle section of Berkenhead's poem takes account of Beaumont's early death in terms familiar from other commendatory poems; Fletcher functions as both men, a process described in absolutist language: "Imperiall FLETCHER! here begins thy Raigne / Scenes flow like Sun-beams from thy glorious Brain" (E2). The middle section's departure from the earlier description of collaboration is signaled by its insistence on a competition between authorial figures ("Brave *Shakespeare* flow'd, yet had his Ebbings too, / Often above Himselfe, sometimes below; / Thou Always Best"), the policing of plagiarism (other playwrights steal from Fletcher's work), and the author's corresponding originality and self-sufficiency: "When did'st *Thou* borrow? . . . / Thou was't thine *owne* Muse" (E2). Comparing Fletcher on a number of bases with other playwrights, the section concludes with a statement that resolutely differentiates Fletcher (and here the apostrophe may mark either contraction or possession): "Thou hadst no Sloath, no Rage, no sullen Fit, / But *Strengh* and *Mirth*, FLETCHER'S a *Sanguin* Wit" (E2^v).

It is something of a surprise, then, that after this lengthy excursus on Fletcher's distinction and difference, the last section of the poem begins with a moment of unearned logical conjunction: "Thus, two great *Consul*–Poets all things swayd, / Till all was *English* Borne or *English* Made" (E2^v). The logically tenuous link between the poem's sections ("Thus") receives emphasis in the construction of Beaumont and

Fletcher as "Consul–Poets." The previous section of the poem had elaborated the power of "Imperiall" Fletcher and his singular "Raigne"; here, though the imperial(ist) theme is retained in making all things English, the rhetoric is not that of absolutist monarchy but of Roman republicanism – "Consuls" being "the two annually elected magistrates who exercised conjointly supreme authority" (*OED*). Etymologically, the word *consul* intersects with *con-*, the prefix closely associated with friendship discourse (as in *con/sult*). The stanza moves immediately to elaborate further the pair's inseparability, finding in their work "*Miter* and *Coyfe* here into One Piece spun, / BEAVMONT a *Judge's*, This a *Prelat's* sonne." This rhetoric both introduces and erases the idea of separate patrimonies; Beaumont and Fletcher unite their fathers' occupations, as symbolized by the head-dress of the church and the law.[46] Union (importantly, at the figure of the father) leads immediately into the final lines of a poem that is, it is useful to recall here, ostensibly written about "the happy Collection of Master *FLETCHER'S* Works":

> What strange Production is at last displaid,
> (Got by Two Fathers, without Female aide)
> Behold, two *Masculines* espous'd each other,
>   *Wit* and the World were born without a *Mother*.   (E2ᵛ)

In this final burst of overdetermination, the poem exhibits the dialectic that has enabled it thus far, the attempt to explain within an increasingly authorial framework the production of collaborative texts. Enlarging on its tracings of patrimony, the poem employs a patriarchal model of textual reproduction; the text is begotten by, and born of, its fathers. Yet, as we have seen implicitly in a number of other texts, the phrase "Got by Two Fathers" – *two* patriarchs, *dual* authorities – is virtually an oxymoron in this period. The *OED* glosses the verb "to get" as "to beget, procreate (said of the male parent)," and the definition's explanatory parenthesis illustrates the problematic of the doubly fathered text at this cultural moment: of *which* male parent may we say this? That "got" was often followed by "on" – that is, that the hierarchy of the patriarchal model of reproduction was often (re)produced at the minute level of a preposition signaling the relative position of differently gendered parents in the reproductive sex act – only further complicates the use of such rhetoric here; the passage glances at this problem (by exempting "Female aide" from the process) but does not offer further clarification.[47] In sum, the poem attempts to perform here what it has unsuccessfully essayed thus far, an absorption of collaborative textual production within the realm of the author.

The difficulty of this consolidation, its apparent novelty, is signaled (as before) by the resonant term *strange*. The word *masculine* may also register here incipient discomfort with male-directed male sexuality in a new context. This appearance of *masculine* actually precedes by five years the *OED*'s first recorded instance of the word as a full-fledged noun meaning a "person of the male sex," but the *OED*'s 1652 quotation (from a tract condemning magicians and astrologers) may signal the extent to which the word marks the increasing notability of such a sexual relation: "If he had abused himselfe with a masculine ... he was forced ... to kill himselfe."[48] As with the word *get*, the difficulty of the phrase "two *Masculines* espous'd" lies in the traditional female-directed action of the verb; as the *OED* makes clear, *espouse* was only occasionally used in a context where the woman was the espous*er* rather than the espoused, and the first recorded use of the term in a reciprocal sense occurs in 1700. "Two Masculines espous'd *each other*" thus avoids the question of hierarchy resident in its very language of betrothal and marriage; at the same time, by keeping its fathers on equal, friend-ly terms, it may gesture toward the language of emergent companionate relations between men and women.[49] The tensions between collaborative and authorial systems are nowhere more striking than in the contradictions, ellisions, and negotiations of these sexual discourses.

As is obvious by this point, Berkenhead's formulations of textual production have radically marginalizing effects on representations of women. In its phrase "Got by Two Fathers, without Female aide," the poem appropriates female generative power for male purposes (this range of meanings is not entirely restricted to a sexual sense, for "to get" also meant "to acquire wealth or property"). Furthermore, the poem aligns two important categories upon which the construction of the folio heavily depends, both art and nature ("Wit and the World"), with male procreation.[50] Stressing the erasure of female generativity ("without Female aide ... without a Mother") in this context implicitly elides the possibility of female authorship; given the earlier notion that Beaumont and Fletcher's father's occupations are united in their sons, the poem's last line may suggest that the sons *and* their texts were "born without a Mother." Texts and authors both seem to be patriarchally generated.

This misogynist fantasy is by no means restricted to Berkenhead's poem; at a number of points in the commendatory verses it is accomplished by the silencing of the female muses ("When did'st *Thou* borrow? ... Thou was't thine *owne* Muse") in contexts that often associate borrowing or textual sharing with effeminacy. George Lisle's poem "To the memory of my most honoured kinsman, Mr. *Francis Beaumont*," for

example, works like Berkenhead's, moving from the singular writer of
the title to a consideration of collaboration, and it culminates in a similar
appropriation of female generativity:

> Behold, here's *FLETCHER* too! the World ne're knew
> Two Potent Witts co-operate till You;
> For still your fancies are so wov'n and knit,
> Twas *FRANCIS-FLETCHER*, or *JOHN BEAUMONT* writ.
> Yet neither borrow'd, nor were so put to't
> To call poore Godds and Goddesses to do't;
> Nor made Nine Girles your *Muses* (you suppose
> Women ne're write, save *Love Letters in prose*)
> But are your owne Inspirers, and have made
> Such pow'rfull Sceanes, as when they please, invade.   (b1)

Like Berkenhead's, this poem collates a number of strands we have been
analyzing: a masculinity allied with discourses of absolute power ("Two
Potent Witts ... pow'rfull Sceanes ... invade"), authorial self-sufficiency
and autonomy ("neither borrow'd"), and the reflexivity of friendship in
the chiastic formulation of the names ("*FRANCIS-FLETCHER*, or *JOHN
BEAUMONT*"). The indeterminacy of the phrase "your owne Inspirers"
may again signal the tension between "co-operation" (the two writers
inspire each other) and authorial self-sufficiency (each inspires his
"owne" work himself). Again: "Thou was't thine *owne* Muse." Yet,
despite its slightly different approach to these issues, this poem parallels
Berkenhead's in carefully policing the gendering of writing, at least in
drama. The "Nine Girles" (this diminution of the usual terminology is
itself significant) are held in abeyance; female writing is relegated to the
decidedly unelevated domain of prose love-letters, and this alternative is
proffered only as a qualification of the generalization that "Women ne're
write." The potentiality of female dramatic authorship in the seventeenth
century is a subject to which we will turn in the final chapter, but here it
is important to note that the exclusion of such writing in this period
occurs not only at the level of material practice (the restriction and
manipulation of literacy, the manifold deprivations Virginia Woolf long
ago identified) but also in the discursive constitution and negotiation of
those material circumstances, the erection and maintenance of generic
boundaries.[51]

Self-estranging artifacts

Thus far I have argued that the Beaumont and Fletcher folio attempts, in
its preliminary materials, to negotiate two modes of textual production
and their related sexual rhetorics. That the volume itself does not

approach this problem with anything resembling a unified, consistent voice should by this point be apparent. At one level, when one compares the multiple texts written by single individuals within the volume, one finds rupture, difference, contradiction; we saw this in Moseley's statements about his texts' provenance, but it is also the case in James Shirley's preface and poem, and William Cartwright's two consecutive poems. At another level, the volume continuously exhibits itself as a collaborative production, in a sense much larger than that proposed by its bracketing of two playwrights on the title page. In addition to the two stationers also listed there (the twin-named Humphrey Moseley and Humphrey Robinson), the volume includes text attributed to: the actors from whom Moseley secured the rights to print the plays after they could no longer make performative use of them;[52] Shirley (a fellow-playwright) in a preface; Moseley in another preface; the thirty-six poets (most living, some dead) who wrote the thirty-seven commendatory verses; the unnamed and unenumerated "others" who (according to Moseley) wrote some of the plays' prologues and epilogues; the volume's "severall Printers" (according to Moseley) – as many as eight (according to R.C. Bald). And then there are the Beaumont–Fletcher plays themselves. Though only one of the preliminary texts is, according to its attribution, collaborative (the multiply signed actors' dedicatory letter, appropriately), a number of the other preliminary materials speak of the relation of Authors to reader–writers in terms familiar from the foregoing discussion. The negotiation of collaboration and authorship is not limited in these preliminary materials to playwrights long dead and only presently resurrected in their texts; the poets of the commendatory verses, inscribing themselves as both readers of and writers about Beaumont and Fletcher's texts, work to figure a relation between themselves and "*Authours* of this *Volume*," in terms familiar from their construction of those Authours themselves. Collaboration and authorship, in other words, are not only in contention in descriptions of prior textual productions, but in those of the volume's present moment as well.

In their poems and the titles attached to those poems, the writers of the folio's commendatory verses employ a number of conflicting terms to describe the vocation and textual produce of Beaumont and Fletcher – for example, "Authour," "writers," "Dramatick Poet," "celebrated Poets and Fellow-writers," "Renowned Twinnes of Poetry"; "plays," "Dramaticall Poems," "Dramaticall Workes," "the Edition," "Dramatick Poems," "Pieces," "Works." These terms – terms that were not used to describe Beaumont and Fletcher and their texts earlier in the century – suggest a movement already charted in the Jonson canon (from plays to poems, from plays to works),[53] but we would want to note in these particular instances the variability of the terms; once again this volume lies in a liminal zone between theatre and poem, playwright and poet. The tendency toward a poetic discourse, however, is much more strongly marked in the *self*-figurations of the commendatory-verse writers; they refer to themselves uniformly in the discourse of poetry, with concomitant reference to singular poetic makers.

But though in general the verse writers tend to inscribe their own roles as authorial (agonistic and competitive, emphasizing a singular poetics over collaborative drama), these inscriptions too are complicated negotiations of sexual discourses. A number of these poets describe textual interactions with Beaumont and/or Fletcher, yet they do so in terms clearly indebted to a patriarchal–absolutist paradigm of agonistic authorship. John Harris writes of the difficulty of commending Fletcher after his death ("Singly we now consult our selves and fame, / Ambitious to twist ours with thy great name" [f3ᵛ]), a situation he figures in strikingly reproductive terms:

> And but [that] thy Male wit like the youthfull Sun
> Strongly begets upon our passion,
> Making our sorrow teeme with Elegie,
> Thou yet unwep'd, and yet unprais'd might'st be.   (f4)

Constructing the belated elegists as female matter fertilized by Fletcher's "Male wit" (they are "strongly begot *upon*"), Harris places current poets in an agonistic relation with Fletcher – desiring but unable to approach his greatness in the very poems that attempt to praise him. Harris furthermore associates the paucity of these poetic inscriptions with female generativity, writing that the poems in Fletcher's praise

> are imperfect births; and such are all
> Produc'd by causes not univocall,
> The scapes of Nature, Passives being unfit,
> And hence our verse speakes only Mother wit.   (f4)

Univocal could describe terms or signs signifying unambiguously (the author as patriarchally constituted would speak with one voice), but "univocal generation" was also the term used to signify reproduction between male and female members of the same species *(OED)*. Harris writes that his textual reproduction with Fletcher is *not* univocal – that is, that they are not members of the same poetic species, a mixture that results in malformed offspring, "scapes of Nature"; *scape*'s contemporary meanings as an error in speech or print and a breach of chastity are clearly resonant here. What immediately follows – Harris's misogynist gendering of his own otherness *in specie* as female – works to mark both the superiority and the patriarchality of Fletcher; in the end, Harris and his contemporaries can produce only "Mother wit" – common sense.

Not content to remain in the effeminized category he has established, however, Harris proceeds immediately to expose again the agonism of this model:

> Oh for a fit o'th Father! for a Spirit
> That might but parcell of thy worth inherit;
> For but a sparke of that diviner fire
> Which thy full breast did animate and inspire ...

Harris here refers back to the inadequacy of his "Mother wit" and puns on the contemporary term for hysteria, "fit of the Mother," which took its name from the supposed wandering of the womb ("the Mother").[54] Harris desires instead a disease that is not one (this is the only occurrence of the term "fit of the father" I have yet found); it is precisely *not* a disease in a patriarchal culture because it might hypothetically be said to consist of a super-abundance of the phallus. The sexual valence of these lines is strengthened by evidence that in contemporary discourse *spirit* often signified both "penis" and "semen" (the "spirit generative").[55] The poem thus inscribes a fantasy in which ensuing poets "inherit" (again, it would seem, "without Female aide") a "spirit" from the author as patriarchally conceived, and the poem aligns this suggestion in a parallel construction with what will in subsequent centuries become a dominant authorial model, the internally generating genius (in incipient form): "a sparke of that diviner fire."

A similar configuration animates T. Palmer's tribute to Fletcher, which concludes, as we saw earlier, in the paradoxical claim that the highest praise of Fletcher lies in labeling him Beaumont's friend. The poem proceeds from there to develop its own moment of imagined collaborative intercourse with Fletcher:

> What shall I doe? all Commendations end,
> In saying only thou wert *BEAUMONTS* Friend?
> Give me thy spirit quickely, for I swell,
> And like a raveing Prophetesse cannot tell
> How to receive thy *Genius* in my breast ...   (f2ᵛ)

Like Harris, Palmer asks for Fletcher's "spirit," but again the apparent homoeroticism of this configuration (a resonance strengthened by the reference to male friendship discourse and what may in this context be a suggestion of phallic swelling) is avoided in a shift that genders the speaker of the poem as a speaking female receptacle for the (quickening) authorial spirit of genius.[56] The conclusion of George Buck's poem, "To the desert of the Author in his most Ingenious Pieces," likewise swerves away from a collaborative model of textual intercourse toward the patriarchal. Comparing Fletcher to other canonized dramatists of the period, Buck writes:

> Let *Shakespeare*, *Chapman*, and applauded *Ben*,
> Weare the Eternall merit of their Pen,
> Here I am love-sicke: and were I to chuse,
> A Mistris corrivall 'tis *Fletcher's* Muse.   (c3)

Having disposed of Shakespeare, Chapman, and Jonson, the sentence would seem logically to require its "love-sicke" writer to choose Fletcher, a formulation that would place the writer in a situation not unlike the ones we examined in chapter 2. Nevertheless, the poem establishes this possibility only to efface it: the proposed partner is not Fletcher but "Fletcher's Muse," and the relation is rendered (gendered) in what we would call heterosexual terms. And yet, we can perhaps see the vestigial traces of the collaborative model in the unusual appearance here of the term "Mistris corrivall"; a *corrival* (or *co-rival*) was a rival suitor, usually male, and Buck's term is in a sense oxymoronic. Though the sentence may thus sketch a configuration in which Shakespeare et al. are gendered as female rival mistresses to Fletcher's muse, there is also the implication (not entirely avoided by the word "Muse") of collaborative male intercourse. And once again a familiar sign of collaborative male friendship (the prefix *co-*) recurs.

In each of these instances, commendatory poets inscribe their relation to the dead Beaumont and Fletcher in the discourses used to figure the relation between the dramatists themselves. But I want also to suggest that these moments in the Beaumont and Fletcher folio make emphatic a notion that has been implicit in the argument of this book from the beginning. We noted in chapters 1 and 2 the tenuousness in a collaborative paradigm of borders between what we now call "individuals," and we saw the ways in which collaborative texts and texts figuring collaboration often slip easily between identities, frustrating modern attempts to discern separate authors, divergent persons, or distinct characters. The authorial paradigm with which we are more familiar, of course, depends upon the construction and policing of the borders of personhood, an identification of the textual parent. "Know you the Charecter? ... It is my Lords."[57] In the Beaumont and Fletcher volume, however, the apparatus guaranteeing the identification of separable individuals and their discrete textual properties is very much in flux. We have noted in passing the occasional appearance of the apostrophe in its new role delimiting textual property; plays are attributed to one writer, the other, or both; Fletcher is said to become Beaumont-and-Fletcher after Beaumont's death. In other words, just as this volume occupies a liminal status between collaboration and authorship, between collective making structured homoerotically and patriarchally individuated textual properties, the book is also situated, in a way I can only suggest here, at a crucial moment in the history of the subject. This applies not only to the complicated emulation and agonism inscribed in the book's com-mendatory-verse writers (who are also of course its readers), but also to the larger book-consuming audience for this volume. Addressing this audience in his preface, James Shirley suggests the instability of the categories: "You may here find passions raised to that excellent pitch and by such insinuating degrees that you shall not chuse but consent, & go along with them, finding your self at last grown insensibly the very same person you read, and then stand admiring the subtile Trackes of your engagement" (A3^v). We might take as a marker of the sort of estrangement Shirley here describes the fact that, as in many early modern texts, the personal pronoun of possession (in this case, *your*) has not yet become inseparably, typographically fused with the "self," and the passage resonates with the sort of self-reflecting "consenting Consort" and "mutuall interchoice" we read earlier in Richard Brathwait, or Montaigne's textual friendship with Boitie.[58] And yet, there are also in this passage hints of a new dispensation of self-possession: the self views its own misleading "engagement"; it stands outside the text, warily, if admiringly, noting the insensibility and "insinuating degrees" of its (momentary) dispossession. The thrill of insensibility, the pleasures of self-identification and momentary self-estrangement, have become a selling point. At the same time, the passage bears a trace of the language of collaborative intercourse we have read elsewhere in the volume: "passions," in/sinuation, "engage-ment." Perhaps a *readership* espous'd.

Although one would want to be careful not to situate too precisely the emergence of a proto-bourgeois individualism in the civil upheavals of this period, the resultant changes in modes of government, and concomitant adjustments in the definition of political "subjects," the shift I am describing can usefully be seen in the context of the tumultuous political events of the 1640s–60s. A number of these poems address implicitly or explicitly the revolution of the 1640s, but one in particular speaks to the subject of the individual in this context. We have already glanced at Roger L'Estrange's poem, "On the Edition of Mr *Francis Beaumonts*, and Mr *John Fletchers* PLAYES never printed before," with its extralineal insertion of Beaumont's name. The poem argues that the Edition it praises is a welcome "cure" for the times, in which "*Nature* her *Selfe* is out of *Tune*; and *Sicke* / Of *Tumult* and *Disorder, Lunatique*" (c1). Arguing that "Just in *this nicke, Fletcher sets the world cleare* / Of all disorder and reformes us here" (c1ᵛ), L'Estrange constructs a concluding catalogue of social types, in which Fletcher acts to rectify all social ills:

> The *severe States-man quits* his *sullen forme*
> Of *Gravity* and *bus'nesse*; The *Luke-warme*
> *Religious* his *Neutrality*; The *hot*
> *Braine-sicke Illuminate* his *zeale*; *The Sot*
> *Stupidity*; The *Souldier* his *Arreares;*
> The *Court* its *Confidence*; The *Plebs* their *feares*;
> *Gallants* their *Apishness* and *Perjurie,*
> *Women* their *Pleasure* and *Inconstancie;*
> *Poets* their *Wine*; the *Vsurer* his *Pelfe;*
> The *World* its *Vanity*; and *I* my *Selfe.*
>
> Roger L'Estrange   (c1ᵛ)

The catalogue is a striking account of how the ostensible excesses of the era are perceived to be mapped upon particular social types, and of how (from a royalist perspective, as we shall see in more detail momentarily) this book could seem to function as a restoration of social order. Yet we should also notice the shift that the last entry in L'Estrange's list encodes. Fletcher's work not only restores balance and order; it also realigns the "self" of the writer. Furthermore, L'Estrange's self-estranging ending may suggest both the extent to which notions of the subject in this period are being renegotiated and accommodated in relation to contemporary events and publications (the solution or "cure" to contemporary difficulties is to "quit" the self as currently constituted), and the way in which notions of identity remain closely tied to the idea of textual inscription: "Fletcher re/formes us here."

Such a notion of the subject in transition accords with what we know of publication and attribution in this period. On the one hand, there is *Areopagitica* (1644) – an argument that, even in its call for textual proliferation, generates an interest in a new textual and authorial identification in language that resonates with patriarchal–absolutist discourses we have been examining: "For Books are not absolutely dead things, but doe contain a *potencie* of life in them to be as active as that soule was whose *progeny* they are; nay they do preserve as in a violl the purest efficacie and extraction of that living intellect that *bred* them."[59] On the other hand(s), there is that promiscuous proliferation – the ricochet of pamphlets, news-sheets, and journals, published anonymously. Writing about three of these journals, Lois Potter has recently provided convincing evidence of the plasticity and plurality of the writing subject: "any attempt to attribute authorship, at least without the aid of computer tests, soon has to break down. All three journals probably had more than one writer, and they were parodied and pirated to such an extent that their styles often ended up being interchangeable" (*Secret Rites*, p. 4). Style, we might say (though Potter does not), is produced in relation and reaction to other texts. Potter has further isolated what she calls "a composite royalist personality" (p. 121) and, in the poetry of the period, a "plural I": "the writer cannot honestly separate his individual voice from those of the authors who, inevitably, have become a part of him" (p. 122). "What lies behind this language," Potter goes on to argue, "is the writer's desire to escape responsibility for his own state... [L]iterary 'borrowing' ... and its creation of the 'composite personality', are ways of hiding oneself in a crowd" (p. 149). Potter's evidence is voluminous and persuasive, but her explanation is only one of several possibilities: instead of positing a self who precedes writing, and then effaces himself and his style, melding into a "composite self," we might instead consider these moments as evidence of the fluctuating nature of the subject and authorship in this era. Where Potter detects a "self" fleeing "responsibility for his own state," we may instead notice the fluctuating notion of the "state" (in the political sense), the concomitant (re)definitions of the "self," and the emergence of the very idea of individual responsibility and accountability. The internalization of self-discipline, as Foucault has suggested and as Francis Barker has argued in connection with Milton's contemporary work, is only beginning to be articulated in this period.[60]

Returning to the apparatus of the Beaumont and Fletcher folio, we can see in Moseley's "post-script" to the preliminary materials the very sort of ambivalence available in Potter's evidence. Moseley writes: "After the *Comedies* and *Tragedies* were wrought off, we were forced (for expedition) to send the *Gentlemens* Verses to severall Printers, which was the occasion of their different Character; but the *Worke* it selfe is one continued Letter ..."(g2). Moseley here accounts for the "different Character" of the commendatory verses – the great variety of typefaces used in the volume's preliminary section. At the same time, however, his rhetoric gestures toward the variability of the "Characters" in those poems (the characters Beaumont and Fletcher there represented, the gentlemanly characters there representing), in contrast to the ostensible uniformity of the "Worke" that follows. The "Worke it selfe," he contends, is all of one piece, "one continued Letter." The text does appear to be so, and yet, as I noted above, Bald has isolated the work of as many as eight different printers in the printing of the ostensibly singular "Worke it selfe." Even without the close bibliographic analysis for which the post-script itself seems to call, the contention that the work that follows is uniform has already been placed in doubt by the doubleness of the title page and frontispiece, and in this same post-script Moseley notes the participation of other writers in addition to Beaumont and Fletcher in the writing of the plays' prologues and epilogues. But what we may see illustrated here in microcosm is the attempted textual *production* of uniformity, the charactering of singular Character, and, at the same time, the emergence of Character thus constituted (and still tenuously plural) out of a collaborative textual practice. This is both the Character to whom Foucault first alerted us, the Author, and the character of whom Jonathan Goldberg writes in his study of a Renaissance cultural graphology:[61] the individual who emerges later in English culture to write "one continued Letter" is here reproduced by many hands.

Our singular good lord

> ... political criticism of court and king was a central urge in the most important plays of Beaumont and Fletcher.
>
> Philip J. Finkelpearl[62]

Much of the twentieth-century criticism of Beaumont and Fletcher has concerned itself less with the contingent place of the 1647 folio within the unfolding events of the decade than with contesting the true political affiliation of the two playwrights. This argument often stages itself as what we might call a royalist binary: Beaumont and Fletcher either were, or were not, servile monarchists; they either served, or critiqued (subtly), the concerns of the Stuarts and their court. (Lawrence B. Wallis and Finkelpearl can serve, respectively, as exemplars of these viewpoints.[63]) This argument is troubling, for so often it reduces to a question of authorial intentionality (the plays demonstrate that Beaumont and Fletcher did, or did not critique, and therefore that they were not, or were, monarchists), and again has as its ultimate object a divination of what the author thought, a tenuous methodology in any case, made more complex by the presence/absence here of two authors thinking the same and/or different thoughts.[64]

This binarism is demonstrably impossible to resolve, and centers on a question that will in the end tell us very little about drama in/and early modern England. What we can, however, investigate are the ways in which Beaumont and Fletcher plays functioned in their culture, how the plays and the playwrights' names were deployed, and it is here that the 1647 folio will be a central document. Not as a recording of biographical facts and political beliefs; the volume's preliminary materials are not simply factual documents of Beaumont and Fletcher's associations (as scholars on either side of the critical binary have treated them), but, rather, texts registering and re/forming the contingencies of politics, preferment, patronage, publishing, authorship, etc.

We have already noted in the previous section the implication of the Beaumont and Fletcher folio in the political events of the 1640s. The volume was, in one rather straightforward material sense, made possible by those events, since, as Bald has demonstrated, it publishes texts that the King's Men had blocked Moseley from publishing a few years earlier but that had lost all utility for them with the closing of the theatres in 1642. The 1647 volume was printed in the very midst of revolution, as Wallis notes:

When Moseley and Robinson entered 30 of these plays in the Stationers' Register on September 4, 1646, the First Civil War was over, and the royalist cause at ebb. King Charles the First had put himself into the hands of the Scotch on May 5, Oxford had yielded seven weeks later, and Raglan Castle had surrendered on August 19. Only at Harlech on the far Welsh coast was the king's flag still flying. In London a Presbyterian parliament, hostile to stage-plays, was in the ascendancy. To the players, the prospect of a legal reopening of the theatres must have seemed more hopeless than ever.[65]

The relation of the folio to the discourses and events of the decade is nevertheless more complex than such a narrative allows, and – with the caveat that, whatever the political allegiances of its contributors and publishers, the folio does not function as a transparent document providing access to genuine political beliefs – we can sketch some of the connections between the volume and the contestation of the monarchy in the 1640s.

Whether the Beaumont and Fletcher plays signified as propaganda or critique of a royalist or absolutist position while they were alive, it is clear that the folio of 1647 functions as a royalist artifact in a number of ways. In her study of mid-century royalist texts, for example, Lois Potter has shown that genre itself carried clear political significations in the period:

there were some literary forms which belonged specifically to the royalists, and which were equally specifically the targets for satire by parliamentarians. These were plays, whose performance had been forbidden by ordinance since August 1642, and romances. Simply to write in either form was to make a statement about one's relation to the party in power. Many royalists managed to do both at once, since the most popular plays of the period were dramatised romances or romantic tragicomedies.[66]

Tragicomedy was the genre most closely associated with Beaumont and Fletcher, and the publication of a weighty collection of these (even if not titled as such),[67] with a masque (a genre with similar ideological markings) tacked on for good measure, was certainly politically meaningful. Prefaced by Moseley, who openly advertised himself as a royalist printer,[68] signed by a group of men once associated with the King's Men (a name that must have had even greater resonance by 1647), and commended by a "muster-role of Cavalier writers in verse,"[69] the volume's printing cannot be extracted from the contestations of royalist politics.

We detailed in the previous chapter the connections between textual authorship and political authority in some texts acted and printed early in the Stuart period, and, given the political affiliations of its participants noted above, it is perhaps no surprise that the folio's preliminary materials make use of that relation. Phrases like the "King of Poets" and "Monarch of Wit" already noted gain an added political charge in this context. The resonance is stronger than this, however, for the writers in the preliminaries frequently suggest an equation of Charles (absent from London at the time of publication) and Fletcher (similarly absent, but represented by the works in folio). Robert Stapylton, Knight, makes an oblique reference to this connection early in the preliminary poems, in his "On the Works of the most excellent Dramatick Poet, Mr. *John Fletcher*":

> Adde to [Fletcher's] Trophies, that a *Poets name*
> (Late growne as odious to our *Moderne states*
> As that of *King* to *Rome*) he vindicates
> From black aspersions, cast upon't by those
> Which only are inspir'd to lye in prose.   (a4ᵛ)

Stapylton comments only indirectly on the political situation (for by 1647 one modern state in particular had at least begun to question not only the name of Poet but also that of King). However, the lines also imply an equation in which England is compared to imperial Rome and Fletcher to Charles, coupled with a concluding derogation of the parliamentarian prose pamphleteers.

Two emphatic examples of this absolutist comparison fall at the end of the commendatory verses. Richard Brome's "To the memory of the

deceased but ever-living *Authour* in these his *Poems*, Mr. JOHN FLETCHER"
is a meditation on its own late position, thirty-fifth (and last but two) in
the sequence, and he constructs himself as the "Porter" to "keepe out"
"the Rowt" of others who seek to "crowd" Fletcher's book with verses.
Brome's position as elite and elitist door-keeper is authorized (and
author-ized) by his well-known connection to his mentor, Ben Jonson, as
he emphasizes here in a complex web of patriarchal affiliation:

> I knew [Fletcher] in his strength; even then, when *He*
> That was the Master of his Art and Me
> Most knowing *Johnson* (proud to call him *Sonne*)
> In friendly Envy swore, He had out-done
> *His very Selfe.*   (g1)

The passage suggests that Brome's "master" Jonson named Fletcher
both his "sonne" and his superior, and its particularly labyrinthine
syntax (the difficulty of ascertaining who "he" is at any given point) may
enact Fletcher's (and Brome's) reproducing of the father/master/author
in filial form. The rhetoric of reproduction may speak as well in the
sexual resonances of the terms "out-*done*" and "Most *knowing.*" The
Jonsonian authorization of Brome's comments and Fletcher's works
leads directly into the poem's royal reference, as Brome works to
historicize Fletcher for royalist purposes:

> In the first yeere, our famous *Fletcher* fell,
> Of good King *Charles* who grac'd these *Poems* well,
> Being then in life of Action: But they [the Poems] dyed
> Since the Kings absence; or were layd aside,
> As is their *Poet.*   (g1)

Brome first establishes a connection between Fletcher and Charles by
dating the playwright's death according to the years of Charles's reign –
or perhaps vice versa, the syntax suggests. Brome then equates the death
of Fletcher, the cessation of play-acting ("then in life of Action"), and
the absence of the king. Salvation (I choose the term deliberately) is not,
however, far off:

>   Now at the Report
> Of the *Kings* second comming to his Court,
> The *Bookes* creepe from the *Presse* to Life not *Action*;
> Crying unto the World, that no protraction
> May hinder *Sacred Majesty* to give
> *Fletcher*, in them, leave on the *Stage* to live.

These overdetermined lines both suggest a connection between Charles
and Jesus Christ ("the Kings second comming") and deepen the connection between Charles and Fletcher's texts. As the King returns to court,

Fletcher's books are published, and they in turn argue for the resumption of play-acting on the stage. At the same time, Brome's description of the publication of the volume for which he writes hints at the language of patriarchal reproduction he had used earlier in connection with Jonson; the infant books "creepe from the Presse to Life," and they "cry" their message "unto the World." Furthermore, the living texts cry that Charles (again aligned with Christ in the phrase "Sacred Majesty") will allow them to "live" again "on the Stage." Finally, the poem makes reference both to the convention of authorial resurrection and to the notion of patriarchal lineage; on the stage, Fletcher will live again, and live through his creeping, crying textual progeny.

The complexity of patriarchal, political, authorial, and religious resonances culminates in the next and penultimate commendatory poem, Shirley's "Upon the Printing of M^r. IOHN FLETCHERS workes." Shirley emphasizes, as do others before him, the impossibility of adequately praising Fletcher without at the same time exposing his own poetic inadequacies by comparison: "this Booke his Resurrection's made, / We bleed our selves to death, and but contrive / By our owne Epitaphs to shew him alive" (g1^v). In the Christian context Brome establishes, the "Booke" as "Resurrection" gains added religious resonance, which Shirley continues to activate in the Apocalyptic conclusion to his poem:

> But let him live and let me prophesie,
> As I goe Swan-like out, Our Peace is nigh;
> A Balme unto the wounded Age I sing,
> And nothing now is wanting but the King.

At what he constructs as his own moment of death (haunted perhaps by the return of a "Swan-like" Shakespearean ghost), Shirley here seems to prophesy a second coming for Charles – a projected moment of "Peace" (imagined in the midst of war) and tranquility, "A Balme unto the wounded Age," a time at which "nothing" will be left "wanting." At the same time, replaying 1625, the year of Fletcher's burial and Charles's accession, Shirley equates Fletcher's "Resurrection" with Charles's return, and, as in Brome's lines, the book by this Author, for which he writes, becomes a substitute for the absent King. The final "Peace," in which Charles returns, may only be "nigh" – a "Report" in Brome's term – but Fletcher's "pieces" (a term used elsewhere in the volume to mean "plays," as in the French) are immediately available – they begin three pages after Shirley's. The Booke becomes the Balme; authorship in an absolutist mode substitutes, as it turns out, with a measure of historical permanence, for the King's absolute political authority.

Brome's and Shirley's poems insist upon the equation of authorship and authority, but, while noting that the folio functions implicitly and explicitly as a royalist artifact, we cannot help but remark upon the ways in which the volume undermines the very goals its organizers seem interested to promote. We have already seen the evidence for this; it is nothing less than the volume's insistent equivocality, the relentless way in which it exposes its own lack of "univocall" generation. "Looke on this Kingdome," Aston Cockain, Baronet, writes of the folio, but elsewhere, the volume suggests that it is in fact a divided kingdom, even perhaps a Commonwealth, and alerts us instead to Beaumont and Fletcher as "Consul-Poets," registering a substantially contradictory model of political and literary authority. Shirley's poem equating political and poetical authority posits Fletcher as the volume's author, but its claim is disassembled by the volume's other text signed "Shirley," which invokes repeatedly "these Authours" (A3^v), a phrase that may still at this date bear the vestigial trace of an oxymoron in making what was once singular (by definition) plural. The volume is both a "Kingdome" and, in collaboration's leveling language, "thy fortunate *concernement* and Companion" (A3^v). This is the story of a volume, and perhaps a nation, that could not make up its mind(s).

Taking a large view of the relation of authorship and political systems in Anglo-American culture since the seventeenth century, one might say, in a formulation that Brome and Shirley make conveniently available, that authorship (that is, author/ity at a local, textual level) *does* substitute for absolutist political authority on the larger historical scale. To put this shift more schematically: textual production seems to move from collective making to individual authorship, while modes of government begin, however slowly, to move from singular authority to more collective action. Or so the fiction goes. Yet, if each (or some) members of a collective government are said to have a voice (to be represented), then each member within this corporate body is individuated, in a way that they were not in the collaborative process of writing as I analyze it in chapters 1 and 2; that is, just as collaboration functions and signifies differently within a system organized around singular authorial production, so too might the idea of the political collective. As the tentativeness of these statements suggests, we have only begun to investigate their implications: in a diachronic view, what are the relations between modes of textual production, systems of government, and modes of subjectivity?

As must be equally clear from Brome's and Shirley's poems, however, this broad historical shift does not transpire in some easily intentional way: those who advocate the monarchy see it as *parallel to*, not *exchange-*

able for, an ideology of individual authorship. And, outside drama,[70] the figure of Milton is a useful reminder that an advocacy of singular authorship, and the rhetorics we have seen accompanying that advocacy, are not restricted to those of the royalist party in this era.[71] Nor are these developments and allegiances clearly mapped through a history of a single material book – the Beaumont and Fletcher folio or a 1645 volume entitled *Poems of Mr. John Milton.* However closely aligned the latter volume might have been said to be to its republican author (it advertises itself not only with an engraved frontispiece of Milton but also as "Printed by his true Copies"), its title page clearly situates the book in a no less royalist context: "The SONGS were set in Musick by Mr. HENRY LAWES Gentleman of the KINGS Chappel, and one of His MAIESTIES Private Musick," and the book is "to be sold at the signe of the Princes Arms." (This "signe," however arbitrary in some sense, must also be "signe" of royal power – not least because, as Nigel Smith notes, "bookshops became important meeting places for those attached to religious or political causes."[72]) If the textual parentage of these poems is somewhat obscured by the stationer's prefatory phrasing – "I shall deserve of the age, by bringing into Light as true a Birth, as the Muses have brought forth since our famous *Spencer* wrote; whose Poems in these English ones are as rarely imitated, as sweetly excell'd" (a4ᵛ) – if, that is, the stationer only "bring[s] into Light" what is doubly "brought forth" by Muses and written by an "Author" invoked principally through his imitation and excelling of another, the discourse is nevertheless recognizably patriarchal–absolutist in its provenance. If, as we briefly noticed in *Areopagitica,* Milton's relation to these discourses is complicatedly republican *and* absolutist, it should perhaps come as no surprise that, less than two years after the *Poems,* this same stationer, Humphrey Moseley, collaborates with the same printer, Ruth Raworth, on another volume whose parentage and politics is likewise marked by significant ambiguity: the Beaumont and Fletcher *Comedies and Tragedies* of 1647.[73]

A partial lover

As we have seen, in attempting to shore up the 1647 folio's interimplicated political and literary authority, Brome's and Shirley's poems both invoke a singular author, Fletcher, and, in concluding our consideration of that volume's complicated reproduction, it is useful to return to Aston Cokain's disclosure that not one but *three* playwrights collaborated in the plays that make up the book – Beaumont, Fletcher, and "my good friend Old Philip Massinger."[74] So Cokain contends in two poems included in his 1658 collection *Small Poems of Divers sorts*. Supported largely by problematic linguistic analysis (discussed in chapter 1), the idea that Massinger's "share" in the Beaumont and Fletcher canon exceeds Beaumont's has become a commonplace of recent criticism.[75]

We noticed in the introduction that Cokain is elsewhere in his collection concerned to emphasize the indistinguishability of collaborators in life, death, and text; of Fletcher and Massinger's double burial he writes: "Playes they did write together, were great friends, / And now one Grave includes them at their ends" (p. 186). What is remarkable about these other poems in Cokain's volume is that their writer seems doubly concerned both to disclose triple authorship and, at least initially, to protect Fletcher's singular interests in the Beaumont and Fletcher folio. In an epigram addressed *"To Mr.* Humphrey Mosley, *and Mr.* Humphrey Robinson," the folio's publishers, he asks:

> In the large book of Playes you late did print
> (In *Beaumonts* and in *Fletchers* name) why in't
> Did you not justice ? give to each his due ?
> For *Beaumont* (of those many) writ in few:
> And *Massinger* in other few; the Main
> Being sole Issues of sweet *Fletchers* brain.   (p. [217])

Cokain stresses Fletcher's singularity in familiar patriarchal rhetoric ("sole Issues of sweet *Fletchers* brain") – a singularity that then makes possible the division of authorial property into three, so central to twentieth-century construals of this canon. At the same time, the poem articulates, in its final lines, an ambiguity now familiar from our readings of the folio, in which the problematic antecedents of the discourse just as surely fail to mark out authorial divisions:

> Ith'next impression therefore justice do,
> And print their old ones in one volume too:
> For *Beaumonts* works, & *Fletchers* should come forth
> With all the right belonging to their worth.   (p. [217])

The separate worth of Beaumont and of Fletcher? The worth of their separate, or collaborative works? Notice too that in the final lines of the epigram, Massinger's claims have again evaporated, registering perhaps the way in which both homoerotic friendship and patriarchal absolutism, as discourses of writing, fail to engage with the idea of a three-way collaborative production. Friendship, as our earlier readings in this book have implicitly suggested, functions as a discourse of monogamy (monoamity?): two masculines espous'd make eventually for strange unimitable intercourse, but three masculines may be literally unimitated, unrepresentable in the available languages of textual intercourse and reproduction.

The monogamy of male friendship seems also to be at stake initially in the other related poem, addressed by Cokain "*To my Cousin Mr.* Charles Cotton." Cokain there marvels that Cotton "would permit / So great an Injury to *Fletcher*'s wit, / Your friend and old Companion," that he would allow Fletcher's plays to be co-attributed in print to Beaumont (p. 91). "They were," Cokain proceeds to announce of Beaumont and Fletcher (echoing, we cannot fail to notice, the Fletcher–Massinger burial poem), "two wits, and friends, and who / Robs from one to glorifie the other, / Of these great memories is a partial Lover" (p. 91). Once again, in its effort equitably to attribute the plays in the volume, Cokain's discourse seems to resist its own divisions; attributing the plays to Beaumont-and-Fletcher-writing-together paradoxically makes one "a partial Lover." Partial to Beaumont (in giving him more than his share)? Or (and? thus?) a lover of only part of the pair? What would it mean, in the *ménage* Cokain seems both to approach and de/part, for Cotton to be *im*partial, a lover of *both*?

The possibility of a such a love-triangle (whether Cotton, Beaumont, and Fletcher, or Massinger, Beaumont, and Fletcher) seems unable to be fully articulated or disentangled, and it is important to notice, finally, that the urge to separate, to produce (as Cokain does in closing this poem) a singular authorial Fletcher who is made, in patriarchalism's language, to be "*Beaumonts* Heir" (p. 93), itself comes from within the complicated self-reflexive enfoldings of friendship discourse. The impetus to write these poems, indeed, the very proprietary knowledge Cokain claims in attempting correctly to attribute the authorship of these plays, emerges only through the circuit of friendship's relations: "But how came I (you ask) so much to know? / *Fletchers* chief bosome-friend inform'd me so" (p. [217]).

This "chief bosome-friend" of the Moseley/Robinson poem is presumably Mr. Cotton, Cokain's gentle kinsman, and we can add these relations to the chain of others Cokain produces, or discloses, in these poems: Beaumont and Fletcher were "two wits, and friends," Fletcher and Massinger "were great friends," Cotton is Fletcher's "friend and old Companion," and Cokain himself is linked to "my good friend Old *Philip Massinger*." If the monogamy of male friendship as we have seen it seems sorely tried by Cokain's poems, we might take this unimitable and seemingly ever-broadening circle of intercourse (a circle that may also include the manifold verse-writers of the 1647 folio, who also see themselves in relation to these several playwrights) to suggest that we may never get, or set, the authorship of this canon straight.

5   Mistris corrivall: Margaret Cavendish's dramatic production

> *Ros.* It is not the fashion to see the Lady the Epilogue . . .
> M^r. William Shakespear's Comedies, Histories, and Tragedies,
the third impression, 1664

> I know there are many Scholastical and Pedantical persons that will
> condemn my writings, because I do not keep strictly to the Masculine
> and Feminine Genders, as they call them, as for example a Lock and a
> Key . . . but I know no reason but that I may as well make them Hees
> for my use, as others did Shees, or Shees as others did Hees.
> <div align="right">Margaret Cavendish, "To the Readers,"
<i>Playes</i>, 1662[1]</div>

We have had ample reason to observe throughout this study the effects
for real and imagined women of the models of textual reproduction
associated with theatrical texts in the late sixteenth and seventeenth
centuries. A woman's entrance into theatrical discourse perceived as a
conversation between men and/or a patriarchal bringing forth was
treacherous and heavily policed; Margaret Cavendish's observations on
the gender of lock and key are more than arbitrary examples in a
grammar lesson and resonate with, for example, the appropriately named
Jailer's Daughter, Antiochus's Daughter, and Elizabeth Cary, apparently
the only woman to publish a play before the closing of the theatres in
1642.[2]

This book concludes by looking briefly at the strategies one woman
used to situate herself within this difficult textual economy. At a time
when male-authored and -organized dramatic collections continued to be
published – between the first and second Beaumont and Fletcher folios,
and between the second and fourth Shakespeare folios – Margaret
Cavendish published two folio volumes of plays. *Playes Written by the
Thrice Noble, Illustrious and Excellent Princess, The Lady Marchioness of
Newcastle*, the first and more elaborate volume on which I will focus, was
published in 1662, and Cavendish's 1668 folio (*Plays, Never before
Printed*) also speaks resonantly in the folio tradition, as its title's
recollection of Beaumont and Fletcher may begin to indicate.[3]

The 1662 *Playes* registers the difficulty of a woman writing and publishing within the genre of drama in elaborate bibliographical fashion. Unlike the Beaumont and Fletcher folio or its famous predecessors, Cavendish's collection includes no succession of male poets commending the plays. The "Epistle Dedicatory" in this volume is addressed by Cavendish to her husband ("My Lord ..."), and, in contrast to the more than thirty commendatory poems assembled at the beginning of the Beaumont and Fletcher volume, the only preliminary verses in Cavendish's book are a poem by her husband and one by Cavendish herself. What is most unusual in this woman's entry into dramatic discourse, however, is the book's elaborate apparatus of self-signed letters "To the Readers" (ten in all). These speak to the extensive preparation required for a reader of a woman's text in a genre unaccustomed to a woman's activity, and culminate in a dramatized scene, "An Introduction," in which three gentlemen enter and discuss whether or not they should attend a play written by a woman. (The recalcitrant gentleman is convinced, and with their exit, the plays begin on the succeeding recto page.)[4] In significant contrast to the letters from acting companies to patrons, the addresses by collectors and stationers to readers, and the commendatory verses from contemporary poets to dramatists that begin the Jonson, Shakespeare, and Beaumont and Fletcher folios, the bulk of the Cavendish preliminary materials, it must be emphasized, is signed by Cavendish herself.

The Cavendish first folio, then, begins with an introductory apparatus nearly as extensive as that of the Beaumont and Fletcher folio, or those of the Shakespeare folios, but that apparatus is significantly different in its arrangement and constitution. What is most striking, however, is its unwillingness to speak the languages of textual reproduction those other volumes register with such persistence. Cavendish does not use the discourses of patriarchal reproduction or absolutism except in describing her male playwright precursors. Though, as some critics have noted, Cavendish did use those discourses to inscribe subjectivity and her own textual practice in other genres,[5] it is crucial to notice that she does not do so here in her introduction of *dramatic* texts. While she routinely describes her own position as that of a servant, it is her husband, notably, who describes her in absolutist terms (regendered female):

> So we are all your Subjects in each Play,
> Unwilling willingly still to obey;
> Or have a thought but what you make or draw
> Us by the power of your wits great law;
> Thus Emperess in Soveraign power yours sits
> Over the wise, and tames Poetick wits.   (no sig.)

While an authorial absolutist model thus does make a brief appearance, we can note at the same time the poem's momentary reluctance to engage this paradigm of readerly obedience, especially in this culturally problematic configuration of husband-to-wife subjection: "we" are subjects "Unwilling willingly."

Cavendish's only reference to her playwrighting within a sexual or reproductive discourse comes in a description of her husband's participation in the volume. "My Lord," she writes,

> was pleased to illustrate my Playes with some Scenes of his own Wit, to which I have set his name, that my Readers may know which are his, as not to Cozen them, in thinking they are mine; also Songs to which my Lords name is set, for being no Lyrick Poet, my Lord supplied the defect of my Braine; thus our Wits join as in Matrimony, my Lords the Masculine, mine the Feminine Wit, which is no small glory to me, that we are Married, Souls, Bodies, and Brains, which is a treble marriage, united in one Love ... (A6)

Read alongside the Beaumont and Fletcher poems of the previous chapter, this passage is interesting for a number of reasons. Cavendish uses the sexualized language of male–male collaboration already marked as "strange" in the Beaumont and Fletcher folio, but here reproduces it within the newly emergent discourse of companionate marriage. The passage is startling to the modern reader acquainted with its discursive pre-texts, for it demonstrates the emergence of male–female collaboration out of the prior discourse of homoerotic friendship that informs the Beaumont and Fletcher volume.[6] That is, the normative mode of textual intercourse in drama in the early decades of the century ("two Masculines espous'd") had become by 1647 "strange Production"; at the same time, what would have signified as *radical* production in, say, Florio's Montaigne (that is, the presumptive impossibility, even perversity, of men and women writing together) is here written into the discourse of companionate marriage: not "two Masculines," but Masculine and Feminine "espous'd."[7] We have seen in the Beaumont and Fletcher volume the relentless, putative masculinity of its "Two Potent Witts," and the magnitude of the Cavendish reconfiguration is perhaps registered here in her positive portrayal of what may have been for seventeenth-century readers a significant oxymoron: "the Feminine Wit."[8]

At the same time that this letter proposes a regendering of dramatic collaboration, however, we can see in it the careful regulation of textual property within the paradigm of singular authorship. Cavendish says she has "set [her husband's] name" to his texts (she does so in the volume that follows), and she suggests that to do otherwise is to "Cozen" her readers. (This is a significant departure from Moseley's practice in the Beaumont and Fletcher folio, or Heminge and Condell's practice in the

Shakespeare folio.)[9] Furthermore, at several points in the preliminary letters, Cavendish uses collaboration as a way to denigrate her precursors and elevate herself within the paradigm of singular authorship. Speaking in a letter "To the Readers" about prior theatrical practice, she writes:

I Have heard that such Poets that write Playes, seldome or never join or sow the several Scenes together; they are two several Professions, at least not usual for rare Poets to take the pains; like as great taylors, the Master only cuts out and shapes, and his Journy-men and Apprentices join and sow them together; but I like as a poor taylor was forced to do all my selfe ... (no sig.)

This statement, like many in the preliminaries to this volume, is in part Cavendish's apology for her admittedly disjointed practice. At the same time, however, this letter constructs her as a "rare Poet," (or rather, *more than* a "rare Poet") and suggests, as elsewhere, her ostensible self-sufficiency, while it attributes to her precursors the supposed insufficiencies of collaboration.

This strategy – deploying modes of textual production disparaged by an emergent ideology of singular authorship to deflate her predecessors and inflate her own position – has as its central locus Cavendish's self-commendatory poem "A General Prologue to all my Playes." Though the resonance that title now has with Chaucer's *Canterbury Tales* was not current for Cavendish and her readers,[10] the title does bring forth the author to present her plays in a prologue, in a way that resonates with staged authorial figures like Gower and Homer (see chapter 2). At the same time, Cavendish begins her poem by differentiating herself from the earliest dramatic author to be published in folio:

> NOBLE Spectators, do not think to see
> Such Playes, that's like *Ben. Johnsons* Alchymie,
> Nor Fox, nor Silent Woman: for those Playes
> Did Crown the Author with exceeding praise;
> They were his Master-pieces, and were wrought
> By Wits Invention, and his labouring thought,
> And his Experience brought Materials store,
> His reading several Authors brought much more ...   (A7)[11]

Cavendish's mode here might be viewed as reproducing Jonson's own in the *Epigrams*, for she seems to praise him at the same time that she implicitly uses his accomplishments to deflate him. In this opening maneuver, the poem equates Jonson's own textual practice with aptly chosen titles from his canon: *The Alchemist, The Fox (Volpone), The Silent Woman (Epicoene)*. Within this schema, the author who constructed himself as such by writing against the ostensibly bogus magic of theatricality[12] himself becomes a practitioner of "Alchymie" – not to mention a fox, and (singularly appropriate to the volume Cavendish constitutes over his dead corpus) a creator of silent women. These lines portray Jonson in the familiar discourse of absolutist authorship (his "Master-pieces" "Crown [their] Author," who is later compared to "Forein Emperors"), but at the same time they hold him accountable in that discourse for his reliance on other texts. Cavendish's opening lines effectively accuse the inventor of plagiarism in English of plagiarism; as she notes later: "Some take great pains to get, and yet are poor, / And some will steal for to increase their store" (A7).[13] The poem proceeds to specify further this allegation, in a catalogue that designates the dramatists printed in the most important seventeenth-century folio collections of drama:

> But Noble Readers, do not think my Playes,
> Are such as have been writ in former daies;
> As *Johnson*, *Shakespear*, *Beamont*, *Fletcher* writ;
> Mine want their Learning, Reading, Language, Wit:
> The Latin phrases, I could never tell,
> But *Johnson* could, which made him write so well.
> Greek, Latin Poets, I could never read,
> Nor their Historians, but our English *Speed*;
> I could not steal their Wit, nor Plots out take;
> All my Playes Plots, my own poor brain did make ...   (A7ᵛ)

These lines are again in apologetic mode, and yet their attack on those below whom Cavendish ostensibly ranks herself is twofold. First, the poem differentiates Cavendish from the other famous folio-authors by emphasizing that they derived their plays from the books of others – the Latin and Greek poets and historians. At the same time, it deploys here a xenophobic strategy that occurs throughout these preliminaries; elsewhere a gentleman in the introduction says that Cavendish "hath neither Language, nor Learning, but what is native and naturall" (B1ᵛ) – a marked contrast to the allusive, learned, foreign ("strange") aspects of her predecessors. In sum, the poem deploys the ideology of singular authorship – the importance of originality and self-inspiration, the derogation (in a sense new to drama) of theft and derivation – against those authors who were, as we have seen, the very sites of authorship's initial construction.

To replace the model of those subjected to her praising critique, Cavendish inscribes an epic simile of her own textual production. In this elaborate description of her playwrighting, Cavendish – "Like those that have a little patch of Land, / Even so much whereon a house may stand" – builds what she calls "a house, though of no shcw, / A Cottage warm and clean, though thatch'd and low" (A7ᵛ). This rhetoric is remarkable on a number of counts. First, as we have noted above, it entirely avoids the discourses we have come to expect in dramatic folios of the seventeenth century. The materials from which Cavendish's cottage is constructed replicate her earlier insistence on the "native and naturall"; not only does her maker build the house himself, without the help of carpenters and masons, but he also refuses to use materials "from forein parts," preferring instead "some sound Tree, which on his ground did grow." The language emphasizes the organicism and "natural" self-inspiration that will become the hallmarks of the author-genius in subsequent English culture.

At the same time, Cavendish's crafted, artisanal description of her writing exhibits itself as a particularly apt metaphor for the self-possessed, proto-bourgeois individual who accompanies the rise of authorship. The individual as Cavendish constitutes him seems to build upon the figure of the English yeoman[14] and to gesture toward the later bourgeois fantasy of self-sufficiency: he "raise[s]" "a house with his own stock" and "lives contentedly of his own labour; / And by his labour he may thrive, and live / To be an old rich man." The metaphor is almost entirely self-contained and -containing: the house is built by the man from organic materials derived from the land he owns, and the man lives in the house thus constituted. We might gain some critical distance on Cavendish's metaphor by noting *its* distance from the socio-economic contingencies of her own life (as volatile as those may have been); this is not the House of the Newcastle family, but a "Cottage," "thatch'd and low."[15] The derivation of the land is not specified – its owner simply "has" it – but, in her application of the metaphor to her own writing, Cavendish says that "the works I have writ, / ... are the buildings of my natural wit; / My owne Inheritance, as Nature's child ..." We might view this statement as a mystification both of the complex position from which Cavendish writes and of authorship itself. Though the title page's advertisement of her class position and the support and collaboration of her husband as announced in the preliminaries would seem to complicate these statements, the poem culminates in a radical fantasy of self-sufficiency: "All the materials in my head did grow, / All is my own, and nothing do I owe" (A8).

Finally, it is important to note the gendered dissonance of vehicle and tenor in Cavendish's simile. Her house-builder is male; her writer (that is, the speaker of the poem, gendered female elsewhere in the preliminaries) is not. This, we might speculate, is a particularly interesting moment in the history of individualism and its corollary, singular authorship, for the simile here exposes the gender asymmetry of possessive individualism's emergence.[16] Even as the text assiduously avoids the sexual and reproductive discourses earlier folio volumes lead us to expect in the construction of dramatic authorship, it registers gender again; even at the moment that Cavendish labors to construct authorship as a category independent of social, economic, and cultural contingencies, and based instead solely within the individual, she does so in a language that is intimately tied to precisely those categories.

Cavendish's *Playes* are a locus at which to isolate (and to note the significant absence of) a variety of discourses surrounding dramatic authorship in the seventeenth century. Her writing both draws on emergent paradigms of authorship – the nascent policing of textual theft and borrowing – and inscribes discourses that have become more familiar in the author's subsequent domain and reign: the self-sufficient, "naturall" organicism of the home-grown genius; authorship as cottage industry. At the same time, Cavendish's texts demonstrate the difficulty of locating a discourse in which women playwrights could write of writing in the seventeenth century. Given authorship's patriarchal–absolutist beginnings, we cannot ignore the radical charge provided by a woman using the terms "Authoress," "Poetress," even occasionally "Author," to describe her vocation.

Frontispiece

I regard not so much the present as future Ages, for which I intend all my Books.

> Margaret Cavendish, "To the Readers,"
> *Plays, Never before Printed* (1668)[17]

The engraved frontispiece to Cavendish's volume serves as an endpiece to this one, for, like the preliminary materials we have examined, it both refers to the history of dramatic authorship traced in seventeenth-century folios and gestures, if tentatively, in the direction of an "author" beginning to split off from its male-collaborative and patriarchal–absolutist past. That splitting off, as I suggested in chapter 3, is registered in the word *author*, which no longer carries for us, as it did well into the seventeenth century, the meanings "father," "begetter," "Creator," and "authority" – as well as "writer."[18] This dissociation is beginning to be marked in one line of the otherwise reproductively focused Beaumont and Fletcher folio ("Man may beget; a Poet can create"), but the separation of textual and sexual modes of reproduction is more strongly embodied in the Cavendish frontispiece (Fig. 11).[19]

The engraving situates Cavendish in an ornate, arched alcove (no thatched cottage, this), between the statues of two classicized figures. Cavendish's biographer Douglas Grant identifies the figures as "Apollo

Here on this Figure Cast a Glance,
But so as if it were by Chance,
Your eyes not fixt, they must not Stay,
Since this like Shadowes to the Day
It only represent's; for Still,
Her Beuty's found beyond the Skill
Of the best Paynter, to Imbrace,
These lovely Lines within her face,
View her Soul's Picture, Judgment, witt,
Then read those Lines which Shee hath writt,
By Fancy's Pencill drawne alone
Which Peece but Shee, can justly owne.

Figure 11   Engraved frontispiece: Margaret Cavendish, *PLAYS, Never before Printed. WRITTEN By the Thrice Noble, Illustrious, and Excellent PRINCESSE, THE Duchess of Newcastle* (London: by A. Maxwell, 1668).

and Minerva,"[20] and his apparent confusion (is he reading left-to-right? vice-versa?) is significant: is the figure on the left female? She seems to have breasts, a feminized tunic, and hair longer (slightly) than the figure on the right. At the same time, she is more like her male fellow-statue than the figure of Cavendish that dominates the engraving; she wears a helmet and carries a staff and shield;[21] and she may also suggest the "herms" – columns with human heads, often of Hermes – common in classical architecture. "She" is, then, at least *ambiguously* gendered, and Grant's seemingly reversed reading (Apollo? Minerva?) begins to have a certain logic; where, after all, does the pedestal below the tunic end and the gendered figure begin?[22] We might go so far as to say that the leftmost figure is "masculine," if not "male," and, we could recall that Pallas/Minerva is called "Man-Maide" in the Aurelian Townshend and Inigo Jones masque *Tempe Restor'd* (1631).[23] Given the preliminary materials' association of classicism in general with male authorship, even a female goddess might register male significations in the context of this volume. Cavendish's Prologue may function as a methodology for reading the engraving:

> The Latin phrases, I could never tell,
> But *Johnson* could, which made him write so well.
> Greek, Latin Poets, I could never read,
> Nor their Historians, but our English *Speed* ...

What might be said to matter, in other words, is not so much the identities of the Greek and Latin faces/phrases in the engraving, as the associations that, in this context, they call forth. Indeed, to seek to identify the classical figures may be to align oneself with a male mode of reading and writing the volume devalues ("*Johnson* could ..."), and to ignore the English figure at its center.[24] More figuratively, the Medusan shield may protect against just this sort of intense ("Scholastical and Pedantical"?) scrutiny.

What, then, is the relation of the classical margins of this engraving to its center – the relation of the author to her frame? Perhaps as if to register at once the difficulty and the boldness, the backward glance and frontal assault this volume poses for dramatic authorship and the male hegemony that has characterized it, the "masculine" figures communicate with each other (two Masculines espous'd, at least in line of sight), while – at once a fashioned and fashioning frontispiece to a later history of textual production, and an unfashionable lady epilogue to its prior histories – the suggestively mobile Cavendish cuts across this exchanged gaze to regard, as if directly, her readerly audience.

Notes

INTRODUCTION: TEXTUAL INTERCOURSE

1 Emily Brontë, *Wuthering Heights*, David Daiches (ed.), Harmondsworth: Penguin Classics, 1987, p. 319.

2 Humphrey Moseley, "The Stationer to the Reader," in COMEDIES AND TRAGEDIES *Written by* FRANCIS BEAVMONT AND IOHN FLETCHER *Gentlemen*, London: for Humphrey Robinson and Humphrey Moseley, 1647, A4ᵛ.

3 Sir Aston Cokain, Epigram 100, *Small* POEMS *of Divers sorts*, London: by Wil. Godbid, 1658, p. 186.

4 On burial fees, see Vanessa Harding, " 'And one more may be laid there': the Location of Burials in Early Modern London," *The London Journal* 14.2 (1989), pp. 112–29.

5 David Cressy, "Death and the Social Order: The Funerary Preferences of Elizabethan Gentlemen," *Continuity and Change* 5.1 (1989), pp. 99–119.

6 See Harding, " 'And one more.' "

7 I use "discourse" in order to distinguish my discussion from the derogatory sense of the term more often used: "The *Cult* of Friendship."

8 On companionate marriage generally, see Lawrence Stone, *The Family, Sex and Marriage in England 1500–1800*, Abridged edition, New York: Harper, 1977, pp. 100–01, 217–18. For an elaboration of the argument that companionate marriage appropriated the vocabulary of male friendship (as a reading of Stone's examples suggests), see Jeffrey Masten, "My Two Dads: Collaboration and the Reproduction of Beaumont and Fletcher," in Jonathan Goldberg (ed.), *Queering the Renaissance*, Durham: Duke University Press, 1994, pp. 280–309.

9 *Shakespeare's Sonnets*, Stephen Booth (ed.), New Haven: Yale University Press, 1977, p. 13 (sonnet 11). Booth details the troping of print and reproduction (p. 151); see also chapter 2 below.

10 *'Brief Lives,' Chiefly of Contemporaries, set down by John Aubrey, between the years 1669 and 1696*, Andrew Clark (ed.), 2 vols., Oxford: Clarendon Press, 1898, I: pp. 95–96.

11 Scott McMillin, *The Elizabethan Theatre and The Book of Sir Thomas More*, Ithaca: Cornell University Press, 1987; Steven Mullaney, *The Place of the Stage: License, Play, and Power in Renaissance England*, Chicago and London: University of Chicago Press, 1988. Gerald Eades Bentley, *The*

Profession of Dramatist in Shakespeare's Time 1590–1642, Princeton: Princeton University Press, 1971; Bentley, *The Profession of Player in Shakespeare's Time 1590–1642*, Princeton: Princeton University Press, 1984. Bentley's two books are, appropriately, now available in a single bound volume.

12 Bentley, *Profession of Player*, p. 7.

13 Qtd. in Bentley, *Profession of Player*, pp. 19–20.

14 There is nevertheless an asymmetry here, and the male–male relations are, at least in Phillips's will, given preeminence: "if the said Anne my wife do at any time marry after my decease that then and from thenceforth she shall cease to be anymore or longer the executrix of this ... and that then and from thenceforth John Hemings, Richard Burbage, William Slye, and Timothy Whithorne shall be fully and wholly my executors of this my last will and testament as though the said Anne had never been named" (Bentley, *Profession of Player*, p. 20). This arrangement may indicate that the husband/wife relation is one of alliance (an alliance that would end with the wife's remarriage), while the relation of male friends is one of affect as well as alliance.

15 In *Profession of Dramatist*, Bentley emphasizes the magnitude of collaboration in the theatre; Stephen Orgel's brief, important essay "What is a Text?" sketches some of the implications for historical and interpretive work and has been formative for this book; see *Research Opportunities in Renaissance Drama* (1981), pp. 2–4. While it engages the discussion of collaborative dramatic texts, Gordon McMullan's *The Politics of Unease in the Plays of John Fletcher*, Amherst: University of Massachusetts Press, 1994, remains largely within the paradigm of singular authorship, as its title begins to suggest.

16 See Arthur F. Marotti, "Shakespeare's Sonnets as Literary Property," in Elizabeth D. Harvey and Katharine Eisaman Maus (eds.), *Soliciting Interpretation: Literary Theory and Seventeenth-Century English Poetry*, Chicago and London: University of Chicago Press, 1990, and *Manuscript, Print, and the English Renaissance Lyric*, Ithaca: Cornell University Press, 1995; J. W. Saunders, "From Manuscript to Print: A Note on the Circulation of Poetic MSS in the Sixteenth Century," *Proceedings of the Leeds Philosophical and Literary Society* (1951), pp. 507–28; Max Thomas, "Reading the Renaissance Commonplace Book: A Question of Authorship?" in Martha Woodmansee and Peter Jaszi (eds.), *The Construction of Authorship: Textual Appropriation in Law and Literature*, Durham: Duke University Press, 1994, pp. 401–15; Wendy Wall, *The Imprint of Gender: Authorship and Publication in the English Renaissance*, Ithaca: Cornell University Press, 1993, pp. 23–109.

17 Gayle Rubin's term for "the set of arrangements by which a society transforms biological sexuality into products of human activity" (p. 159); "The Traffic in Women: Notes on the 'Political Economy' of Sex," in Rayna Reiter (ed.), *Toward an Anthropology of Women*, New York: Monthly Review Press, 1975, pp. 157–210.

18 In *Profession of Player*, Bentley finds that one role women did occupy in the theatre was that of "box-holder," the person responsible for collecting admission fees (pp. 94–95).

19 Mr. John Fletcher and Mr. William Shakspeare. Gent., THE TWO NOBLE
   KINSMEN, London: Tho. Cotes for Iohn Waterson, 1634.

20 Some important exceptions in drama are Margreta de Grazia's discussion of
   the "filiated" Shakespeare first folio preliminaries in *Shakespeare Verbatim:
   The Reproduction of Authenticity and the 1790 Apparatus*, Oxford: Clarendon
   Press, 1991; Peter Stallybrass, "Shakespeare, the Individual, and the Text," in
   Lawrence Grossberg, Cary Nelson, and Paula Treichler (eds.), with Linda
   Baughman, and with assistance from John Macgregor Wise, *Cultural Studies*,
   New York: Routledge, 1992, pp. 593–610; Elizabeth Pittenger, "Dispatch
   Quickly: The Mechanical Reproduction of Pages," *Shakespeare Quarterly* 42
   (1991), pp. 389–408. Wendy Wall's *Imprint of Gender* performs a similar
   function for early modern poetry in discussing the relation of printed textual
   apparatus, gender, and social class. See also Jonathan Goldberg's discussion
   of authorial attribution, gender, and sexuality in *Sodometries: Renaissance
   Texts, Modern Sexualities*, Stanford: Stanford University Press, 1992, pp.
   81–101. Because women's access to print, handwriting, education, and literacy
   were often highly regulated, investigations of women's writing in the period
   have often been in a better position to confront the conjunction of sex/gender
   and textual production. See for example: Margaret J.M. Ezell, *The Patriarch's
   Wife: Literary Evidence and the History of the Family*, Chapel Hill: University
   of North Carolina Press, 1987; Margaret W. Ferguson, "A Room Not Their
   Own: Renaissance Women as Readers and Writers," in Clayton Koelb and
   Susan Noakes (eds.), *The Comparative Perspective on Literature: Approaches
   to Theory and Practice*, Ithaca: Cornell University Press, 1988, pp. 93–116;
   Ann Rosalind Jones, *The Currency of Eros: Women's Love Lyric in Europe,
   1540–1620*, Bloomington: Indiana University Press, 1990; Barbara Lewalski,
   Writing Women in Jacobean England, Cambridge: Harvard University Press,
   1993; and Jeffrey Masten, " 'Shall I turne blabb?': Circulation, Gender, and
   Subjectivity in Wroth's Sonnets," in Naomi Miller and Gary Waller (eds.),
   Reading Mary Wroth: Representing Alternatives in Early Modern England,
   Knoxville: University of Tennessee Press, 1991, pp. 67–87. For a psychoanalytic discussion of collaborative writing and homosexuality in the nine-
   teenth and twentieth centuries, see Wayne Koestenbaum, *Double Talk: The
   Erotics of Male Literary Collaboration*, New York and London: Routledge,
   1989.

21 I am gesturing toward Eve Kosofsky Sedgwick's phrase: *Between Men:
   English Literature and Male Homosocial Desire*, New York: Columbia
   University Press, 1985. Along with Rubin's argument, Sedgwick's formulation of the homosocial continuum is central to my understanding of sex/
   gender, although it will become clear in the pages that follow that both these
   schemas must necessarily be revised and adapted to the historical particula-
   rities of the sixteenth and seventeenth centuries in England.

22 Patricia Parker's exemplary readings of early modern discourses and rhetorics
   across modern disciplinary divides have enabled my analyses in the chapters
   that follow; see *Literary Fat Ladies: Rhetoric, Gender, Property*, London and
   New York: Methuen, 1987.

23 Michel Foucault, *The History of Sexuality, Volume I: An Introduction*, New
   York: Vintage, 1980.

24 David M. Halperin, *One Hundred Years of Homosexuality and Other Essays on Greek Love*, New York and London: Routledge, 1990, pp. 17–18.

25 Goldberg, *Sodometries*, pp. 68–71, 129.

26 Though Alan Bray resists (most prominently in his title) the conclusions of his own research, he has shown persuasively that there is no *Homosexuality in Renaissance England*, London: Gay Men's Press, 1982. See also Jonathan Goldberg's critique of Bray in "Colin to Hobbinol: Spenser's Familiar Letters," *South Atlantic Quarterly* 88.1 (1989), pp. 107–26; and Bray's revision of his views in "Homosexuality and the Signs of Male Friendship in Elizabethan England," in Goldberg (ed.), *Queering the Renaissance*, pp. 40–61. Halperin argues that homosexuality as we conceptualize it did not exist for the Greeks either. Bruce Smith sees more continuity between past and present than these critics, though he also locates a number of "myths" of male relations – what I would call multiple *sites* or *structures* of homoeroticism, though not homosexuality; see *Homosexual Desire in Shakespeare's England: A Cultural Poetics*, Chicago: University of Chicago Press, 1991.

27 This risk has been most persuasively articulated in the work of John Boswell, for example, "Revolutions, Universals, and Sexual Categories," *Salmagundi* 58–59 (1982–83), pp. 89–113.

28 For a critique of this position with regard to recent work in the field, see Jeffrey Masten, "Designing Sodomies" (review of Claude Summers [ed.], *Homosexuality in Renaissance and Enlightenment England: Literary Representations in Historical Context*, New York: Haworth, 1992, and Goldberg, *Sodometries*), *Lesbian and Gay Studies Newsletter* (July 1993).

29 Halperin, *One Hundred Years*, p. 2.

30 The preceding paragraphs may suggest the extent of my differences with Koestenbaum's *Double Talk*, a book that has usefully opened up a discussion of collaborative erotics. As Koestenbaum makes clear in his introduction, however, he is not particularly interested in the historicity and materiality of authorship, collaboration, the individual, and sexuality (pp. 8–10). A number of the categories central to his analysis – the psychoanalyzable subject, the "integrity of the author" – are largely inappropriate to the Renaissance, though he argues for the extension of his method transhistorically (p. 12). In considering the historical contingency of "the closet" and its relation to distinctly modern notions of public/private, I am indebted to Jay Grossman, "'The evangel-poem of comrades and of love': Revising Whitman's Republicanism," *American Transcendental Quarterly* 4.3 (1990), pp. 210–18; D. A. Miller, *The Novel and the Police*, Berkeley: University of California Press, 1988; and Eve Kosofsky Sedgwick, *Epistemology of the Closet*, Berkeley: University of California Press, 1990.

31 The seventeenth-century argument for what will in this century be called Massinger's "share" in the Beaumont and Fletcher volume is made by Cokain in two 1658 poems (one addressed to the folio's publishers); as I suggest at the end of chapter 4, the poems and the attributional knowledge they claim are situated within the circuit of homoerotic male friendship discussed above and analyzed in detail below. (On the poem to the publishers and Massinger's collaboration more generally, see General Introduction, *The Plays and Poems of Philip Massinger*, Philip Edwards and Colin Gibson [eds.],

Oxford: Clarendon, 1976, I: pp. xix–xx.) The basis of the twentieth-century argument for Massinger's collaboration with Fletcher – Cyrus Hoy's linguistic sorting – is the subject of chapter 1 below.

32 Beaumont and Fletcher, *COMEDIES AND TRAGEDIES*, E2ᵛ.

33 One of the few plays by a woman in the early seventeenth century, Elizabeth Cary's *THE TRAGEDIE OF MARIAM, THE FAIRE Queene of Iewry*, London: by Thomas Creede, for Richard Hawkins, 1613, seemingly confronts the transgressive potential of women writing drama in its first line: "How oft have I with publike voyce runne on?"

34 Beaumont and Fletcher, *COMEDIES AND TRAGEDIES*, E2v.

35 Foucault of course first pointed to the necessity of historicizing *both* authorship and sexuality, though as distinct projects.

36 The primary locus of this argument has been the sonnets. See Booth's admirably balanced but notably modern comment in "Facts and Theories about Shakespeare's Sonnets": "William Shakespeare was almost certainly homosexual, bisexual, or heterosexual. The sonnets provide no evidence on the matter" (*Shakespeare's Sonnets*, p. 548). For a view that allies Shakespearean homosexuality with a canonical project, see Joseph Pequigney, *Such is My Love: A Study of Shakespeare's Sonnets*, Chicago: University of Chicago Press, 1985. On the installation of a homo/hetero binary at the founding moment of the sonnets' editing, canonization, and criticism in the eighteenth century, see de Grazia, "The Scandal of Shakespeare's Sonnets," *Shakespeare Survey* 46 (1993), pp. 35–49.

37 See Sedgwick's analysis of this issue in "Introduction: Axiomatic," *Epistemology of the Closet*.

38 See de Grazia, *Shakespeare Verbatim*.

39 See the essays in *The Division of the Kingdoms: Shakespeare's Two Versions of King Lear* (Gary Taylor and Michael Warren [eds.], Oxford: Clarendon, 1983), especially Stanley Wells's "Introduction" (pp. 1–22), which produces Shakespeare as a revising romanticist on the model of Wordsworth and Tchaikovsky. (I'm indebted to Jay Grossman for pointing out the anachronism of Wells's analogies.) Grace Ioppolo's *Revising Shakespeare*, Cambridge, MA: Harvard University Press, 1991, applies this restricted mode of revision to the Shakespeare canon at large.

40 Stephen Greenblatt, *Shakespearean Negotiations: The Circulation of Social Energy in Renaissance England*, Berkeley: University of California Press, 1988, p. 4.

41 "(Re)consideration," for prior considerations of Shakespeare as collaborator have tended to reify rather than disperse the notion of "Shakespeare," by separating him from and elevating him over his collaborators, or by quarantining play-texts thought collaborative from the rest of the canon. Modern editions often reproduce this critical perspective: the Riverside edition prints only the "Shakespearean" scenes of *Sir Thomas More*, and the Arden series has not to this date published an edition of *The Two Noble Kinsmen*.

42 Michel Foucault, "What Is an Author?" in Paul Rabinow (ed.), *The Foucault Reader*, New York: Pantheon, 1984, p. 119.

43 It might be more historically appropriate, for example, to compile a much more widely inclusive canon of play-texts, organizing it by acting company

(*The Complete Play-texts of the King's Men*) or by year of first production and/or later revival.

44 I am aware that the risks of returning to Shakespeare are significant; see, for example, Marjorie Garber, "Shakespeare as Fetish," *Shakespeare Quarterly* 41.2 (1990), pp. 242–50.

45 There are clearly logistical limits to this practice; I would prefer to follow the example of Randall McLeod and "photoquote" all quotations of text. But even such fidelity to the textual exemplar cannot reproduce other material aspects of these texts, some of which may be arguably crucial in any given instance. For more on the importance of materiality, see Margreta de Grazia and Peter Stallybrass, "The Materiality of the Shakespearean Text," *Shakespeare Quarterly* 44 (1993), pp. 255–83; and D. F. McKenzie, *What's Past is Prologue: The Bibliographical Society and the History of the Book,* Bibliographical Society Centenary Lecture, 14 July 1992, Hearthstone Publications, 1993.

46 Only recently has technology made searching and retrieving information via other categories feasible.

I SEEING DOUBLE: COLLABORATION AND THE INTERPRETATION OF RENAISSANCE DRAMA

1 Richard Whitlock, ZOOTOMIA, *or Observations on the Present Manners of the English: Briefly Anatomizing the Living by the Dead*, London: Tho. Roycroft and Humphrey Moseley, 1654, p. 208.

2 Michel Foucault, "What Is an Author?" in Paul Rabinow (ed.), *The Foucault Reader*, New York: Pantheon, 1984, p. 101; subsequent references will be parenthetical.

3 A survey of seventeenth-century reference materials shows that, even in this limited meaning, *anonymous* rarely appeared in hard-word-lists and translation dictionaries. An exception, the scholarly *Riders Dictionarie*, 3rd edition, Oxford: Joseph Barnes, 1612, translates the English *Namelesse* into the Latin *Anonymus*, but, significantly, not vice versa – a suggestion that the word had not gained currency as an English word beyond a scholarly, Latinate context. This is the case as late as 1677, in Elisha Coles's *A Dictionary, English–Latin, and Latin–English*, London: by John Richardson, for Peter Parker ... And Thomas and John Guy. Iohn Minsheu's *Ductor in Linguas, THE GVIDE INTO TONGVES*, London: Iohn Browne, 1617, translates the Latin *Anonymus* into English as "Vnnamed." In none of the other "dictionaries" in which it appears does the word connect persons with texts; the unanimous gloss is simply "nameless."

4 For methodological reasons (the *OED*'s limited quotation-sources) as well as theoretical reasons (the notion of word "coinage" is readily historicized within a capitalist context), we must read *OED*'s dates not as solid markers of a word's invention or origin but, more flexibly, as an indication of meanings in circulation at any given time. The related forms of *anonymous* (*anonymity, anonymously, anonymousness*) emerge even later, in the eighteenth and nineteenth centuries.

5 See especially chapters 3 and 4. See also Marjorie Garber, *Shakespeare's Ghost Writers: Literature as Uncanny Causality*, New York: Methuen, 1987.

6 Roland Barthes, "The Death of the Author," in *Image, Music, Text*, trans. Stephen Heath, New York: Hill and Wang, 1977.

7 For a characterization of anonymity related but alternative to the one I have sketched above, see Virginia Woolf's posthumously published essay "ANON.," *Twentieth-Century Literature* 25 (1975), pp. 382–98. Although Woolf too identifies a shift in English culture from nameless to named texts, her construal romanticizes "Anon" as a free and nameless individual; the central strategy of the essay is in some sense to identify and individualize the writer she identifies as nameless. In Woolf's scheme, the named author *replaces* (rather than emerges with) "Anon."

8 Gerald Eades Bentley, *The Profession of Dramatist in Shakespeare's Time 1590–1642*, Princeton: Princeton University Press, 1971, p. 199.

9 *Ibid.*, p. 263. Recent considerations of revised texts in the Shakespeare canon have worked to dissolve the notion of the single text, but continue to insist anachronistically upon the notion of a singular revising authorial consciousness; see Gary Taylor and Michael Warren (eds.), *The Division of the Kingdoms: Shakespeare's Two Versions of King Lear*, Oxford: Clarendon, 1983; Grace Ioppolo, *Revising Shakespeare*, Cambridge, MA: Harvard University Press, 1991. In contrast, Scott McMillin usefully explores revision as a deconstruction of authorial individuality in the *Sir Thomas More* manuscript; *The Elizabethan Theatre and The Book of Sir Thomas More*, Ithaca: Cornell University Press, 1987, pp. 153–59.

10 Bentley, *Profession of Dramatist*, p. 198. See also Stephen Orgel's important discussion of Bentley in "What is a Text?," *Research Opportunities in Renaissance Drama* (1981), pp. 2–4.

11 This is to say nothing of the manifold collaborations that generated a play-text when/if it was eventually printed. On book-holders, see William B. Long, "Bookkeepers and Playhouse Manuscripts: A Peek at the Evidence," *Shakespeare Newsletter* 44 (1994), p. 3; and Long, "Stage Directions: A Misinterpreted Factor in Determining Textual Provenance," *TEXT* 2 (1985), pp. 121–37. Largely, of course, the participation in textual production of agents other than "the" playwright has been viewed as intrusive and corruptive, rather than collaborative.

12 Jean-Christophe Agnew, *Worlds Apart: The Market and the Theater in Anglo-American Thought, 1550–1750*, Cambridge: Cambridge University Press, 1986, p. 111. Cf. Woolf: "the play was a common product, written by one hand, but so moulded in transition that the author had no sense of property in it. It was in part the work of the audience" ("ANON.," p. 395). It is important to notice that (in a way to which I will return below) Woolf insists upon the singlehandedness of textual production in this period, even as she stresses the collaborative role of the audience.

13 [William Shakespeare], AN EXCELLENT conceited Tragedie OF Romeo and *Iuliet*, London: by Iohn Danter, 1597.

14 Mr. John Fletcher and William Shakspeare. Gent., THE TWO NOBLE KINSMEN, London: Tho. Cotes for Iohn Waterson, 1634. See Agnew's discussion of the handshake's emerging contractual significance (*Worlds Apart*, pp. 86–89).

15 See Annabel Patterson, *Censorship and Interpretation: The Conditions of*

Writing and Reading in Early Modern England, Madison: University of Wisconsin Press, 1984.

16 For a summary, see T. H. Howard-Hill, "The Author as Scribe or Reviser?: Middleton's Intentions in *A Game at Chess*," *Transactions of the Society for Textual Scholarship* 3, New York: AMS, 1987, pp. 305–18.

17 See McMillin's chapter "Locations," in *The Elizabethan Theatre*.

18 AN EXCELLENT conceited Tragedie OF Romeo and Iuliet, title page, my emphasis.

19 For further analysis of play-text quartos, see chapter 4.

20 Cyrus Hoy, "The Shares of Fletcher and his Collaborators in the Beaumont and Fletcher Canon (I)," *Studies in Bibliography* 8 (1956), p. 130.

21 *Ibid.*

22 Hoy, "The Shares of Fletcher and his Collaborators in the Beaumont and Fletcher Canon (III)," *Studies in Bibliography* 11 (1958), p. 86.

23 Hoy, "Shares (I)," p. 142.

24 *Ibid.*, p. 130. It is worth noting that Hoy's project was begun in 1952 and published between 1956 and 1962, and thus may in its discourse and epistemology bear (however unintentionally) the traces of a culture experiencing an explosion of interest in the visible signs and detection of homosexuality and homosexual practices. On this, see Lee Edelman, "Tearooms and Sympathy; or, The Epistemology of the Water Closet," in *Homographesis: Essays in Gay Literary and Cultural Theory*, New York: Routledge, 1994, pp. 148–70.

25 Though he is largely engaged in the same project as Hoy, R. C. Bald demonstrates that distinguishing ostensible scribal and authorial pronoun preferences is fraught with difficulties: *Bibliographical Studies in the Beaumont and Fletcher Folio of 1647*, Supplement to the Bibliographical Society's Transactions, no. 13, Oxford: Oxford University Press for the Bibliographical Society, 1938 (for 1937), pp. 93–102.

26 Sheldon P. Zitner (ed.), *The Knight of the Burning Pestle*, by Francis Beaumont, The Revels Plays, Manchester: Manchester University Press, 1984, p. 10.

27 See Martha Woodmansee's indispensable consideration of these issues: "The Genius and the Copyright: Economic and Legal Conditions of the Emergence of the 'Author,'" *Eighteenth-Century Studies* 17 (1984), pp. 425–48. For a historicization of handwriting and the signature, see Jonathan Goldberg, *Writing Matter: From the Hands of the English Renaissance*, Stanford: Stanford University Press, 1990.

28 Gordon McMullan's interpretation of this phrase as referring to *authorial* differences is apparently the central point of his critique of an earlier published version of this chapter (*The Politics of Unease in the Plays of John Fletcher*, Amherst: University of Massachusetts Press, 1994, p. 154).

29 Hoy, "Shares (III)," p. 87.

30 On the individuation of Shakespeare, see Margreta de Grazia, *Shakespeare Verbatim: The Reproduction of Authenticity and the 1790 Apparatus*, Oxford: Clarendon Press, 1991. Shakespeare's style (whether protean or utterly, brilliantly predictable) figured prominently – and was deployed by all sides – in the controversy surrounding Gary Taylor's (re)attribution of the ms. poem

"Shall I die?" to Shakespeare. See Taylor, "A New Shakespeare Poem?," *TLS* (20 December 1985), pp. 1447–48, and "'Shall I die?' Immortalized?," *TLS* (31 January 1986), pp. 123–24. For responses, see *TLS* letters, 27 December 1985 through 7 March 1986. See also Stephen Orgel, "The Authentic Shakespeare," *Representations* 21 (1988), pp. 1–25.

31 And the model and basis for extensive (and similarly compromised) work on Massinger, Middleton, and others; see David J. Lake, *The Canon of Thomas Middleton's Plays: Internal Evidence for the Major Problems of Authorship*, London: Cambridge University Press, 1975; MacD. P. Jackson, *Studies in Attribution: Middleton and Shakespeare*, Salzburg Studies in English Literature, Salzburg: Universität Salzburg, 1979.

32 See Hoy, "The Shares of Fletcher and his Collaborators in the Beaumont and Fletcher Canon (VII)," *Studies in Bibliography* 15 (1962), p. 88.

33 Fredson Bowers, foreword, *The Dramatic Works in the Beaumont and Fletcher Canon*, Cambridge: Cambridge University Press, 1966, vol. I: p. vii; Cyrus Hoy, "Critical and Aesthetic Problems of Collaboration in Renaissance Drama," *Research Opportunities in Renaissance Drama* 19 (1976), p. 4 (my emphasis). Cf. McMullan's nearly identical statement, where the ground is simply shifted from aesthetics to politics: "For the political interpretation of plays in a collaborative canon, understanding of the processes and division of collaborative work is essential, since inappropriate readings may result from inadequate textual knowledge" (*Politics of Unease*, p. 149).

34 Literary-critical essays often move to "settle" questions of authorship before moving on to their central interpretive purposes. Take, as an example of this process, the following initial footnote to an article on tragicomedy: "In order to avoid the minefield of the authorship of the Beaumont and Fletcher canon, I am using 'Fletcher' to refer to plays by Fletcher and his collaborators" (Kathleen McLuskie, "'A maidenhead, *Amintor*, at my yeares': Chastity and Tragicomedy in the Fletcher Plays," in Gordon McMullan and Jonathan Hope [eds.], *The Politics of Tragicomedy: Shakespeare and After*, London: Routledge, 1992, p. 120).

35 As his title begins to suggest, Wayne Koestenbaum's *Double Talk: The Erotics of Male Literary Collaboration*, New York and London: Routledge, 1989, works within this paradigm of doubling.

36 See Jerome J. McGann's critique of the editing/interpreting distinction in "The Monks and the Giants: Textual and Bibliographical Studies and the Interpretation of Literary Works," in McGann (ed.), *Textual Criticism and Literary Interpretation*, Chicago and London: University of Chicago Press, 1985, pp. 180–99. De Grazia demonstrates how the editorial apparatus itself functions to shape and constrain interpretation in editions of the Shakespeare canon; see *Shakespeare Verbatim*.

37 Bowers, foreword, in *Dramatic Works*, I: p. vii, my emphasis.

38 On "verbal corruption" and actors' "interpolations" in *Hamlet*, see Harold Jenkins's Arden edition, London: Methuen, 1982, pp. 62–63.

39 William Shake-speare, THE *Tragicall Historie of* HAMLET *Prince of Denmarke* (Q1), London: for N.L. and Iohn Trundell, 1603, E4^v.

40 William Shakespeare, THE *Tragicall Historie of* HAMLET, *Prince of Denmarke* (Q2), London: by I.R. for N.L., 1604, title page.

41 McGann argues that even the text that seems to have been materially produced by one person exists fundamentally in the realm of the social; revision in authorial manuscripts, he argues, "reflect[s] social interactions and purposes." See *A Critique of Modern Textual Criticism*, Chicago and London: University of Chicago Press, 1983, p. 62.

42 Stephen Greenblatt makes a related point in his discussion of "the *collective* making of distinct cultural practices and inquiry into the relations among these practices," though I would note that, in the next sentence, he returns to singular "making" in labeling his subject "plays by Shakespeare" (*Shakespearean Negotiations: The Circulation of Social Energy in Renaissance England*, Berkeley: University of California Press, 1988, p. 5, my emphasis).

43 Morse Peckham, "Reflections on the Foundations of Modern Textual Editing," *Proof* 1 (1971), pp. 122–55.

44 In other words, we would not want to rely too heavily on Jonson's attitude toward collaboration alone; for an alternative interpretation of dramatic collaboration in this mode, see Donald K. Hedrick, " 'Be Rough With Me': The Collaborative Arenas of *The Two Noble Kinsmen*," in Charles H. Frey (ed.), *Shakespeare, Fletcher, and The Two Noble Kinsmen*, Columbia: University of Missouri Press, 1989, pp. 45–77.

45 *THE KNIGHT OF the Burning Pestle* (Q1), London: for Walter Burre, 1613, A2.

46 Francis Beaumont and Iohn Fletcher. Gent., *THE KNIGHT Of the BVRNING PESTLE* (Q2), London: N.O. for I.S., 1635, A3. The third quarto, often supposed to be a later reprint despite its stated date of 1635, is most easily distinguished from Q2 by its spelling of "Beamount" on the title page: Francis Beamount and Iohn Fletcher, *THE KNIGHT Of the BVRNING PESTLE* (Q3), London: N.O. for I.S., 1635.

47 *THE KNIGHT* (Q2), A4.

48 *THE KNIGHT* (Q1), A2ᵛ.

49 Reprinted in Zitner, (ed.), *The Knight*, pp. 163–64.

50 For example: John Doebler's edition in the Regents Renaissance Drama series, Lincoln: University of Nebraska Press, 1967; Andrew Gurr's edition for Fountainwell Drama Texts, Edinburgh: Oliver and Boyd, 1968; Michael Hattaway's New Mermaids edition, London: Ernest Benn, 1969; and Zitner's 1984 Revels Plays edition. All of these followed the 1966 publication of the play's "standard" edition (as edited by Hoy) in *The Dramatic Works* supervised by Bowers and cited above.

51 Eugene M. Waith's influential study of *The Pattern of Tragicomedy in Beaumont and Fletcher*, New Haven: Yale University Press, 1952, for example, discounts *The Knight* as uncharacteristic before it proceeds to an analysis of the rest of the canon (p. 5).

52 For reasons explored above, I quote not from an edition of *The Knight* governed by anachronistic notions of authorship, but rather from Q1, providing page references to that text. Joseph Loewenstein notes acting companies' use of the first-person plural in "The Script in the Marketplace," in Stephen Greenblatt (ed.), *Representing the English Renaissance*, Berkeley: University of California Press, 1988, p. 266; my understanding of drama's eventual emergence as textual property is greatly indebted to this article.

53 Barthes, "The Death of the Author," p. 146.

54 The source-tracing textual glosses and commentary in the editions mentioned above – upon which I rely heavily in the discussion of "quotation" that follows – are themselves voluminously symptomatic and constitutive of the twentieth-century preoccupation with authorship and the transmission of textual property. For an important critique of the traditional relation of "source" to play-text, see Jonathan Goldberg, "Speculations: Macbeth and Source," in Jean E. Howard and Marion F. O'Connor (eds.), *Shakespeare Reproduced: The Text in History and Ideology*, New York and London: Methuen, 1987, pp. 242–64.

55 The relation of *The Knight* to *Don Quixote* is a matter of some controversy, especially if one is concerned about "Beaumont's" "originality"; see Zitner's edition, pp. 39–42, for a summary of the issues.

56 See Zitner (ed.), *The Knight*, pp. 28–31.

57 In *The Pattern of Tragicomedy*, Waith quarantines the play from this possibility by labeling it "Beaumont's"; see note 51 above.

58 Zitner (ed.), *The Knight*, p. 173.

59 *Hamlet*'s Arden editor, Harold Jenkins, calls these O's "theatrical accretions to Shakespeare's dialogue" (p. 62). Terence Hawkes's perceptive essay "That Shakespeherian Rag," in his book of the same title (London: Methuen, 1986), first brought Hamlet's dying O's to my attention.

60 Lee Bliss, "'Plot Mee No Plots': The Life of Drama and the Drama of Life in *The Knight of the Burning Pestle*," *Modern Language Quarterly* 45.1 (1984), pp. 13 and 3.

61 Again, comparison with Woolf's romanticized character "Anon." is instructive.

62 The complexity of social class in this play is often too easily simplified by critics siding unselfconsciously with the actors and upper-class audience against the citizens' supposed lack of sophistication and their "naive" interventions in "art." Bliss, for example, derides the citizens because they "demolish the independent aesthetic status of the playwright's work and overturn the traditional ideal of drama as a clarifying mirror of men and their relation to their world" ("'Plot Mee No Plots,'" p. 4).

63 Alexander Nehamas, "Writer, Text, Work, Author," in Anthony J. Cascardi (ed.), *Literature and the Question of Philosophy*, Baltimore: Johns Hopkins University Press, 1987, p. 286 (first quotation); "The Postulated Author: Critical Monism as a Regulative Ideal," *Critical Inquiry* (1981), p. 145 (second quotation).

64 Or defies, I might add, the limitations of my own dyadic rhetoric here: "seeing *double*." The implications of three-way collaboration and attribution are explored briefly in the last section of chapter 4.

2 BETWEEN GENTLEMEN: HOMOEROTICISM, COLLABORATION, AND THE DISCOURSE OF FRIENDSHIP

1 Richard Brathwait, THE *English Gentleman*, London: by Iohn Haviland [for] Robert Bostock, 1630.

2 *Ibid.*, title page.

3 Brathwait, THE ENGLISH GENTLEMAN, 2nd edition, London: Felix Kyngston

for Robert Bostocke, 1633. Only some copies of the 1630 edition (e.g. the Newberry Library copy) include the engraved title page and "Draught" shown in Fig. 1.

4 See Raymond Williams, *Keywords: A Vocabulary of Culture and Society*, New York: Oxford, 1976, pp. 133–36; Peter Stallybrass, "Shakespeare, the Individual, and the Text," in Lawrence Grossberg, Cary Nelson, and Paula Treichler (eds.), with Linda Baughman, and with assistance from John Macgregor Wise, *Cultural Studies*, New York: Routledge, 1992, pp. 593–610.

5 I am indebted to David Boyd for his assistance in exploring the range of possible translations.

6 See Lawrence Stone, *The Family, Sex and Marriage in England 1500–1800*, Abridged edition, New York: Harper, 1977, pp. 100–02, 217–18. Though *The English Gentleman*'s first and third editions are separated by only eleven years, it is tempting to see in the details of its publication history a shift in the sex/gender system in microcosm. In the 1641 edition, the 1633 gloss ("[a]lluding properly to those *Peeces* engraven in former Editions") is retained, but the *Gentleman*'s engravings are different; where the earlier editions depicted "acquaintance" as two men hugging, the 1641 engraving substitutes two disembodied hands shaking. The 1641 edition furthermore brings together *The English Gentleman* and *The English Gentlewoman* in one volume; it seems to perform a textual marriage of male and female companion volumes, the word made one flesh – or in the words of the title: THE ENGLISH GENTLEMAN; AND THE ENGLISH GENTLEVVOMAN, BOTH *In one* VOLVME *couched*, London: by Iohn Dawson, 1641. That Brathwait speaks even in the early editions of a wife as a variety of "acquaintance," however, also suggests the simultaneous circulation of differing sex/gender discourses in a culture (in a single text) – a situation that a word like "shift" too easily simplifies. For an analogous argument about the late nineteenth and early twentieth centuries, see Eve Kosofsky Sedgwick, *Epistemology of the Closet*, Berkeley: University of California Press, 1990; my view of the problematics of *shift* as a central and problematic term in new historicist work generally is indebted to conversations with Tyler Smith.

7 Edmund Spenser, "A Letter of the Authors expounding his whole intention in the course of this worke," THE FAERIE QVEENE. *Disposed into twelve books, Fashioning* XII. *Morall vertues*, London: for William Ponsonbie, 1590), p. 591. See Ruth Kelso's extensive bibliography and redaction of conduct books, *The Doctrine of the English Gentleman in the Sixteenth Century*, Gloucester, MA: Peter Smith, 1964. Lauren J. Mills, *One Soule in Bodies Twain: Friendship in Tudor Literature and Stuart Drama*, Bloomington, IN: Principia, 1937, traces classical precedents and Renaissance reincarnations.

8 See Lawrence Stone, "Social Mobility in England, 1500–1700," *Past and Present* 33 (1966); Frank Whigham, "Courtesy Literature and Social Change," chapter 1, *Ambition and Privilege: The Social Tropes of Elizabethan Courtesy Theory*, Berkeley: University of California Press, 1984, p. 5.

9 Whigham, *Ambition and Privilege*, pp. 18–19.

10 Parenthetical references to Florio's Montaigne are to THE ESSAYES OR *Morall, Politike and Millitairie Discourses of Lo: Michaell de Montaigne ... now done into English*, London: by Val. Sims for Edward Blount, 1603. A reprint of the

1632 text is widely available: *The Essays of Montaigne*, with an introduction by George Saintsbury, 3 vols., London: David Nutt, 1892; rpt. New York: AMS, 1967.

11 The title page of the 1613 (second) edition: ESSAYES WRITTEN IN French By MICHAEL Lord of Montaigne ... DONE INTO ENGLISH, according to the last French edition, by IOHN FLORIO ..., London: by Melch. Bradvvood for Edvvard Blovnt and William Barret, 1613.

12 Though Montaigne's essays are of course significant in the original French cultural context, I am here concerned not with Montaigne "himself" or the French text of "*De l'amitié*," but, instead, with what the translated essay puts into circulation in England. In other words, my focus is not the particular meanings the French text conveys, what Montaigne might have intended in that text, its connection with Montaigne's life, or the "fidelity" of the translation, but rather Florio's text as a cultural document in its own right and its participation in English discourses of friendship and homoeroticism. For these reasons, my references are to the 1603 Florio edition; I retain Florio's spellings (including the indeterminacy of Boitie/Boetie) and his translations of Montaigne's classical quotations. For an important and related reading of the politics and erotics of "voluntary servitude" in the French text of the essay, see forthcoming work by Marc Schachter (unpublished paper given at MLA 1995).

13 The Boetie essay was never printed in *Essayes* but was replaced by his sonnets in some French editions. In the 1603, 1613, and 1632 Florio editions, the place of the poems is held by Montaigne's letter dedicating the sonnets "to the Ladie of Grammont" (1603, p. 97). A similar text on friendship and the pleasures of textual exchange is Francis Beaumont's letter to Thomas Speght, begging him to publish Chaucer's texts; the letter is addressed (in the 1598 edition) "F. B. to his very louing friend, T. S." (no sig.). Beaumont thanks Speght for giving him "of your Copies [of Chaucer] to vse priuatly for mine owne pleasure," and urges, in conclusion: "Wherein [by publishing Chaucer] you shall not onely satisfie that conceit which I haue many yeares carried of your vnfained loue towards me: but pleasure many who daylie expect your paines herein, and perfourme vnto *Chaucer* great part of that honour that he most worthely deserueth ... *Your assured and euer louing friend, Francis Beaumont*" (THE *Workes of our Antient and Learned English Poet*, GEFFREY CHAVCER, *newly Printed*, London: by Adam Islip at the charges of Bonham Norton, 1598, no sig.).

14 This material (routinely elided from modern reprints of Florio's translation) derives from the first edition (1603), A2–A2^v.

15 *Translation* could signify a transformation of both languages and persons in the Renaissance; a familiar example: "Bottom ... Thou art translated" (William Shakespeare, *A Midsommer nights dreame*, London: for Thomas Fisher, 1600, D2^v). For the relation of translation, "transport," and metaphor in Renaissance rhetoric, see Patricia Parker, *Literary Fat Ladies: Rhetoric, Gender, Property*, London and New York: Methuen, 1987, pp. 93 and 36–53. In an unpublished essay ("Authoring Renaissance Translations: Marie de Gournay and John Florio"), Doug Trevor has demonstrated that even prior to English translation, what we call "Montaigne" is itself a complex fabrica-

tion produced through manifold editions, revisions, and additions, only some of which are attributable to Montaigne.

16 i.e. *lose*, but since *loose* and *lose* were interchangeable, both modern meanings are possible here.

17 Notably, Florio retains "jovissance" to describe friendship but substitutes "enjoying" for (apparently) sexual activity; in the French text "jouissance" is used in both instances. Early modern French *jouissance* did not have the playfulness of Barthes' *jouissance* and apparently did not mean "orgasm" in either French or English at the time. It is nevertheless apparent from context (in both the French and English texts) as well as from historical dictionaries that *jouissance/enjoying* signified sexually and meant "*having sex*" quite literally, with emphasis on the having/possession, usually of a woman by a man. Minsheu defines *enjoy* as: "*to* **Enioy** *or haue the possession of*, à G. [= French] Iouir, *quod deduci videtur à Lat*: gaudere ... *Vi. to* **Possesse**"; Iohn Minsheu, *Ductor in Linguas, THE GUIDE INTO TONGUES*, London: Iohn Browne, 1617, p. 174. For more on sexual *enjoying*, see Stephen Booth (ed.), *Shakespeare's Sonnets*, New Haven: Yale University Press, 1977, pp. 444–45.

18 For an exploration of a culture in which sexual relations were constructed on precisely these hierarchies, see David M. Halperin, *One Hundred Years of Homosexuality and Other Essays on Greek Love*, New York and London: Routledge, 1990. Brathwait uses "Offices" in the term "Conjugall Offices" ("A Supplement" to the 1641 edition [cited above], sig. Aaa3, p. 5). Henry Abelove has suggested to me the resonance of this term and the passage generally within republican rhetoric.

19 This catalogue is from Stephen Booth's indispensable commentary to *Shakespeare's Sonnets*, p. 466.

20 The early use of *concurrence* to signify meetings of liquids as well as persons may even suggest here a sort of simultaneous orgasm/ejaculation (*OED*). The presence of *semblable* adds to that sense, although it is not related (at least etymologically) to *semen*. I am indebted to Margreta de Grazia and Jay Grossman for suggesting this resonance.

21 On the opposition of the prefixes *di-* and *con-* in the French text, see Robert D. Cottrell, *Sexuality/Textuality: A Study of the Fabric of Montaigne's Essais*, Columbus: Ohio State University Press, 1981, p. 130.

22 Brathwait, *English Gentleman* (1630), p. 302.

23 Or other transgressions of rank/hierarchy. Alan Bray, *Homosexuality in Renaissance England*, London: Gay Men's Press, 1982. In Jonathan Goldberg's terms, sodomy is fundamentally a structural category: "sodometries, relational structures precariously available to prevailing discourses"; see *Sodometries: Renaissance Texts, Modern Sexualities*, Stanford: Stanford University Press, 1992, p. 20.

24 For the divergence of sodomy and friendship as discourses of homoeroticism, see Alan Bray's important article "Homosexuality and the Signs of Male Friendship in Elizabethan England," *History Workshop Journal* 29 (1990), pp. 1–19 (rpt. in Jonathan Goldberg [ed.], *Queering the Renaissance*, Durham: Duke University Press, 1994). Bray's revisionary treatment in this article of his own work in *Homosexuality in Renaissance England* suggests the extent to

which "homosexuality" in both titles must be placed under historical erasure. Bray's article first brought the Brathwait engraving to my attention.

25 Mr. John Fletcher and Mr. William Shakspeare. Gent., THE TWO NOBLE KINSMEN, London: Tho. Cotes for Iohn Waterson, 1634, title page and verso. Subsequent references to this play will cite this quarto's page numbers.

26 See for example Eugene M. Waith's otherwise helpful discussion of Renaissance/classical friendship in his introduction to *The Two Noble Kinsmen*, Oxford Shakespeare, Oxford and New York: Oxford University Press, 1989, pp. 49–52; also Mills, *One Soule in Bodies Twain.* That early modern friendship is often referred to as a "Cult" registers both the critical desire for distance from it and the desire to mark its seeming aberrance in relation to modern male relations.

27 The play thus mystifies the contemporary social tensions over whether gentlemen are born or made; see Whigham, Introduction, *Ambition and Privilege.*

28 My quotations (including the spelling "Protheus") derive from MR. WILLIAM SHAKESPEARES COMEDIES, HISTORIES, & TRAGEDIES, London: Isaac Iaggard and Ed. Blount, 1623, as edited by Charlton Hinman and reprinted in *The Norton Facsimile*, New York: Norton, 1968. Unless otherwise noted, emphases are the folio's. Through-line numbering (TLN) will appear parenthetically.

29 The term, now commonplace, is Eve Kosofsky Sedgwick's; see *Between Men: English Literature and Male Homosocial Desire*, New York: Columbia University Press, 1985. Sedgwick's initial definition – "'Homosocial' ... describes social bonds between persons of the same sex" (p. 1) – is modified in her larger introduction; as I begin to suggest by revising her title in naming this chapter, I am relying upon, but also specifying in what I hope is a consistently more historicist way, the terms of Sedgwick's influential argument.

30 For a thematic reading of education in the play, see Peter Lindenbaum, "Education in *The Two Gentlemen of Verona*," *Studies in English Literature* 15 (1975), pp. 229–44.

31 I avoid the term *heterosexual* here, for, as Halperin demonstrates and as my discussion of Montaigne above suggests, it is as much in need of historicization as its counterpart; see *One Hundred Years*, pp. 17–18. To designate what may seem (to modern eyes) to be straightforward "heterosexual" love, I use the term *Petrarchan*, both because it is more historically defensible (that is, it suggests the conventionality of a rhetoric of gender arrangements at a specific point in English history) and because the term highlights the textuality of the sexual. (This is not to say that Petrarchism does not eventually participate in the construction of modern heterosexuality; as any number of modern song lyrics demonstrate, it is still much with us. On the persistence of Petrarchism, I'm indebted to conversations with Nancy Vickers and Roland Greene, and to Greene's *Post-Petrarchism: Origins and Innovations of the Western Lyric Sequence*, Princeton: Princeton University Press, 1991.)

32 Juliet Fleming notes the early modern use of *conversation* for meanings we would now attach to *intercourse*: "in 1581 the possible meanings of 'conversation' included 'dwelling', 'dwelling with or among', social dealings, the exchange of words and ideas, and the act of sex. The word which now covers these meanings, 'intercourse', did not develop its sexual connotation until the

eighteenth century ... " Juliet Fleming, "The Ladies' Man and the Age of Elizabeth," in James Grantham Turner (ed.), *Sexuality and Gender in Early Modern Europe: Institutions, Texts, Images*, Cambridge: Cambridge University Press, 1993, p. 160. See also *OED*.

33 Jonathan Goldberg, "Shakespearian Characters: the Generation of Silvia," *Voice Terminal Echo: Postmodernism and English Renaissance Texts*, New York and London: Methuen, 1986, pp. 68–100.

34 Christopher Marlowe, *Hero and Leander* (II.226), in Fredson Bowers (ed.), *The Complete Works of Christopher Marlowe*, vol. II, Cambridge: Cambridge University Press, 1973. Though *The Two Gentlemen of Verona* is often thought to have been composed in 1592–93 on stylistic grounds, the first mention of the play is in Meres's *Palladis Tamia* (1598) and the text of the play was not published until 1623. There is thus no difficulty in associating the play with *Hero and Leander*, the earliest known edition of which is also dated 1598. Furthermore, the poem was entered in the Stationers' Register in 1593 and was undoubtedly written prior to Marlowe's death earlier that same year. Gregory W. Bredbeck provides a reading of the Neptune passage that emphasizes its homoeroticism; see *Sodomy and Interpretation*, Ithaca: Cornell University Press, 1991, pp. 131–34. Though Bredbeck and others disregard/ disparage the importance of the poem's publication history, it is relevant to my argument here that *Hero and Leander* was widely read in the period as a *collaborative* text – a poem by Marlowe with Chapman's continuation and his arguments to the "sestyads." Q1 (1598) publishes the Marlowe fragment; Q2 and subsequent editions publish Marlowe with Chapman's continuation. My thinking about textual issues in the poem has been influenced by Judith Haber's essay " 'True-loves blood': Narrative and Desire in *Hero and Leander*" (forthcoming in *English Literary Renaissance*).

35 For relevant discussions of mimetic desire, see René Girard, "The Politics of Desire in *Troilus and Cressida*," in Patricia Parker and Geoffrey Hartman (eds.), *Shakespeare and the Question of Theory*, New York and London: Methuen, 1985, pp. 188–209; and Sedgwick, *Between Men*, pp. 21–27.

36 The discursive enjambment of friendship and love is illuminated by the *OED*: *friend* meant at the time of this play both "one joined to another in mutual benevolence and intimacy," and "a lover or paramour of either sex." Likewise, *lover* could mean both "a friend or well-wisher" and "one who is in love with ... a person of the opposite sex." *Shake-speares Sonnets* 144 provides an example of the two used interchangeably, and Booth comments on sonnet 126: " 'Lover' meant 'friend' in context of a friendship, and this is such a context; 'lover' meant 'paramour' in context of a love affair, and by literary kind this is such a context" (*Shakespeare's Sonnets*, p. 432).

37 Parker, *Literary Fat Ladies*, pp. 69–73.

38 Qtd. in *ibid.*, p. 70.

39 See Parker's connection of the doublet, *copia*, and print (*ibid.*, p. 73).

40 Goldberg, "Shakespearian Characters," p. 72.

41 Except for the word *Siluia* these emphases are mine. In the folio, the text of the poem is set off from the Duke's speech and printed in italic, the "hand" of nobility; the very typeface of the text may thus mark Valentine's class-climbing. (I have not reproduced this arrangement here.) It is important to

note, however, that italic also had other meanings in printed texts, that a printed text does not necessarily simply reproduce the hand(s) of a manuscript, and that the manuscript of this play would not necessarily encode high-class texts using the conventions of their inscription elsewhere in the culture. Jonathan Goldberg's "Hamlet's Hand," *Shakespeare Quarterly* 39 (1988), suggestively raises these issues without, I think, fully acknowledging some of the problematics of reading handwriting conventions over into printed texts.

42 Arthur F. Marotti, "'Love is not love': Elizabethan Sonnet Sequences and the Social Order," *ELH* 49 (1982), p. 399.

43 On the intersection of these terms in *Astrophil and Stella*, see Ann Rosalind Jones and Peter Stallybrass, "The Politics of *Astrophil and Stella*," *SEL* 24 (1984), pp. 53–68. Mary Wroth's sonnets, the exception to this rule, are the earliest known examples of sonnets by an English woman.

44 J. W. Saunders, "From Manuscript to Print: A Note on the Circulation of Poetic MSS in the Sixteenth Century," *Proceedings of the Leeds Philosophical and Literary Society* (1951), pp. 507–28; see also Wendy Wall, *The Imprint of Gender: Authorship and Publication in the English Renaissance*, Ithaca: Cornell University Press, 1993, pp. 23–109; Max Thomas, "Reading the Renaissance Commonplace Book: A Question of Authorship?" in Martha Woodmansee and Peter Jaszi (eds.), *The Construction of Authorship: Textual Appropriation in Law and Literature*, Durham: Duke University Press, 1993, pp. 401–15.

45 Clara Gebert (ed.), *An Anthology of Elizabethan Dedications and Prefaces*, Philadelphia: University of Pennsylvania Press, 1933, p. 107.

46 See Wall, *Imprint of Gender*, pp. 189–90.

47 My argument here is related to Sedgwick's (*Between Men*, pp. 33–36), though I am attempting to draw attention to the historical specificity of discourses figuring male reproduction and to illustrate their intersection with the material practices of sonnet circulation and publication.

48 *SHAKE-SPEARES SONNETS*, London: G. Eld for T. T., 1609.

49 In an unpublished essay, William Fisher details the ways in which discourses of usury, sodomy, and reproduction are often coterminous in this period; "Queer Money," circulated in "The Politics of Pleasure" seminar, Shakespeare Association of America, Albuquerque, 1994.

50 On this, see Arthur F. Marotti, "Shakespeare's Sonnets as Literary Property," in Elizabeth D. Harvey and Katharine Eisaman Maus (eds.), *Soliciting Interpretation: Literary Theory and Seventeenth-Century English Poetry*, Chicago and London: University of Chicago Press, 1990, p. 146.

51 By positing a collaborative reading of the sonnets, I do not mean to efface what Montaigne/Florio might call the "disparitie and difference" in the language and practice of patronage; I would argue instead that sonnets and their dedicatory apparatus often stage collaboration to efface class differences and empower their writers. For an analysis of sonnets and social mobility, see Wall, *Imprint of Gender*, pp. 74–180, to which this discussion is greatly indebted. For a reading of the sonnets that insists anachronistically on their homosexuality in a modern psychoanalytic sense, see Joseph Pequigney, *Such is My Love: A Study of Shakespeare's Sonnets*, Chicago: University of Chicago Press, 1985.

52 Arthur Quiller-Couch, Introduction, in Quiller-Couch and John Dover

Wilson (eds.), *The Two Gentlemen of Verona*, New Cambridge Shakespeare, New York: Macmillan, 1921, p. xiv. Subsequent citations will be parenthetical.

53 That is, what Foucault, Halperin (*One Hundred Years*, p. 17), and others see as the modern emergence of distinct hetero- and homosexualities. Sedgwick, however, argues against the "notion that 'homosexuality as we conceive of it today' itself comprises a coherent definitional field rather than a space of overlapping, contradictory, and conflictual definitional forces" (*Epistemology*, pp. 44–48).

54 Hereward T. Price, "Shakespeare as Critic," *Philological Quarterly* 20 (1941), pp. 390–99. "Any explanation of this scene that implies that Shakespeare was serious does rather less than justice to Shakespeare's sense of humor." Clifford Leech's introduction to the Arden edition of the play (London and New York: Methuen, 1969) largely concurs with this view (p. lxxiv).

55 Anne Barton, Introduction to *The Two Gentlemen of Verona*, in G. Blakemore Evans et al. (eds.), *The Riverside Shakespeare*, New York: Houghton Mifflin, 1974, p. 143.

56 For the arguments that *The Two Gentlemen of Verona* is, to a greater or lesser extent, a collaboration, see Leech's Arden edition. Though Leech denies that his is "a 'revision theory' in the customary sense of the term" (p. xxx), he proposes that the text was revised by Shakespeare, "working on a play and modifying his original conception as the work grew under his hands" (p. xxxi).

57 That Valentine can be rewritten as "well deriu'd" suggests again this play's mystification of sixteenth- and seventeenth-century tensions over gentlemen born and gentlemen made. See Whigham, *Ambition and Privilege*.

58 This is of course a situation that reproduces this theatre's mode of production. Julia's last action of the play is her exposure of the ring plot and (thus) her identity and gender; as Protheus's ring moves from him to Julia and back again, it traces a homosocial circuit (like Valentine's letter to himself) and, as elsewhere in the period, functions metonymically as female gender and genitalia. (For a more familiar example, see the concluding lines of *The Merchant of Venice*.) Julia and the ring are both restored to Protheus.

59 Though again, it is important to acknowledge Sedgwick's caveat that modern sexualities are hardly unconflicted, fully stable, or always binarized. See note 53 above.

60 William Shakespeare, *A Midsommer nights dreame*, F2^v.

61 *THE ESSAYES OR COVNSELS, CIVILL AND MORALL, OF FRANCIS LO. VERVLAM, VIS-COVNT ST. ALBAN*, London: Iohn Haviland for Hanna Barret, 1625; rpt. London: Oxford University Press, 1966, p. 116.

62 Other narratives of friendship and/vs. male–female love that resolve thus symmetrically include Sidney's *Arcadia* and, most elaborately, *The Faerie Queene*, Book IV.

63 Social class ostensibly bars the Jailer's Daughter from marrying Palamon; however, her "mad" speeches constantly expose this restriction to critique. She imagines at one point that she can only marry Palamon at "th end o'th world," where "we shall finde / Some blind Priest for the purpose" (p. 78). The play thus both gestures toward a subversion of class distinction and suggests the theatrical construction (and thus performativity) of social class

by marrying her to a version of Palamon acted by the otherwise nameless Wooer.

64 See for example C. L. Barber, " 'Thou that beget'st him that did thee beget': Transformation in 'Pericles' and 'The Winter's Tale,' " *Shakespeare Survey* 22 (1969): "The primary motive which is transformed in *The Winter's Tale* ... is the affection of Leontes for Polixenes, *whatever name one gives it*. The resolution becomes possible because the affection is consummated, *as it could not otherwise be*, through Perdita and Florizel" (p. 65, my emphasis).

65 As Steven Mullaney notes in his resonant chapter "The Rehearsal of Cultures," the distinction I've made here between rehearsal and performance is a modern one, usually not observed in early modern rhetoric. And yet, as I hope my sentence suggests, the use of the term here has something in common with what Mullaney cites as the lone exception to this rule: "A rehearsal was fully distinct from public performance when it took place at the Office of Revels," a rehearsal, that is, "performed under the gaze of jurisprudence *for purposes of cultural review*" (*The Place of the Stage: License, Play, and Power in Renaissance England*, Chicago and London: University of Chicago Press, 1988, p. 70, my emphasis).

66 In its particulars, this passage is syntactically problematic and often heavily emended in modern editions; the general sense, I hope, is clear.

67 Stallybrass suggests the implications of this passage for seventeenth-century subjectivity and "individuality" ("Shakespeare, the Individual, and the Text"). See also Valerie Traub's indispensable discussion of female friendship, "The (In)Significance of 'Lesbian' Desire in Early Modern England," in Goldberg (ed.), *Queering the Renaissance*, pp. 62–83.

68 Noel R. Blincoe restricts the line to this context in her " 'Sex Individual' as Used in *The Two Noble Kinsmen*," *Notes and Queries* 35.4 (1988), pp. 484–85. Blincoe argues that the play prefers "the holy love of marriage ... to the love of friendship."

69 See note 17 above.

70 A difficult passage; I would suggest reading "values shortnes" as a parenthetical appositive: "Their nobleness gives the prejudice of disparity (value's shortness) to any lady breathing."

71 *THE ARTE OF ENGLISH POESIE*, London: by Richard Field, 1589, Lib. II, pp. 78–79. For an alternative characterization of the contest, see Donald K. Hedrick, " 'Be Rough With Me': The Collaborative Arenas of *The Two Noble Kinsmen*," in Charles H. Frey (ed.), *Shakespeare, Fletcher, and The Two Noble Kinsmen*, Columbia: University of Missouri Press, 1989, pp. 45–77.

72 This is Hedrick's thesis; it becomes clear in the course of the argument that his sense of collaboration-as-competition is in the service of a larger biographical allegorization in which Fletcher and Field contend for Shakespeare's approval and position. This competitive view of dramatic collaboration is supported throughout by evidence from Ben Jonson alone; as Bentley and others have shown, Jonson is hardly a representative figure for the early modern dramatist (*The Profession of Dramatist in Shakespeare's Time 1590– 1642*, Princeton: Princeton University Press, 1971).

73 Bibliographic presentation may support the idea that the prologue is a later addition: it is printed separately from the rest of the play, on the verso of the

title page, implying that it is not the "beginning" of the play, which commences on the facing recto. There the title is restated and the play begins with "Actus Primus." Bentley argues that any play in repertory for more than ten years without reaching print was probably augmented or otherwise revised (*Profession of Dramatist*, p. 263). For further theories about multi-layered composition, see Richard Proudfoot, "Shakespeare and the New Dramatists of the King's Men," in J. R. Brown and B. Harris (eds.), *Later Shakespeare*, London: Arnold, 1966, pp. 250–51; and Lois Potter, "Topicality or Politics? *The Two Noble Kinsmen*, 1613–34" in Gordon McMullan and Jonathan Hope (eds.), *The Politics of Tragicomedy: Shakespeare and After*, London: Routledge, 1992, pp. 77–91. Potter's nuanced account of the play's possible early revivals is a reminder that, whatever the date or dates of composition, the play takes on new "topical" meanings each time it is restaged.

74 This and subsequent quotations from the prologue and epilogue transcribe the quarto's italic print as roman.

75 Though it will become clear that I differ with some of her conclusions, Lois Potter asks some of these same questions in concluding the article cited above.

76 See Bentley, *Profession of Dramatist*. Editors routinely (and silently) emend "wrighter" to "writer."

77 Though *his* and *its* were at one time interchangeable in English (that is, *his* could be used for a neuter possessive), they had already begun to be differentiated in the sixteenth century. See Booth, *Shakespeare's Sonnets*, pp. 259–60 and *OED*.

78 The preceding chapter suggests some of the ways in which *The Knight of the Burning Pestle* figures this type of collaborative practice. Charles H. Frey's reading of the prologue finds a collaboration between performance and audience similar to the one I articulate here, but his audience is universal (rather than historical), and the object of his reading is a privileging of "our own psychosomatic, helping-hands response," rather than a reimmersion in the material practice of the collaborative Renaissance theatre. As the visionary and romanticizing ending to his essay makes clear, the object of critical desire is a communion with Shakespeare (Fletcher and the company of actors conspicuously drop out of this analysis): "Let Shakespeare collaborate and merge with his colaborers. Let us collaborate and colabor with Shakespeare." The essay thus collaborates (in the more recent and sinister sense of that term) with a romanticized ideology of the author and of Shakespeare that is, I hope, the antithesis of my project here. See "Collaborating with Shakespeare," in Charles H. Frey (ed.), *Shakespeare, Fletcher, and The Two Noble Kinsmen*, Columbia: University of Missouri Press, 1989.

79 The fanciful coda to Hedrick's "'Be Rough With Me'" provides such a correspondence and suggests the extent to which his earlier reading of the play is governed by a desire to identify its writers.

80 See Waith, Introduction, pp. 1–2; Potter, "Topicality," p. 79.

81 THE *Compleat Gentleman*, London: for Francis Constable, 1622, p. 44. Peacham's notion of "style," and his attempt to teach it to others, illustrates how pedagogical texts from this period militate against the nineteenth- and twentieth-century practice of distinguishing individual's shares in collabora-

tive texts from this period on the basis of a more modern, individuated conception of style; chapter 1 treats this issue in detail. See also Potter, "Topicality," p. 91.

82 Florio, Montaigne's *Essayes* (1603), A2.

83 *'Brief Lives,' Chiefly of Contemporaries, set down by John Aubrey, between the years 1669 and 1696*, Andrew Clark (ed.), 2 vols. (Oxford: Clarendon Press, 1898), I: pp. 95–96. My ellipsis between "lay together" and "had one wench" elides only Aubrey's attribution of his source.

84 Foucault has made a related point about friendship; see "An Interview: Sex, Power and the Politics of Identity," *The Advocate* (7 Aug. 1984), p. 30.

85 Bray provides examples from court records (*Homosexuality*, pp. 47–48); see also his "Friendship" article. See also *Othello* 3.3.419–432, where Iago stages for Othello a scene in which he sleeps with Cassio and plays Desdemona's part in Cassio's erotic dream, discussed in Bruce Smith, *Homosexual Desire in Shakespeare's England: A Cultural Poetics*, Chicago: University of Chicago Press, 1991, pp. 61–62.

86 *Wench* denoted a range of meanings: young woman, maid-servant, working-class girl or woman, mistress, and "daughter, wife, or sweetheart" as a "familiar or endearing form of address" (*OED*).

3 REPRESENTING AUTHORITY: PATRIARCHALISM, ABSOLUTISM, AND THE AUTHOR ON STAGE

1 *THE HOLY BIBLE, Conteyning the Old Testament, and the New: Newly Translated out of the Originall Tongues ... by his Maiesties speciall Comandement*, London: by Robert Barker, Printer to the Kings most Excellent Maiestie, 1611, A2^v.

2 Citations of plays in MR. WILLIAM SHAKESPEARES COMEDIES, HISTORIES & TRAGEDIES (1623) are taken from *The Norton Facsimile*, ed. Charlton Hinman, New York: Norton, 1968, and refer to that edition's through-line numbering (TLN 1165).

3 *THE Workes of our Antient and Learned English Poet*, GEFFREY CHAVCER, *newly Printed*, London: by Adam Islip at the charges of Bonham Norton, 1598.

4 See for example Sandra Gilbert and Susan Gubar's discussion of "the metaphor of literary paternity" in the first chapter of *The Madwoman in the Attic: The Woman Writer and the Nineteenth-Century Literary Imagination*, New Haven and London: Yale University Press, 1984, and their opening question: "Is a pen a metaphorical penis?" Also Marshall Grossman's insistence on "metaphor" in his important study of *Paradise Lost: "Authors to Themselves": Milton and the Revelation of History*, Cambridge: Cambridge University Press, 1987; the entry for "authorship" in Grossman's index, for example, reads: "see metaphor" (p. 239).

5 *Minor Prose Works of King James VI and I*, eds. James Craigie and Alexander Law, Edinburgh: Scottish Text Society, 1982, p. 70; sig. C7 in the 1598 text.

6 *Oxford American Dictionary*, New York and Oxford: Oxford University Press, 1980. Unless otherwise noted, all other definitions derive from the *Oxford English Dictionary*.

7 Here I rely on, but also expand, discussions of *author* in Gilbert and Gubar, *Madwoman*; Edward Said, *Beginnings: Intention and Method*, New York: Basic Books, 1975; and Grossman, *"Authors to Themselves,"* pp. 1–2.

8 The first and last recorded date for this meaning is 1382.

9 For clarity, I have eliminated the yogh character which begins the word "If."

10 THE WORKES OF THE MOST HIGH AND MIGHTY PRINCE, IAMES, *By the grace of God Kinge of Great Brittaine France & Ireland Defendor of ye Faith &c.*, London: Iames, Bishop of Winton, 1616; subsequent parenthetical citations will refer to signatures in this volume. For a more detailed description and interpretation of this title page (to which my reading is indebted), see Margery Corbett and Ronald Lightbown, *The Comely Frontispiece: The Emblematic Title-Page in England 1550–1660*, London: Routledge & Kegan Paul, 1979, pp. 137–42.

11 See also Leah Marcus, *Puzzling Shakespeare: Local Reading and its Discontents*, Berkeley: University of California Press, 1988, pp. 2–3, though I take issue with her puzzling suggestion that the title page is emblematic while the portrait is not.

12 *Patriarchal* has often been used in contemporary feminist discourse to signify any gender-stratified social system that is male-dominated. Throughout this chapter, I follow Gayle Rubin in restricting its use here to a specific sex/gender system, one headed by a patriarch; see Rubin, "The Traffic in Women: Notes on the 'Political Economy' of Sex," in Rayna Reiter (ed.), *Toward an Anthropology of Women*, New York: Monthly Review Press, 1975, pp. 166–68. For a more specific analysis of patriarchal systems in Renaissance England, see Susan Dwyer Amussen, *An Ordered Society: Gender and Class in Early Modern England*, Oxford and New York: Basil Blackwell, 1988.

13 This example disputes the *OED*'s claim that this meaning was obsolete by 1616. See note 8 above.

14 Winton also writes: "Let these *Workes*, therefore, most gracious *Prince*, lie before you as a Patterne; you cannot haue a better: Neither doeth the Honour of a good Sonne consist in any thing more, then in immitating the good Presidents of a good Father … " (James I, THE WORKES, a4). The spelling "Presidents" clearly suggests that the father/precedent is also a father who *presides*.

15 See *OED*'s entries for *abiliment* and (especially) *habiliment*.

16 The preface is set in italic, with roman emphases, which I have reversed.

17 Amussen, *Ordered Society*, p. 55.

18 Gordon J. Schochet, *Patriarchalism in Political Thought: The Authoritarian Family and Political Speculation and Attitudes Especially in Seventeenth-Century England*, Oxford: Basil Blackwell, 1975; Jonathan Goldberg, *James I and the Politics of Literature: Jonson, Shakespeare, Donne, and Their Contemporaries*, Baltimore: Johns Hopkins University Press, 1983, and "Fatherly Authority: The Politics of Stuart Family Images," in Margaret W. Ferguson, Maureen Quilligan, and Nancy J. Vickers (eds.), *Rewriting the Renaissance: The Discourses of Sexual Difference in Early Modern Europe*, Chicago and London: University of Chicago Press, 1986, pp. 3–32.

19 GOD and the King: Or, *A Dialogue shewing that our Soueraigne Lord King*

IAMES, being immediate vnder God within his DOMINIONS, Doth rightfully claime whatsoeuer is required by the Oath of ALLEAGEANCE, London: Imprinted by his Maiesties Speciall priuiledge and command, 1615, p. 61, emphasis original. The text is often said to be by Richard Mocket; for analysis of the text and its influence, see Amussen, *Ordered Society*, p. 55, and Schochet, *Patriarchalism*, pp. 88–90. The slippage between the commandment's father and mother and the political theory's singular emphasis on fathers has often been noted, especially in conjunction with Robert Filmer's later *Patriarcha*.

20 Goldberg may suggest this possibility when he writes, "in family portraits in which self-portraiture is involved, the matrix of family images can serve as an image of artistic authority, too" ("Fatherly Authority," p. 27), but his discussion confines itself to analysis of painterly (not textual) authorship. Furthermore, I would want to note that use of the familial model for authorship need not be limited to self-depictions.

21 James I, *Minor Prose Works*, p. 74 (D3).

22 According to *OED*'s entry for *one*, the modern pronunciation "won" only became standard in the late seventeenth century. *One* and *own* were also often spelled interchangeably. Randall McLeod first brought this to my attention.

23 "James's real contribution to Divine Right theory lay in identifying his prerogative with the production of a legitimate male successor" (Goldberg, *James I*, p. 84).

24 Goldberg "Fatherly Authority," and Catherine Belsey, "Disrupting Sexual Difference: Meaning and Gender in the Comedies," in John Drakakis (ed.), *Alternative Shakespeares*, London and New York: Methuen, 1985, pp. 166–90.

25 This paragraph summarizes material covered more fully in: G. E. Bentley, *The Profession of Dramatist in Shakespeare's Time 1590–1642*, Princeton: Princeton University Press, 1971; Stephen Orgel, "What is a Text?", *Research Opportunities in Renaissance Drama* (1981); and chapter 1 above.

26 Timothy Murray, *Theatrical Legitimation: Allegories of Genius in Seventeenth-Century England and France*, New York and Oxford: Oxford University Press, 1987, p. 70.

27 In "Shakespeare's Gower and the Role of the Authorial Presenter," *Philological Quarterly* 54 (1975), pp. 434–43, Walter F. Eggers, Jr., provides a useful but by no means complete list of choric figures and "authorial presenters." Eggers does not attempt to engage a history of authorship but presumes instead that, for reasons he does not provide, the authorial presenter began at a certain point in time to represent the already extant author.

28 Page references to the Ages plays are to *The Dramatic Works of Thomas Heywood Now First Collected with Illustrative Notes and a Memoir of the Author in Six Volumes*, New York: Russell and Russell, 1964 (rpt. of 1874), volume III.

29 *THE LATE, And much admired Play, Called Pericles, Prince of Tyre*, London: for Henry Gosson, 1609, A2. All subsequent references to signatures in this quarto will appear parenthetically.

30 See Bentley, *Profession of Dramatist*. For a skeptical reading of the *Henry V* chorus, to which I am indebted, see Phyllis Rackin, *Stages of History:*

Shakespeare's English Chronicles, Ithaca and New York: Cornell University Press, 1990, pp. 82–85.

31 Compare Robert Weimann's formulation that authority in Renaissance texts is problematic because "[t]raditional ... institutions were economically, politically, and culturally uprooted without having as yet been superseded by the more modern forms" ("History and the Issue of Authority in Representation: The Elizabethan Theater and the Reformation," *New Literary History* 17 [1986], p. 468).

32 Michel Foucault, "What Is an Author?," in Paul Rabinow (ed.), *The Foucault Reader*, New York: Pantheon, 1984, p. 105.

33 See F. D. Hoeniger's introductory discussion in the Arden *Pericles*, London: Methuen, 1963, pp. xiii–xix; subsequent references will be parenthetical. See also Geoffrey Bullough, *Narrative and Dramatic Sources of Shakespeare*, New York: Columbia University Press, 1966, vol. VI, pp. 349–74. Discussing the relation of "Theatre and Literary Culture," an essay by Barbara A. Mowat makes some related points about *Pericles'* intertextual appropriations ("Theatre and Literary Culture," in John D. Cox and David Scott Kastan (eds.), *A New History of Early English Drama*, New York: Columbia University Press, forthcoming, 1996).

34 In *Shakespeare's Romances and the Royal Family*, Lawrence, Kansas: University Press of Kansas, 1985, David M. Bergeron convincingly proposes the life of the Jacobean royal family as another "source" for the play.

35 See Steven Mullaney's general commentary on the play's sources, *The Place of the Stage: License, Play, and Power in Renaissance England*, Chicago and London: University of Chicago Press, 1988, p. 148. While my analysis here in part parallels Mullaney's highly condensed discussion of Gower, I will emphasize both the complexity and the discursively conservative formulation of what we both see as the "emerging figure of the author" in this play.

36 For a discussion of the "necromantic metaphor," see Thomas M. Greene, *The Light in Troy: Imitation and Discovery in Renaissance Poetry*, New Haven and London: Yale University Press, 1982, pp. 32–34, 37–43.

37 George Wilkins, *The Painfull Adventures of Pericles Prince of Tyre* (1608), as reprinted in Bullough, *Narrative and Dramatic Sources*, p. 494, my emphasis. Like the play-text, the precise derivation of the Wilkins "novel" (as it is often called) is unknown, and hotly contested. The text closely follows the play and Twine, sometimes verbatim, and most modern editors conjecture that Wilkins's novel is a memorial reconstruction of the play or was composed with reference to a copy of the script. Wilkins would not have read the play in quarto, since it was published after his text, but, as the quotation above illustrates, the novel capitalizes on the theatrical production. See F. D. Hoeniger's introduction to the Arden edition, which, despite its widespread anti-theatrical and ahistorical assumptions, remains an important gathering of the relevant information. See also Mowat, "Theatre and Literary Culture."

38 Gower can be constructed as introductory only to (what these editions designate as) the first three acts; in the last two, Gower's mid-act speeches are usually simply given separate scenes. The Arden, but not the Riverside, designates Gower's final speech as "[EPILOGUE]."

39 Gower's second and third speeches in the play are preceded in the quarto text by a single horizontal line. The meaning of this unusual device is uncertain and has been the object of little scholarly scrutiny.

40 Phyllis Gorfain, "Puzzle and Artifice: The Riddle as Metapoetry in Pericles," *Shakespeare Survey* 29 (1976), p. 13.

41 Under this definition, *OED* supplies the line from *Pericles* and – though too late to be more than merely resonant in this context of patriarchal author/ity – a use of *mould* in *Paradise Lost* x.744: "Did I request thee, Maker, from my Clay To mould me Man."

42 *Mould* as a noun could mean "a hollow form or matrix into which fluid or plastic material is cast or pressed ... so as to form an object of a particular shape or pattern" (sb.³, 1.2.). The play's figuration of reproduction here accords with an Aristotelian notion of conception. See Angus McLaren, *Reproductive Rituals: The Perception of Fertility in England from the Sixteenth Century to the Nineteenth Century*, London and New York: Methuen, 1984, pp. 16–17. As McLaren makes clear, the Aristotelian theory of reproduction was by no means the only model in circulation in the Renaissance. Ann Rosalind Jones and Peter Stallybrass have recently argued that it is important not to grant medical discourses in this period the privileged place they now enjoy (as "science") in our own discursive universe; see "Fetishizing Gender: Constructing the Hermaphrodite in Renaissance Europe," in Julia Epstein and Kristina Straub (eds.), *Body Guards: The Cultural Politics of Gender Ambiguity*, New York: Routledge, 1991.

43 Mullaney, *Place of the Stage*, p. 145.

44 In addition to *ibid.*, pp. 143–47, see Jean-Christophe Agnew's formative exploration of the relation of market and theatre in *Worlds Apart: The Market and the Theater in Anglo-American Thought, 1550–1750*, Cambridge: Cambridge University Press, 1986.

45 Marjorie Garber, *Shakespeare's Ghost Writers: Literature as Uncanny Causality*, New York: Methuen, 1987, p. 26.

46 I am adopting here the second quarto's reading "Yon" for the first quarto's "You."

47 *The Riverside Shakespeare*, G. Blakemore Evans et al. (eds.), Boston: Houghton Mifflin, 1974, p. 1489.

48 On the perceived need to settle questions of authorship prior to interpretation, see chapter 1, p. 18.

49 Kenneth Muir, "The Problem of *Pericles*," *English Studies* 30 (1949), pp. 65–83; Philip Edwards, "An Approach to the Problem of *Pericles*," *Shakespeare Survey* 5 (1952), pp. 25–49. Subsequent references will be parenthetical.

50 The recent Oxford *Complete Works* edition not only "yearns" for a lost original but actually "reconstructs" one. On the text as ravished maiden, see Wendy Wall, *The Imprint of Gender: Authorship and Publication in the English Renaissance*, Ithaca: Cornell University Press, 1993, chapter 3.

51 Alfred W. Pollard, *Shakespeare's Fight with the Pirates and the Problems of the Transmission of His Text*, 2nd edition revised with introduction, Cambridge: Cambridge University Press, 1920.

52 M^R. *WILLIAM SHAKESPEAR'S Comedies, Histories, and Tragedies*, London: for P.C., 1664.

53 Alfred W. Pollard, *Shakespeare Folios and Quartos: A Study of the Bibliography of Shakespeare's Plays 1594–1685*, London: Methuen, 1909, p. 159.

54 I am not altogether certain it is possible or advisable to do this; that is, I'm not sure that the typical New Bibliographic narrative of compositors and reporters is not itself generated out of a moral crusade for the purity of the singular author, or the attempt to separate the unchaste and perverted text from the ostensible purity of the author's original.

55 Mowat, "Theatre and Literary Culture," makes an important argument on the basis of records first noted by Charles J. Sisson ("Shakespeare Quartos as Prompt-Copies, With Some Account of Cholmeley's Players and a New Shakespeare Allusion," *Review of English Studies* 18 [1942], pp. 129–143): *Pericles* was acted early in its history from the same printed text now almost universally maligned as "Bad." This seems to me a strong historical reason for freeing the 1609 text from New Bibliography's moral tag and the subsequent heavy editorial interventions of, for example, the Arden edition and the new Oxford's "reconstruction."

56 For a similar point about the first folio, see Margreta de Grazia, *Shakespeare Verbatim: The Reproduction of Authenticity and the 1790 Apparatus*, Oxford: Clarendon, 1991, p. 11.

57 For a discussion of the *Cyropedia*'s relation to *A King and no King* in standard text/source terms, see Robert K. Turner, Jr., Introduction, *A King and No King*, Regents Renaissance Drama Series, Lincoln: University of Nebraska Press, 1963, pp. xiv–xv; Philip J. Finkelpearl, *Court and Country Politics in the Plays of Beaumont and Fletcher*, Princeton: Princeton University Press, 1990, pp. 168–69; Lee Bliss, *Francis Beaumont*, Boston: Twayne, 1987, pp. 107–08.

58 Dedicatory letter from Henry Holland to King Charles I, in Xenophon, *CYRUPÆDIA. THE INSTITVTION AND LIFE OF CYRUS*, trans. Philemon Holland, London: J.L. for Robert Allot, 1632.

59 Though he emphasizes the importance of *Cyropedia* to James I, Finkelpearl oddly elides any consideration of its contemporary circulation by citing a modern translation of the text. See also Bliss, *Francis Beaumont*, pp. 107–08.

60 Parenthetical page references are to the first quarto of *A King and no King*, London: for Thomas Walkley, 1619.

61 Note Finkelpearl's incorrect assertion that Arbaces is "reared as the heir when the queen feared she was sterile" (p. 178). Gobrius makes clear that the queen and "almost all the Land" fear the *king* is "past" the age of reproduction (p. 84). On the absence of mothers in representations of early modern English culture, see Mary Beth Rose, "Where are the Mothers in Shakespeare? Options for Gender Representation in the English Renaissance," *Shakespeare Quarterly* 42.3 (1991), pp. 291–314, and Stephen Orgel, "Prospero's Wife," in Ferguson, Quilligan, and Vickers (eds.), *Rewriting the Renaissance*.

62 For a discussion of this play's "tyrant" in the context of Renaissance humanist rhetoric, see Rebecca W. Bushnell, *Tragedies of Tyrants: Political Thought and Theater in the English Renaissance*, Ithaca and London: Cornell University Press, 1990, pp. 160–71.

63 Finkelpearl stabilizes the engraving's meaning; since the royal scepter can be seen lying on the ground, he argues, this engraving represents Arbaces's de-

crowning (*Court and Country*, p. 179). Like the title of the play and Gobrius's plot, I think the engraving has it both ways.

64 Rubin, "Traffic," pp. 171–77.

65 The difficulty of what I'm calling here an "easy fit" is illustrated by Lee Bliss's identification of Gobrius as the "tragicomic playwright" in her book that acknowledges collaboration but is entitled *Francis Beaumont*.

66 Parenthetical through-line-numbers refer to Hinman (ed.), *The Norton Facsimile* of the first folio text.

67 See for example Stephen Greenblatt, *Shakespearean Negotiations: The Circulation of Social Energy in Renaissance England*, Berkeley: University of California Press, 1988, p. 142.

68 See Stephen Orgel's important meditation on the absent mother and the structures of patriarchal relations in the play, "Prospero's Wife." See also Garber's commentary on this passage (*Shakespeare's Ghost Writers*, p. 133), and Rose, "Where are the Mothers in Shakespeare?"

69 That Crane is taken to have written or rewritten many of the stage directions in the published *Tempest* may suggest: (1) the way in which Prospero's author/ity is itself a collaborative production of playwright, actors, scribe(s), and others; and (2) the way in which Crane provides an early modern "reading" of Prospero's author/ity as he saw it registered in the text he was copying/augmenting, and/or as he may have seen it on stage. While I would not want to efface the participation of scribes and theatrical book-holders in the collaborative production of play-texts in this period, the identification of *individual* scribes on the basis of "scribal peculiarities" like spelling, punctuation, etc., seems to me susceptible to the critique of linguistic evidence for identifying collaborators I attempt in chapter 1. On Ralph Crane's participation in the production of some folio texts, see T. H. Howard-Hill, *Ralph Crane and Some Shakespeare First Folio Comedies*, Charlottesville: University of Virginia Press, 1972. On *The Tempest*, see Howard-Hill; Jeanne Addison Roberts, "Ralph Crane and the Text of *The Tempest*," *Shakespeare Studies* 13 (1980), pp. 213–33; and Stephen Orgel's review and analysis of the arguments in his Oxford edition of the play, Oxford and New York: Oxford University Press, 1987, pp. 56–61.

70 Frank Kermode (ed.), *The Tempest*, Arden Shakespeare, London and New York: Routledge, 1954, p. 123.

71 See also *OED*'s entry for *discoverer*. As Patricia Parker has demonstrated, colonial discovery is not unrelated to gendered discourse in this period: *Literary Fat Ladies: Rhetoric, Gender, Property*, London and New York: Methuen, 1987, p. 142. For an example of Miranda's commodification in related terms, see Prospero's conversation at the beginning of Act IV.

72 Francis Barker and Peter Hulme, "Nymphs and Reapers Heavily Vanish: the Discursive Con-texts of *The Tempest*," in Drakakis (ed.), *Alternative Shakespeares*, pp. 191–205. Paul Brown's essay treats similar issues and was published at about the same time: " 'This thing of darkness I acknowledge mine': *The Tempest* and the Discourse of Colonialism," in Jonathan Dollimore and Alan Sinfield (eds.), *Political Shakespeare: New Essays in Cultural Materialism*, Ithaca and London: Cornell University Press, 1985, pp. 48–71.

73 See also: Alvin B. Kernan's romanticizing interpretation, " 'The Great Globe

Itself': The Public Playhouse and the Ideal Theater of *The Tempest*," chapter 6 of *The Playwright as Magician: Shakespeare's Image of the Poet in the English Public Theater*, New Haven and London: Yale University Press, 1979, pp. 129–45; Peter Greenaway's film *Prospero's Books*.

74 Orgel (ed.) *The Tempest*, Oxford Shakespeare edition, p. 49.

75 On the widespread use of *fellows* to refer to members of acting companies, see G. E. Bentley, *The Profession of Player in Shakespeare's Time 1590–1642*, Princeton: Princeton University Press, 1984, p. 25.

76 On actors' disruption of sumptuary laws, see for example Louis A. Montrose, "The Purpose of Playing: Reflections on a Shakespearean Anthropology," *Helios* 7 (1980), pp. 51–74; Peter Stallybrass, "Worn Worlds: Clothes and Identity on the Renaissance Stage," paper delivered at the Center for Literary and Cultural Studies, Harvard University, November 1993.

77 Ben Jonson, BARTHOLMEW FAYRE: A COMEDIE ACTED IN THE YEARE, *1614*, London: by I.B. for Robert Allot, 1631, A5. Subsequent references to signatures in this volume will appear parenthetically.

78 John Dryden, OF DRAMATICK *Poesie*, AN ESSAY, London: for Henry Herringman, 1668, pp. 49–50.

79 Greenblatt, *Shakespearean Negotiations*, pp. vii and 142.

80 See too Orgel's radical questioning of the assumption that the *The Winter's Tale* was written before *The Tempest* (Oxford Shakespeare edition, pp. 63–64).

81 Marcus connects the play's initiating place in the folio with its encoding of "a fantasy of near-total authorial power and control" and with Heminge and Condell's prefatory argument that "Shakespeare's thought and utterance are fully available on the unblotted page" (*Puzzling Shakespeare*, p. 49). However, other moments in Marcus's argument demonstrate her assumption that authorship in this period is an expression of already extant authorial desires, rather than (as I am arguing), an emergent, constitutive discourse: "Authors wanted to be recognized as individuals with their own identifying attributes" (p. 29), or later, "the construction of a transcendent, independent place for art was a project that empowered seventeenth-century authors and opened up a whole range of new possibilities for their lives and work" (p. 30). For a reading of the folio preliminaries as constitutive, rather than factual and/or mimetic, see the first chapter of de Grazia, *Shakespeare Verbatim*.

82 For examples of this approach, see David Sundelson's and Coppélia Kahn's contributions to Murray M. Schwartz and Coppélia Kahn (eds.), *Representing Shakespeare: New Psychoanalytic Essays*, Baltimore and London: Johns Hopkins University Press, 1980.

83 Though he begins by contesting the idea that *The Tempest* is a colonial play, Jeffrey Knapp's injection of the play into a period discussion of the place of the colonial project in England supports my larger point: whatever its "actual" location, *The Tempest* speaks in, addresses, contests, the languages of the colonial projects and the debates surrounding them; "Distraction in *The Tempest*," chapter 6 of *An Empire Nowhere: England, America, and Literature from Utopia to The Tempest*, Berkeley: University of California Press, 1992, pp. 220–42.

84 The overdetermination of colonization in this play is one of Brown's observa-

tions ("'This thing of darkness'"). As work in this area has begun to show, the intersection of theatre and colonialism was immensely culturally productive. In particular, I've been influenced by Rebecca Bach's analysis of John Smith's "staging" of colonialism in the rhetoric of theatricality; "Producing the 'New World': The Colonial Stages of Ben Jonson and Captain John Smith," Ph.D. thesis, University of Pennsylvania, 1994.

85 See Knapp's comment on this conjunction (*Empire Nowhere*, p. 229).

86 Three important discussions of this induction to which I am indebted: Peter Stallybrass and Allon White, "The Fair, the Pig, Authorship," chapter 1 of *The Politics and Poetics of Transgression*, Ithaca: Cornell University Press, 1986, pp. 27–79; Joseph Loewenstein, "The Script in the Marketplace," *Representations* 12 (1985), pp. 101–14; Timothy Murray, *Theatrical Legitimation*.

87 See Bentley's analysis of this contract (*Profession of Dramatist*, pp. 111–44).

88 On this reversal, see Margreta de Grazia, "*The Tempest*: Gratuitous Movement or Action Without Kibes and Pinches," *Shakespeare Studies* 14 (1981), p. 263.

89 For a complicating reading of pardon discourse and the possibilities for subversion at the end of the play, see Greenblatt, *Shakespearean Negotiations*, p. 157.

90 R. A. Gent., THE VALIANT VVELSHMAN, *Or* THE TRVE CHRONICLE *History of the life and valiant deedes of Caradoc the Great, King of Cambria, now called Wales*, London: by George Purslowe for Robert Lownes, 1615, I4^v.

91 The "we" of the acting company themselves speak an ensuing "EPILOGVE" in which they describe themselves as "Tenants" of the theatre, "your Lands" – terms that, by making the theatre an economically contested territory, resonate with the colonialism of *The Tempest*.

92 G. Wilson Knight, *The Crown of Life: Essays in Interpretation of Shakespeare's Final Plays*, London: Oxford University Press, 1947, p. 220.

93 David Sundelson, "'So Rare a Wonder'd Father': Prospero's *Tempest*," in Schwartz and Kahn (eds.), *Representing Shakespeare*, p. 34.

94 On the oppositional definition of Jonson and Shakespeare as a booksellers' tactic, rather than as an authorial projection, see de Grazia, *Shakespeare Verbatim*, pp. 46–47. For a defense of Shakespeare as agonistic author, see Joseph Loewenstein, "Plays Agonistic and Competitive: The Textual Approach to Elsinore," *Renaissance Drama* 19 (1988), pp. 63–96.

4 REPRODUCING WORKS: DRAMATIC QUARTOS AND FOLIOS IN THE SEVENTEENTH CENTURY

1 Quoted in Lois Potter, *Secret Rites and Secret Writing: Royalist literature, 1641-1660*, Cambridge: University Press, 1989, p. 151. Potter attributes this to Samuel Sheppard, although she elsewhere discusses the virtual impossibility of attributing anonymous texts in this period. Subsequent references to Potter will appear parenthetically.

2 *The true Tragedie of Richard Duke of Yorke, and the death of good King Henrie the Sixt*, London: by P.S. for Thomas Millington, 1595.

3 THE LATE, *And much admired Play, Called Pericles, Prince of Tyre*, London:

for Henry Gosson, 1609; THE Tragicall Historie of HAMLET Prince of Denmarke, London: for N.L. and Iohn Trundell, 1603.

4 Elizabeth Eisenstein, *The Printing Press as an Agent of Change: Communications and Cultural Transformations in Early-Modern Europe*, Cambridge: Cambridge University Press, 1979, p. 59.

5 Peter W. M. Blayney, "Shakespeare in St. Paul's Churchyard," Shakespeare Association of America Annual Meeting, Vancouver, 23 March 1991. See also Scott McMillin's important discussion of locations in *The Elizabethan Theatre and the Book of Sir Thomas More*, Ithaca: Cornell University Press, 1987.

6 *Pericles*, title page.

7 See G. E. Bentley, *The Profession of Dramatist in Shakespeare's Time 1590–1642*, Princeton: Princeton University Press, 1971, p. 87.

8 William Shakespeare, *The most excellent Historie of the Merchant of Venice*, London: by I. R. for Thomas Heyes, 1600; THE CRONICLE History of Henry the fift, London: by Thomas Creede, for Tho. Millington, and Iohn Busby, 1600; *A most pleasant and merie nevv Comedie, Intituled, A Knacke to knowe a Knaue*, London: by Richard Iones, 1594.

9 Robert Armin, THE *History of the two Maids of More-clacke*, London: N.O. for Thomas Archer, 1609.

10 Quoted in Bentley, *Profession of Dramatist*, pp. 52–53.

11 I place "same" in quotation marks both because, as is beginning to be recognized, there are in many cases substantial differences between quarto and folio versions of similarly titled texts in the Shakespeare canon and because, even if there were not, a text printed in folio takes on an entirely different set of meanings in that format. For the argument that bibliographic form was at issue in the Bodleian's exclusion and later inclusion of Shakespeare texts, see Margreta de Grazia, *Shakespeare Verbatim: The Reproduction of Authenticity and the 1790 Apparatus*, Oxford: Clarendon Press, 1991, pp. 32–33; I am suggesting not only that quartos do not have the physical monumentality (and thus social weight) of other books, as de Grazia argues, but also that their title pages constructed further differences from other books, allying them instead with a theatrical presentation and audience experience.

12 For a recent statement of what may be taken as a commonplace of New Bibliography, see Fredson Bowers, "Authority, Copy, and Transmission in Shakespeare's Texts," in Georgianna Ziegler (ed.), *Shakespeare Study Today*, New York: AMS, 1986: "Shakespearean textual criticism rests on the determination of authority, an investigation that leads from the general to the specific" (p. 17).

13 Peter Stallybrass, "Shakespeare, the Individual, and the Text," in Lawrence Grossberg, Cary Nelson, and Paula Treichler (eds.), with Linda Baughman, and with assistance from John Macgregor Wise, *Cultural Studies*, New York: Routledge, 1992, pp. 593–610. Alternatively, as David Kastan has suggested to me, the publisher Butter may be making prominent Shakespeare's name on the *Lear* title page in order to extend the vendibility of a name he had also attached to *The London Prodigall* in 1605.

14 The Beaumont and Fletcher canon is usually defined as those plays printed in the 1679 *Fifty Comedies and Tragedies*, excluding *The Coronation*, often

attributed to James Shirley. I include that play in the discussion here because it first appeared in a 1640 quarto attributed to "J. Fletcher."

15 Since the 1647 folio printed only plays "never before printed," none of the plays tabulated here appeared in folio until 1679, except for *The Masque of the Inner Temple and Grayes Inne*. My figures are based on my examination of quarto title pages and information in the revised *A Short-Title Catalogue of Books Printed in England, Scotland, and Ireland, and of English Books Printed Abroad, 1475–1640*, Katharine F. Pantzer (ed.), London: the Bibliographical Society, 1976–91.

16 See Fredson Bowers's discussion of the two title pages in *The Dramatic Works in the Beaumont and Fletcher Canon*, Cambridge: Cambridge University Press, 1966, vol. I, p. 113.

17 I am tempted to see these strange initials as somehow signifying a collaborative conflation of Ben Jonson and John Fletcher. Another version of this play, *The Tragoedy of ROLLO Duke of Normandy* appeared in 1640, "Written by John Fletcher Gent."

18 Francis Beamont & Iohn Fletcher Gent., *A KING, and NO KING*, London: by A.M. for Richard Hawkins, 1631.

19 *PHYLASTER*, London: for Thomas Walkley, 1620; 1622; *PHYLASTER*, London: A.M. for Richard Hawkins, 1628.

20 *MONSIEVR THOMAS*, London: by Thomas Harper, for Iohn Waterson, 1639, A–A2.

21 Iohn Fletcher Gent., *THE ELDER BROTHER ... Printed according to the true Copie*, London: by F.K. for J.W. and J.B., 1637, "Prologue," in italics. The page is unsigned and occurs on the verso of a sheet that prints "*The Speakers of the Play*," followed by a couplet to the readers ("Lectori").

22 To group these studies is *not* to say that they agree, especially on the question of who it is that thus organizes texts under an authorial rubric, or how that idea came into being. On the Jonson folio, see Peter Stallybrass and Allon White, "The Fair, the Pig, Authorship," chapter 1 of *The Politics and Poetics of Transgression*, Ithaca: Cornell University Press, 1986, pp. 27–79; Joseph Loewenstein, "The Script in the Marketplace," *Representations* 12 (1985), pp. 101–14; Timothy Murray, *Theatrical Legitimation: Allegories of Genius in Seventeenth-Century England and France*, New York and Oxford: Oxford University Press, 1987; and the various essays in the recent anthology *Ben Jonson's 1616 Folio*, eds. Jennifer Brady and W.H. Herendeen, Newark: University of Delaware Press, 1991. On the Shakespeare folio, Peter W.M. Blayney, *The First Folio of Shakespeare*, Washington, DC: Folger Library Publications, 1991; Margreta de Grazia, *Shakespeare Verbatim*; Leah Marcus, *Puzzling Shakespeare: Local Reading and Its Discontents*, Berkeley: University of California Press, 1988.

23 Marcus, *Puzzling Shakespeare*, pp. 29–30. I find it problematic to attribute even to Jonson a transparent agency or self-selected authorial ideology, as Sara van den Berg apparently does: "Analysis of Jonson's poetry and portraits reveals that the ideology of authorship offered him an aesthetic solution to the problem of identity that confronts the individual person in a culture of individualism" ("Ben Jonson and the Ideology of Authorship," in Brady and Herendeen, eds., *1616 Folio*, p. 114).

24 For example, not enough has been made of Bentley's significant argument

that Jonson, the figure around whom so much of the analysis of dramatic authorship's emergence revolves, was not dependent on the commercial theatres after 1602 and did not function as an "attached or regular professional" (*Profession of Dramatist*, pp. 31–32).

25 de Grazia, *Shakespeare Verbatim*, p. 39.

26 See Loewenstein, "The Script," and Murray, *Theatrical Legitimation*.

27 Francis Beavmont and Iohn Fletcher Gentlemen, COMEDIES AND TRAGEDIES, London: for Humphrey Robinson and Humphrey Moseley, 1647. All subsequent references to signatures in this volume will appear parenthetically. In transcribing the typography of the volume's preliminaries (about which both Moseley and I will have more to say), I have often reversed the usual transcription of italic and roman text (to avoid persistent italicization) – especially where the folio's "default" font is italic. Though many of the contributors to the commendatory verses are well known from other contexts, I have retained throughout the names and spellings as provided in the folio text; the re-presentations of those names (and attached titles) is, I would suggest, significant in ways I will not fully analyze here, particularly in the context of royalist and republican rhetorics, and should be made available. It cannot be assumed that the titles of particular commendatory poems were, or were not, written by the poets to whom the verses are attributed, or by Moseley, or by someone else.

28 De Grazia has argued that the portrait encodes a collation of art and nature, organizing tropes in the folio's two important predecessors, the Jonson and Shakespeare folios, respectively (*Shakespeare Verbatim*, pp. 46–47).

29 See chapter 1, pp. 21–22.

30 On the terms and contexts of Cokain's allegation, see the final section of this chapter.

31 MR. WILLIAM SHAKESPEARES COMEDIES, HISTORIES, & TRAGEDIES, London: by Isaac Iaggard, and Ed. Blount, 1623. Subsequent citations will appear parenthetically.

32 de Grazia, *Shakespeare Verbatim*, p. 44.

33 For a vindication of Moseley, an effort to correlate his statements with the bibliographical evidence that is clearly in the familiar New Bibliographic genre of defenses of Shakespeare's collectors Heminge and Condell, see R.C. Bald, *Bibliographical Studies in the Beaumont and Fletcher Folio of 1647*, Supplement to the Bibliographical Society's Transactions, no. 13, Oxford: Oxford University Press for the Bibliographical Society, 1938 (for 1937) – in particular the study's concluding paragraph (p. 114).

34 On Fletcher's burial with Massinger, see the introduction, pp. 1–3.

35 See Bentley, *Profession of Dramatist*, pp. 235–63.

36 All the plays previously printed in quarto (i.e. those discussed earlier in this chapter) were added to the second folio collection of 1679. The extent to which "complete" is an important term for Moseley is illustrated by the fact that he elides mention of the one text that *had* been printed earlier, the *Masque*.

37 See Stallybrass and White, *Politics and Poetics*, pp. 76–77; also Loewenstein, "The Script"; and Murray, *Theatrical Legitimation*.

38 The term is resonant both as republican discourse and as theatrical geography; for the latter, see Steven Mullaney, *The Place of the Stage: License,*

Play, and Power in Renaissance England, Chicago and London: University of Chicago Press, 1988, chapters 1–2.

39 See Potter's useful summary in *Secret Rites,* pp. 4–5, and Nigel Smith, *Literature and Revolution in England 1640-1660,* New Haven: Yale University Press, 1994.

40 See chapter 3, p. 74.

41 The *OED* cites 1798 as the first usage of *intercourse* in a sexual sense, but also restricts that usage to intercourse between differently sexed persons. 1799 is the first recorded use of *sexual intercourse* and it is useful to recall here that *sexual* first meant what we now call "gender" or "sexual difference." That is, when the term *sexual intercourse* was first used, it apparently applied only to heterosexual activity. As is well known, sexual activity between men was no new thing in the Renaissance; it only came to be labeled as new and different, as many following Foucault have argued, later, around the time this terminology emerged. (See, for example, Alan Bray's chapter, "Molly" in *Homosexuality in Renaissance England,* London: Gay Men's Press, 1982, and Henry Abelove's important rethinking of the history of [non]reproductive sex in "Some Speculations on the History of 'Sexual Intercourse' During the 'Long Eighteenth Century' in England," in Andrew Parker, Mary Russo, Doris Sommer, and Patricia Yeager [eds.], *Nationalisms and Sexualities,* New York: Routledge, 1992, pp. 335–42.) It therefore seems possible, on the basis of this accumulated evidence, that *intercourse* had a same-sexual valence in 1647, though I know of no examples.

42 See Bray's suggestive remarks on travel narratives (*Homosexuality in Renaissance England,* p. 75), and the imprisonment of a black man, Domingo Cassedon Drago, for "a buggery" in 1647 (pp. 72–73).

43 Michael Warner, "New English Sodom," in Jonathan Goldberg (ed.), *Queering the Renaissance,* Durham: Duke University Press, 1994, pp. 330–58, especially pp. 335–36.

44 Lawrence Stone provides evidence for (without analyzing) the terminological intersection I am describing (*The Family, Sex and Marriage in England 1500–1800,* Abridged edition, New York: Harper, 1977, pp. 218–19). Foucault makes a related suggestion when he argues that sex between men only comes to be viewed as problematic with the demise of a certain type of "intense" male friendship: "As long as friendship was something important, was socially accepted, nobody realized men had sex together. You couldn't say that men *didn't have* sex together – it just didn't matter ... the disappearance of friendship as a social relation, and the declaration of homosexuality as a social/political/medical problem, are the same process" ("An Interview: Sex, Power and the Politics of Identity," *The Advocate* [7 Aug. 1984], p. 30).

45 See chapter 1, pp. 16–20.

46 This (re)union of church and state has an obvious currency within absolutist discourse at the moment of its greatest contestation in English history.

47 That is, the poem raises, then evades, the question of what Montaigne/Florio calls "office" and what we would call – in a way that has little in common with eroticized friendship's anti-hierarchalism – the language of *top/bottom* or *active/passive.* See chapter 2 above.

48 See *OED masculine* (sb.2). The quotation is from John Gaule's THE MAG-

ASTRO-MANCER, OR THE Magical-Astrologicall-Diviner Posed, and Puzzled, London: for Joshua Kirton, 1652, p. 265. A discussion of diverse sexual practices in different cultures (examples that disprove the astrologer's contention that stars govern all human behavior), the passage also cites the ancient Greeks, who "were not ashamed to pursue specious boyes."

49 I am suggesting, in other words, the co-existence and contestation of discourses of hierarchical (patriarchal) marriage, male friendship, and companionate marriage.

50 On the volume as an attempt to consolidate "art" and "nature," see de Grazia, *Shakespeare Verbatim*, pp. 46–47.

51 Virginia Woolf, *A Room of One's Own*, San Diego: HBJ, 1929. On the relation of the material practices of handwriting in this period and their discursive constitution, see Jonathan Goldberg's important study, *Writing Matter: From the Hands of the English Renaissance*, Stanford: Stanford University Press, 1990.

52 On this, see Bald, *Beaumont and Fletcher Folio*, pp. 5–10.

53 Several critics have recently demonstrated the crucial role of poetry, as a high-cultural discourse with resonances of classicism, in the construction of Jonsonian authorship over and against the theatre earlier in the century; see in particular Stallybrass and White, *Politics and Poetics*, pp. 76–77; Murray, *Theatrical Legitimation*; and Richard Helgerson, *Self-Crowned Laureates: Spenser, Jonson, Milton and the Literary System*, Berkeley: University of California Press, 1983, chapter 3. The shift intended or registered by the terms used in the Beaumont and Fletcher folio may be suggested by recalling that Milton subtitles *Samson Agonistes* (a "work [that] never was intended" for "the Stage") "A Dramatic Poem" (Merritt Y. Hughes [ed.], *John Milton: Complete Poems and Major Prose*, New York: Odyssey, 1957, p. 549). Depending on when one dates *Samson*, this subtitle may be contemporaneous with the Beaumont and Fletcher publication.

54 *OED* and Thomas Laqueur, *Making Sex: Body and Gender from the Greeks to Freud*, Cambridge: Harvard University Press, 1990, pp. 108–10.

55 See Stephen Booth (ed.), *Shakespeare's Sonnets*, New Haven: Yale University Press, 1977, pp. 441–43.

56 This is a move that has both sexual–political and politico-religious implications in the historical context; on female prophets, see Phyllis Mack, *Visionary Women: Ecstatic Prophecy in Seventeenth-Century England*, Berkeley: University of California Press, 1992.

57 William Shakespeare, *Pericles*, F1.

58 See chapter 2.

59 *AREOPAGITICA; A SPEECH OF M*^{r}*. JOHN MILTON For the Liberty of Vnlicenc'd PRINTING, To the Parlament of ENGLAND*, London, 1644, p. 4, my emphasis.

60 Francis Barker, *The Tremulous Private Body: Essays on Subjection*, London: Methuen, 1984, pp. 45–49; Michel Foucault, *The History of Sexuality, Volume I: An Introduction*, New York: Vintage, 1980, and *Discipline and Punish: The Birth of the Prison*, trans. Alan Sheridan, New York: Pantheon, 1977. On the emergence of new forms of subjectivity in the period, through old and new literary forms, see also Nigel Smith, *Literature and Revolution in England 1640–1660*, New Haven: Yale University Press, 1994, pp. 232–33.

61 Goldberg, *Writing Matter*.
62 Philip J. Finkelpearl, *Court and Country Politics in the Plays of Beaumont and Fletcher*, Princeton: Princeton University Press, 1990, p. 7.
63 Lawrence B. Wallis, *Fletcher, Beaumont and Company: Entertainers to the Jacobean Gentry*, New York: Octagon, 1968.
64 For an attempt to separate out the politics of a Fletcher/Massinger collaboration, see Gordon McMullan, *The Politics of Unease in the Plays of John Fletcher*, Amherst: University of Massachusetts Press, 1994, p. 153.
65 Wallis, *Fletcher, Beaumont and Company*, p. 14.
66 Potter, *Secret Rites*, p. 74.
67 Potter's brief reference to the volume overstates its significance for her argument by mis-identifying it as *Comedies and Tragicomedies* (*ibid.*, p. 82).
68 On Moseley's politics, see *ibid.*, pp. 19–22; on Moseley more generally, see John Curtis Reed, "Humphrey Moseley, Publisher," *Oxford Bibliographical Society Proceedings and Papers* 2 (1930), pp. 57–142. Peter Lindenbaum has argued that Moseley refigured Shirley and Milton alike in an authorial guise of his own design ("Milton's Contract," in Martha Woodmansee and Peter Jaszi [eds.], *The Construction of Authorship: Textual Appropriation in Law and Literature*, Durham: Duke University Press, 1994, pp. 175–90).
69 Wallis, *Fletcher, Beaumont and Company*, p. 13.
70 As this chapter has suggested in passing, the differentiation of theatrical texts from other forms of the literary is beginning to collapse in this period; at a time when the theatres are closed, the terminological intersection of, for example, the "Dramatic Poem" *Samson* and the "Dramatick Poems" of the Beaumont and Fletcher folio is significant (see note 53 above).
71 On the emergent fiction of self-authorship as a governing trope in *Paradise Lost*, for example, see Marshall Grossman, *"Authors to Themselves": Milton and the Revelation of History*, Cambridge: Cambridge University Press, 1987.
72 Smith, *Literature and Revolution*, p. 24.
73 POEMS OF Mr. *John Milton*, BOTH ENGLISH and LATIN, *Compos'd at several times*, London: by Ruth Raworth for Humphrey Moseley, 1645. The preface quoted above is printed in italics, with roman emphases.
74 Aston Cokain, *"To my Cousin Mr.* Charles Cotton," poem 7 of "Letters to divers Persons," in *Small POEMS of Divers sorts*, London: by Wil. Godbid, 1658, pp. 91–92. Subsequent page numbers refer to this volume, which was also published and circulated under the title A CHAIN OF GOLDEN POEMS, *Embellished with* WIT, MIRTH and ELOQUENCE, London: by W.G. [for] Isaac Pridmore, 1658. Out-of-sequence pagination in this volume has been emended in my citations, for ease of reference.
75 The point is not to confirm or deny that Massinger collaborated widely in these plays (an array of seventeenth-century evidence suggests that he did), but rather to analyze the terms in which such attributions of collaboration and authorship circulate around these plays. For Cyrus Hoy's conclusions about Massinger, see "The Shares of Fletcher and his Collaborators in the Beaumont and Fletcher Canon (VII)," *Studies in Bibliography* 15 (1962), pp. 85–88; other discussions, also largely based on internal evidence of "style," include: Philip Edwards and Colin Gibson (eds.), *The Plays and Poems of Philip Massinger*, vol. I, Oxford: Clarendon, 1976, pp. xx–xxxi;

Donald S. Lawless, *Philip Massinger and His Associates*, Ball State Mono-graph no. 10, Muncie, IN: Ball State University, 1967, pp. 18–25.

5 MISTRIS CORRIVALL: MARGARET CAVENDISH'S DRAMATIC PRODUCTION

The chapter title alludes to a poem in the Beaumont and Fletcher folio; see chapter 4, p. 142.

1 *PLAYES Written by the Thrice NOBLE, ILLUSTRIOUS AND Excellent Princess, THE LADY MARCHIONESS OF NEWCASTLE*, London: by A. Warren for John Martyn, James Allestry, and Tho. Dicas, 1662, no sig. In the University of Pennsylvania, Harvard University, and Newberry Library copies I have examined, some preliminary sheets without page-signatures appear in different order. Subsequent references to signatures in the 1662 volume will appear parenthetically.

2 Elizabeth Cary, *THE TRAGEDIE OF MARIAM, THE FAIRE Queene of Iewry*, London: by Thomas Creede, for Richard Hawkins, 1613. As many have noted, this play is itself centrally concerned with women and public speech.

3 *PLAYS, Never before Printed. WRITTEN By the Thrice Noble, Illustrious, and Excellent PRINCESSE, THE Duchess of Newcastle*, London: by A. Maxwell, 1668.

4 Kathleen Jones attributes the Introduction to Cavendish's husband; *A Glorious Fame: The Life of Margaret Cavendish, Duchess of Newcastle, 1623–1673*, London: Bloomsbury, 1988, p. 130.

5 See for example Catherine Gallagher, "Embracing the Absolute: The Politics of the Female Subject in Seventeenth-Century England," *Genders* 1 (1988), pp. 24–39, and Douglas Grant, *Margaret the First: A Biography of Margaret Cavendish Duchess of Newcastle 1623–1673*, London: Rupert Hart-Davis, 1957.

6 On companionate marriage, see Lawrence Stone, *The Family, Sex and Marriage in England 1500–1800*, Abridged edition, New York: Harper, 1977, pp. 100–01, 217–18. Stone provides evidence that supports the terminological intersection of marriage and male friendship I am describing here (pp. 218–19); I argue for this conjunction in more detail in "My Two Dads: Collaboration and the Reproduction of Beaumont and Fletcher," in Jonathan Goldberg (ed.), *Queering the Renaissance*, Durham: Duke University Press, 1994, pp. 280–309.

7 I'm referring in particular to the highly gender-specific collaborative textual production figured in Montaigne's "Of Friendship," as described in chapter 2. I mean "perversity" here to be culturally specific; for a sense of "perverse" collaboration between men and women at about the time I am thinking of (that is, roughly eighty years before Cavendish's plays), see the rhetoric of monstrous birth, co-parenting, and collaborative authorship in Philip Sidney's dedication of *The Countess of Pembroke's Arcadia* to his sister. The letter has recently been introduced into a resonant context by Jonathan Goldberg in *Sodometries: Renaissance Texts, Modern Sexualities*, Stanford: Stanford University Press, 1992, pp. 99–100.

8 See, e.g., Stephen Booth (ed.), *Shakespeare's Sonnets*, New Haven: Yale

University Press, 1977, p. 177; the potential transgressiveness of a "woman's wit" is registered in *As You Like It* (4.1.159ff.).

9 While merely indicating the possibility of collaborative texts in the Shakespeare folio is of course controversial, I mean here to indicate passages – for example, parts of *Macbeth* – attributed in the period to other writers.

10 Editions of Chaucer in use in the seventeenth century (1598, 1602, 1687) use the term "The Prologues of the Canterbury tales" to refer to the introductory section of the collection.

11 The original is printed in italic with roman emphases; in quotations from this poem, I have reversed these.

12 See Timothy Murray, *Theatrical Legitimation: Allegories of Genius in Seventeenth-Century England and France*, New York and Oxford: Oxford University Press, 1987; and Peter Stallybrass and Allon White, *The Politics and Poetics of Transgression*, Ithaca: Cornell University Press, 1986.

13 Jonson is one of the first recorded users of *plagiary* (and related words) in English (1601); see *OED*.

14 I'm indebted to Peter Stallybrass for this suggestion.

15 See Grant, *Margaret the First*, and Jones, *A Glorious Fame*. Even in exile, and despite massive debts, the Cavendishes lived in a style to which their class position had accustomed them; in Antwerp, their renting of Peter Paul Rubens's mansion (*Margaret the First*, pp. 133–35) suggests a model and situation of artistic production somewhat different from the low cottage of the poem.

16 On this asymmetry, see in particular Catherine Belsey, *The Subject of Tragedy*, London and New York: Methuen, 1985; and Peter Stallybrass: "If radical males defined their individuality against the subjecthood of dependents, those whom they still defined as dependents remained subjects. Individuality for the male citizen; subjectivity for the female daughter and wife" ("Shakespeare, Milton and the Individual," paper delivered at the English Institute, Harvard University, 1990).

17 No sig.

18 Chapter 3 describes the splitting off of "strands" of meaning out of the earlier undifferentiated term *author* (pp. 64–66).

19 The same frontispiece appeared in both the 1662 and 1668 folios, although it is missing from a number of the copies I have examined. Grant identifies the frontispiece as having appeared in *The World's Olio* (*Margaret the First*, p. 142), an attribution that does not accord, at least, with the copy at the Folger Library, but which I have been otherwise unable to confirm; he does not connect it with the volumes of plays. Photograph courtesy of Houghton Library, Harvard University.

20 Grant, *Margaret the First*, p. 142.

21 The Medusa shield has been identified with both Zeus and Athena. Marjorie Garber argues that, furthermore, it may be associated with Perseus' shield; see "Macbeth: the Male Medusa," chapter 5 in *Shakespeare's Ghost Writers: Literature as Uncanny Causality*, New York: Methuen, 1987, pp. 122–23.

22 We might ask, quoting Garber quoting Fruit of the Loom: "Whose underwear is under there?"; *Vested Interests: Cross-Dressing and Cultural Anxiety*, New York: HarperCollins, 1993, p. 118.

23 *Tempe Restor'd*, in *The Poems and Masques of Aurelian Townshend with Music by Henry Lawes and William Webb*, ed. Cedric C. Brown, Reading: Whiteknights Press, 1983, p. 102.

24 One could argue that such a methodology (reading like Jonson, reading with the expectations one takes to drama produced earlier in the century) is, in fact, the reason Cavendish's dramatic production has been overlooked (under-read), even by those who read and write about her other texts. See, for example, the deprecating comments of both Kathleen Jones ("The plays are disappointing [and] episodic, with no attempt to create dramatic tensions," *Glorious Fame*, p. 130) and Douglas Grant ("length is the least of their failings. They are nothing more than a collection of disconnected scenes," *Margaret the First*, p. 161). Neither critic makes a case for a reading of the plays on other grounds. Henry Ten Eyck Perry's early, relatively feminist account of Cavendish similarly concludes of the plays: "They are closet drama indeed – but closet drama so lifeless and so dull that one shrinks from it even on the printed page. They mark the lowest ebb of their authoress's literary production"; *The First Duchess of Newcastle and Her Husband as Figures in Literary History*, Harvard Studies in English IV, Boston and London: Ginn and Company, 1918, p. 214.

Bibliography

Note: For reasons addressed at the end of the Introduction, this bibliography arranges early modern texts by year (and within years, by early modern authorial attribution, if any); modern texts and modern editions of early modern texts are arranged by author/editor. In printed book titles, early modern capitalization has been followed where possible in the notes and bibliography, though not in the text proper; original typefaces in citations of titles, authors, and publishers have not been replicated.

EARLY MODERN TEXTS

THE ARTE OF ENGLISH POESIE, London: by Richard Field, 1589.

Edmund Spenser, *THE FAERIE QVEENE. Disposed into twelve books, Fashioning* XII. *Morall vertues*, London: for William Ponsonbie, 1590.

A most pleasant and merie nevv Comedie, Intituled, A Knacke to knowe a Knaue, London: by Richard Iones, 1594.

The true Tragedie of Richard Duke of Yorke, and the death of good King Henrie the Sixt, London: by P. S. for Thomas Millington, 1595.

AN EXCELLENT conceited Tragedie OF Romeo and Iuliet, London: by Iohn Danter, 1597.

The Workes of our Antient and Learned English Poet, GEFFREY CHAVCER, newly Printed, London: by Adam Islip at the charges of Bonham Norton, 1598.

THE CRONICLE History of Henry the fift, London: by Thomas Creede, for Tho. Millington, and Iohn Busby, 1600.

William Shakespeare, *A Midsommer nights dreame*, London: for Thomas Fisher, 1600.

William Shakespeare, *The most excellent Historie of the Merchant of Venice*, London: by I. R. for Thomas Heyes, 1600.

THE ESSAYES Or Morall, Politike and Millitairie Discourses of Lo: Michaell de Montaigne ... now done into English, trans. John Florio, London: by Val. Sims for Edward Blount, 1603.

William Shake-speare, *THE Tragicall Historie of HAMLET Prince of Denmarke*, London: for N. L. and Iohn Trundell, 1603.

William Shakespeare, *THE Tragicall Historie of HAMLET , Prince of Denmarke*, London: by I. R. for N. L., 1604.

SHAKE-SPEARES SONNETS, London: G. Eld for T.T., 1609.

Robert Armin, THE History of the two Maids of More-clacke, London: by N.O. for Thomas Archer, 1609.

William Shakespeare, THE LATE, And much admired Play, Called Pericles, Prince of Tyre, London: for Henry Gosson, 1609.

THE HOLY BIBLE, Conteyning the Old Testament, and the New: Newly Translated out of the Originall Tongues ... by his Maiesties speciall Comandement, London: by Robert Barker, Printer to the Kings most Excellent Maiestie, 1611.

Riders Dictionarie, 3rd edition, Oxford: Joseph Barnes, 1612.

THE KNIGHT OF the Burning Pestle, London: for Walter Burre, 1613.

E. C., THE TRAGEDIE OF MARIAM, THE FAIRE Queene of Iewry, London: by Thomas Creede, for Richard Hawkins, 1613.

ESSAYES WRITTEN IN French By MICHAEL Lord of Montaigne ... DONE INTO ENGLISH, according to the last French edition, by IOHN FLORIO ..., London: by Melch. Bradvvood for Edvvard Blovnt and William Barret, 1613.

GOD and the King: Or, A Dialogue shewing that our Soueraigne Lord King IAMES, being immediate vnder God within his DOMINIONS, Doth rightfully claime whatsoeuer is required by the Oath of ALLEAGEANCE, London: Imprinted by his Maiesties Speciall priuiledge and command, 1615.

R. A. Gent., THE VALIANT VVELSHMAN, Or THE TRVE CHRONICLE History of the life and valiant deedes of CARADOC the Great, King of Cambria, now called WALES, London: by George Purslowe for Robert Lownes, 1615.

THE WORKES OF THE MOST HIGH AND MIGHTY PRINCE, IAMES, By the grace of God Kinge of Great Brittaine France & Ireland Defendor of ye Faith &c., London: Iames, Bishop of Winton, 1616.

Iohn Minsheu, Ductor in Linguas, THE GUIDE INTO TONGUES, London: Iohn Browne, 1617.

Francis Beamount, and Iohn Flecher, A King and no King, London: for Thomas Walkley, 1619.

Francis Baymont and Iohn Fletcher. Gent., PHYLASTER. OR, Loue lyes a Bleeding, London: for Thomas Walkley, 1620.

Francis Beaumont. and Iohn Fletcher. Gent., PHILASTER. OR, Loue lies a Bleeding. London: for Thomas Walkley, 1622.

Henry Peacham, THE Compleat Gentleman, London: for Francis Constable, 1622.

MR. WILLIAM SHAKESPEARES COMEDIES, HISTORIES, & TRAGEDIES, London: Isaac Iaggard and Ed. Blount, 1623.

THE ESSAYES OR COVNSELS, CIVILL AND MORALL, OF FRANCIS LO. VERVLAM, VISCOVNT ST. ALBAN, London: Iohn Haviland for Hanna Barret, 1625; rpt. London: Oxford University Press, 1966.

Francis Beaumont, and Iohn Fletcher Gentlemen, PHYLASTER. OR, Loue lies a Bleeding, London: A. M. for Richard Hawkins, 1628.

Richard Brathwait, THE English Gentleman, London: by Iohn Haviland [for] Robert Bostock, 1630.

Francis Beamont & Iohn Fletcher Gent., A KING, and NO KING, London: by A. M. for Richard Hawkins, 1631.

Ben Jonson, BARTHOLMEW FAYRE: A COMEDIE ACTED IN THE YEARE, 1614, London: by I. B. for Robert Allot, 1631.

Xenophon, CYRUPAEDIA, THE INSITVTION AND LIFE OF CYRVS, trans. Philemon Holland, London: J. L. for Robert Allot, 1632.

Richard Brathwait, *THE ENGLISH GENTLEMAN*, London: Felix Kyngston for Robert Bostocke, 1633.

Mr. John Fletcher, and William Shakspeare. Gent., *THE TWO NOBLE KINSMEN*, London: Tho. Cotes for Iohn Waterson, 1634.

Francis Beaumont and Iohn Fletcher. Gent., *THE KNIGHT Of the BVRNING PESTLE*, London: N. O. for I. S., 1635.

Francis Beamount and Iohn Fletcher, *THE KNIGHT Of the BVRNING PESTLE*, London: N. O. for I. S., 1635.

Iohn Fletcher Gent., *THE ELDER BROTHER … Printed according to the true copie*, London: by F. K. for J. W. and J. B., 1637.

MONSIEVR THOMAS, London: by Thomas Harper, for Iohn Waterson, 1639.

John Fletcher Gent., *The Tragoedy of ROLLO Duke of Normandy*, Oxford: by Leonard Lichfield, 1640.

THE ENGLISH GENTLEMAN; AND THE ENGLISH GENTLEVVOMAN, Both In one VOLVME couched, London: by Iohn Dawson, 1641.

AREOPAGITICA; A SPEECH OF Mʳ. JOHN MILTON For the Liberty of Vnlicenc'd PRINTING, To the Parlament of ENGLAND, London, 1644.

POEMS OF Mr. John Milton, BOTH ENGLISH and LATIN, Compos'd at several times, London: by Ruth Raworth for Humphrey Moseley, 1645.

Francis Beavmont and Iohn Fletcher Gentlemen, *COMEDIES AND TRAGEDIES*, London: for Humphrey Robinson and Humphrey Moseley, 1647.

John Gaule, *THE MAG-ASTRO-MANCER, or THE Magical-Astrologicall-Diviner Posed, and Puzzled*, London: for Joshua Kirton, 1652.

Richard Whitlock, *ZOOTOMIA, or Observations on the Present Manners of the English: Briefly Anatomizing the Living by the Dead*, London: Tho. Roycroft and Humphrey Moseley, 1654.

Aston Cokain, *Small POEMS of Divers sorts*, London: by Wil. Godbid, 1658.

Aston Cokain, *A CHAIN OF GOLDEN POEMS Embellished with WIT, MIRTH and ELOQUENCE*, London: by W. G. (for) Isaac Pridmore, 1658.

PLAYES Written by the Thrice NOBLE, ILLUSTRIOUS AND Excellent Princess, THE LADY MARCHIONESS OF NEWCASTLE, London: by A. Warren for John Martyn, James Allestry, and Tho. Dicas, 1662.

Mᴿ. WILLIAM SHAKESPEAR'S Comedies, Histories, and Tragedies, London: for P. C., 1664.

PLAYS, Never before Printed. WRITTEN By the Thrice Noble, Illustrious, and Excellent PRINCESSE, THE Duchess of Newcastle, London: by A. Maxwell, 1668.

John Dryden, *OF DRAMATICK Poesie, AN ESSAY*, London: for Henry Herringman, 1668.

Elisha Coles, *A Dictionary, English–Latin, and Latin–English*, London: by John Richardson, for Peter Parker … and Thomas and John Guy, 1677.

MODERN TEXTS AND MODERN EDITIONS OF EARLY MODERN TEXTS

Abelove, Henry, "Some Speculations on the History of 'Sexual Intercourse' During the 'Long Eighteenth Century' in England," in Andrew Parker,

Mary Russo, Doris Sommer, and Patricia Yeager (eds.), *Nationalisms and Sexualities*, New York: Routledge, 1992, pp. 335–42.

Agnew, Jean-Christophe, *Worlds Apart: The Market and the Theater in Anglo-American Thought, 1550–1750*, Cambridge: Cambridge University Press, 1986.

Amussen, Susan Dwyer, *An Ordered Society: Gender and Class in Early Modern England*, Oxford and New York: Basil Blackwell, 1988.

Aubrey, John, *'Brief Lives,' Chiefly of Contemporaries, set down by John Aubrey, between the years 1669 and 1696*, Andrew Clark (ed.), 2 vols., Oxford: Clarendon Press, 1898.

Bach, Rebecca, "Producing the 'New World': The Colonial Stages of Ben Jonson and Captain John Smith," Ph.D. thesis, University of Pennsylvania, 1994.

Bacon, Francis, *The Essayes or Covnsels, Civill and Morall, of Francis Lo. Vervlam, Viscovnt St. Alban*, London: Iohn Haviland for Hanna Barret, 1625; rpt. London: Oxford University Press, 1966.

Bald, R. C., *Bibliographical Studies in the Beaumont and Fletcher Folio of 1647*, Supplement to the Bibliographical Society's Transactions, no. 13, Oxford: Oxford University Press for the Bibliographical Society, 1938 (for 1937).

Barber, C. L., " 'Thou that beget'st him that did thee beget': Transformation in 'Pericles' and 'The Winter's Tale,' " *Shakespeare Survey* 22 (1969), pp. 59–67.

Barker, Francis, *The Tremulous Private Body: Essays on Subjection*, London: Methuen, 1984.

Barker, Francis, and Hulme, Peter, "Nymphs and Reapers Heavily Vanish: the Discursive Con-texts of *The Tempest*," in John Drakakis (ed.), *Alternative Shakespeares*, London: Methuen, 1985, pp. 191–205.

Barthes, Roland, "The Death of the Author," in *Image, Music, Text*, trans. Stephen Heath, New York: Hill and Wang, 1977.

Barton, Anne, Introduction, *The Two Gentlemen of Verona*, in G. Blakemore Evans et al. (eds.), *The Riverside Shakespeare*, pp. 143–46.

Belsey, Catherine, "Disrupting Sexual Difference: Meaning and Gender in the Comedies," in John Drakakis (ed.), *Alternative Shakespeares*, London and New York: Methuen, 1985, pp. 166–90.

The Subject of Tragedy, London and New York: Methuen, 1985.

Bentley, Gerald Eades, *The Profession of Dramatist in Shakespeare's Time 1590–1642*, Princeton: Princeton University Press, 1971.

The Profession of Player in Shakespeare's Time 1590–1642, Princeton: Princeton University Press, 1984.

Bergeron, David M., *Shakespeare's Romances and the Royal Family*, Lawrence, Kansas: University Press of Kansas, 1985.

Blayney, Peter W. M., *The First Folio of Shakespeare*, Washington, DC: Folger Library Publications, 1991.

"Shakespeare in St. Paul's Churchyard," Shakespeare Association of America Annual Meeting, Vancouver, 23 March 1991.

Blincoe, Noel R., " 'Sex Individual' as Used in *The Two Noble Kinsmen*," *Notes and Queries* 35.4 (1988), pp. 484–85.

Bliss, Lee, *Francis Beaumont*, Boston: Twayne, 1987.

" 'Plot Mee No Plots': The Life of Drama and the Drama of Life in *The Knight of the Burning Pestle*," *Modern Language Quarterly* 45.1 (1984), pp. 3–21.

Booth, Stephen (ed.), *Shakespeare's Sonnets*, New Haven: Yale University Press, 1977.

Boswell, John, "Revolutions, Universals, and Sexual Categories," *Salmagundi* 58–59 (1982–83), pp. 89–113.

Bowers, Fredson, "Authority, Copy, and Transmission in Shakespeare's Texts," in Georgianna Ziegler (ed.), *Shakespeare Study Today*, New York: AMS, 1986, pp. 7–36.

(ed.), *The Complete Works of Christopher Marlowe*, vol. II, Cambridge: Cambridge University Press, 1973.

(ed.), *The Dramatic Works in the Beaumont and Fletcher Canon*, vol. I, Cambridge: Cambridge University Press.

Brady, Jennifer, and Herendeen, W. H. (eds.), *Ben Jonson's 1616 Folio*, Newark: University of Delaware Press, 1991.

Bray, Alan, "Homosexuality and the Signs of Male Friendship in Elizabethan England," *History Workshop Journal* 29 (1990), 1–19; rpt. in Jonathan Goldberg (ed.), *Queering the Renaissance*, pp. 40–61.

Homosexuality in Renaissance England, London: Gay Men's Press, 1982.

Bredbeck, Gregory W., *Sodomy and Interpretation*, Ithaca: Cornell University Press, 1991.

Brontë, Emily, *Wuthering Heights*, David Daiches (ed.), Harmondsworth: Penguin Classics, 1987.

Brown, Paul, " 'This thing of darkness I acknowledge mine': *The Tempest* and the Discourse of Colonialism," in Jonathan Dollimore and Alan Sinfield (eds.), *Political Shakespeare: New Essays in Cultural Materialism*, Ithaca and London: Cornell University Press, 1985, pp. 48–71.

Bullough, Geoffrey, *Narrative and Dramatic Sources of Shakespeare*, vol. VI, New York: Columbia University Press, 1966.

Bushnell, Rebecca W., *Tragedies of Tyrants: Political Thought and Theater in the English Renaissance*, Ithaca and London: Cornell University Press, 1990.

Corbett, Margery, and Lightbown, Ronald, *The Comely Frontispiece: The Emblematic Title-Page in England 1550–1660*, London: Routledge & Kegan Paul, 1979.

Cottrell, Robert D., *Sexuality/Textuality: A Study of the Fabric of Montaigne's Essais*, Columbus: Ohio State University Press, 1981.

Cressy, David, "Death and the Social Order: The Funerary Preferences of Elizabethan Gentlemen," *Continuity and Change* 5.1 (1989), pp. 99–119.

de Grazia, Margreta, "The Scandal of Shakespeare's Sonnets," *Shakespeare Survey* 46 (1993), pp. 35–49.

Shakespeare Verbatim: The Reproduction of Authenticity and the 1790 Apparatus, Oxford: Clarendon Press, 1991.

"*The Tempest*: Gratuitous Movement or Action Without Kibes and Pinches," *Shakespeare Studies* 14 (1981), pp. 249–65.

de Grazia, Margreta, and Stallybrass, Peter, "The Materiality of the Shakespearean Text," *Shakespeare Quarterly* 44 (1993), pp. 255–83.

Doebler, John (ed.), *The Knight of the Burning Pestle*, Regents Renaissance Drama, Lincoln: University of Nebraska Press, 1967.

Edelman, Lee, "Tearooms and Sympathy; or, The Epistemology of the Water Closet," in *Homographesis: Essays in Gay Literary and Cultural Theory*, New York: Routledge, 1994, pp. 148–70.

Edwards, Philip, "An Approach to the Problem of *Pericles*," *Shakespeare Survey* 5 (1952), pp. 25–49.

Edwards, Philip, and Gibson, Colin (eds.), *The Plays and Poems of Philip Massinger*, vol. I, Oxford: Clarendon, 1976.

Eggers, Jr., Walter F., "Shakespeare's Gower and the Role of the Authorial Presenter," *Philological Quarterly* 54 (1975), pp. 434–43.

Eisenstein, Elizabeth, *The Printing Press as an Agent of Change: Communications and Cultural Transformations in Early-Modern Europe*, Cambridge: Cambridge University Press, 1979.

Evans, G. Blakemore, et al. (eds.), *The Riverside Shakespeare*, Boston: Houghton Mifflin, 1974.

Ezell, Margaret J. M., *The Patriarch's Wife: Literary Evidence and the History of the Family*, Chapel Hill: University of North Carolina Press, 1987.

Ferguson, Margaret W., "A Room Not Their Own: Renaissance Women as Readers and Writers," in Clayton Koelb and Susan Noakes (eds.), *The Comparative Perspective on Literature: Approaches to Theory and Practice*, Ithaca: Cornell University Press, 1988, pp. 93–116.

Finkelpearl, Philip J., *Court and Country Politics in the Plays of Beaumont and Fletcher*, Princeton: Princeton University Press, 1990.

Fisher, William, "Queer Money," unpublished essay, "The Politics of Pleasure" seminar, Shakespeare Association of America, Albuquerque, 1994.

Fleming, Juliet, "The Ladies' Man and the Age of Elizabeth," in James Grantham Turner (ed.), *Sexuality and Gender in Early Modern Europe: Institutions, Texts, Images*, Cambridge: Cambridge University Press, 1993, pp. 158–81.

Foucault, Michel, "An Interview: Sex, Power and the Politics of Identity," *The Advocate* (7 Aug. 1984), pp. 26–58.

  Discipline and Punish: The Birth of the Prison, trans. Alan Sheridan, New York: Pantheon, 1977.

  The History of Sexuality, Volume I: An Introduction, New York: Vintage, 1980.

  "What Is an Author?" in Paul Rabinow (ed.), *The Foucault Reader*, New York: Pantheon, 1984, pp. 101–20.

Frey, Charles H., "Collaborating with Shakespeare," in Charles H. Frey (ed.), *Shakespeare, Fletcher, and The Two Noble Kinsmen*, Columbia: University of Missouri Press, 1989, pp. 31–44.

Gallagher, Catherine, "Embracing the Absolute: The Politics of the Female Subject in Seventeenth-Century England," *Genders* 1 (1988), pp. 24–39.

Garber, Marjorie, "Shakespeare as Fetish," *Shakespeare Quarterly* 41.2 (1990), pp. 242–50.

  Shakespeare's Ghost Writers: Literature as Uncanny Causality, New York: Methuen, 1987.

  Vested Interests: Cross-Dressing and Cultural Anxiety, New York: Harper Collins, 1993.

Gebert, Clara (ed.), *An Anthology of Elizabethan Dedications and Prefaces*, Philadelphia: University of Pennsylvania Press, 1933.

Gilbert, Sandra, and Gubar, Susan, *The Madwoman in the Attic: The Woman Writer and the Nineteenth-Century Literary Imagination*, New Haven and London: Yale University Press, 1984.

Girard, René, "The Politics of Desire in *Troilus and Cressida*," in Patricia Parker and Geoffrey Hartman (eds.), *Shakespeare and the Question of Theory*, New York and London: Methuen, 1985, pp. 188–209.

Goldberg, Jonathan, "Colin to Hobbinol: Spenser's Familiar Letters," *South Atlantic Quarterly* 88.1 (1989), pp. 107–26.

"Fatherly Authority: The Politics of Stuart Family Images," in Margaret W. Ferguson, Maureen Quilligan, and Nancy J. Vickers (eds.), *Rewriting the Renaissance: The Discourses of Sexual Difference in Early Modern Europe*, Chicago and London: University of Chicago Press, 1986, pp. 3–32.

"Hamlet's Hand," *Shakespeare Quarterly* 39 (1988), pp. 307–27.

James I and the Politics of Literature: Jonson, Shakespeare, Donne, and Their Contemporaries, Baltimore: Johns Hopkins University Press, 1983.

Sodometries: Renaissance Texts, Modern Sexualities, Stanford: Stanford University Press, 1992.

"Speculations: Macbeth and Source," in Jean E. Howard and Marion F. O'Connor (eds.), *Shakespeare Reproduced: The Text in History and Ideology*, New York and London: Methuen, 1987, pp. 242–64.

Voice Terminal Echo: Postmodernism and English Renaissance Texts, New York and London: Methuen, 1986.

Writing Matter: From the Hands of the English Renaissance, Stanford: Stanford University Press, 1990.

(ed.), *Queering the Renaissance*, Durham: Duke University Press, 1994.

Gorfain, Phyllis, "Puzzle and Artifice: The Riddle as Metapoetry in Pericles," *Shakespeare Survey* 29 (1976), pp. 11–20.

Grant, Douglas, *Margaret the First: A Biography of Margaret Cavendish Duchess of Newcastle 1623–1673*, London: Rupert Hart-Davis, 1957.

Greenaway, Peter, *Prospero's Books*, a Miramax Films Release, 1992.

Greenblatt, Stephen, *Shakespearean Negotiations: The Circulation of Social Energy in Renaissance England*, Berkeley: University of California Press, 1988.

Greene, Roland, *Post-Petrarchism: Origins and Innovations of the Western Lyric Sequence*, Princeton: Princeton University Press, 1991.

Greene, Thomas M., *The Light in Troy: Imitation and Discovery in Renaissance Poetry*, New Haven and London: Yale University Press, 1982.

Grossman, Jay, " 'The evangel-poem of comrades and of love': Revising Whitman's Republicanism," *American Transcendental Quarterly* 4.3 (1990), pp. 210–18.

Grossman, Marshall, *"Authors to Themselves": Milton and the Revelation of History*, Cambridge: Cambridge University Press, 1987.

Gurr, Andrew (ed.), *The Knight of the Burning Pestle*, Fountainwell Drama Texts, Edinburgh: Oliver and Boyd, 1968.

Halperin, David M., *One Hundred Years of Homosexuality and Other Essays on Greek Love*, New York and London: Routledge, 1990.

Harding, Vanessa, " 'And one more may be laid there': the Location of Burials in Early Modern London," *The London Journal* 14.2 (1989), pp. 112–29.

Hattaway, Michael (ed.), *The Knight of the Burning Pestle*, New Mermaids edition, London: Ernest Benn, 1969.

Hawkes, Terence, "That Shakespeherian Rag," in *That Shakespeherian Rag*, London: Methuen, 1986.

Hedrick, Donald K., " 'Be Rough With Me': The Collaborative Arenas of *The Two Noble Kinsmen*," in Charles H. Frey (ed.), *Shakespeare, Fletcher, and The Two Noble Kinsmen*, Columbia: University of Missouri Press, 1989, pp. 45–77.

Helgerson, Richard, *Self-Crowned Laureates: Spenser, Jonson, Milton and the Literary System*, Berkeley: University of California Press, 1983.

Heywood, Thomas, *The Dramatic Works of Thomas Heywood Now First Collected with Illustrative Notes and a Memoir of the Author in Six Volumes*, vol. III, New York: Russell and Russell, 1964 (rpt. of 1874 edition).

Hinman, Charlton (ed.), *The Norton Facsimile: The First Folio of Shakespeare*, New York: Norton, 1968.

Hoeniger, F. D. (ed.), *Pericles*, Arden Shakespeare, London: Methuen, 1963.

Howard-Hill, T. H., "The Author as Scribe or Reviser?: Middleton's Intentions in *A Game at Chess*," *Transactions of the Society for Textual Scholarship* 3, New York: AMS, 1987, pp. 305–18.

Ralph Crane and Some Shakespeare First Folio Comedies, Charlottesville: University of Virginia Press, 1972.

Hoy, Cyrus, "Critical and Aesthetic Problems of Collaboration in Renaissance Drama," *Research Opportunities in Renaissance Drama* 19 (1976), pp. 3–6.

"The Shares of Fletcher and his Collaborators in the Beaumont and Fletcher Canon (I)," *Studies in Bibliography* 8 (1956), pp. 129–46.

"The Shares of Fletcher and his Collaborators in the Beaumont and Fletcher Canon (III)," *Studies in Bibliography* 11 (1958), pp. 85–106.

"The Shares of Fletcher and his Collaborators in the Beaumont and Fletcher Canon (VII)," *Studies in Bibliography* 15 (1962), pp. 71–90.

(ed.), *The Knight of the Burning Pestle*, in Fredson Bowers (gen. ed.), *The Dramatic Works in the Beaumont and Fletcher Canon*, vol. I, pp. 1–110.

Hughes, Merritt Y. (ed.), *John Milton: Complete Poems and Major Prose*, New York: Odyssey, 1957.

Ioppolo, Grace, *Revising Shakespeare*, Cambridge: Harvard University Press, 1991.

Jackson, MacD. P., *Studies in Attribution: Middleton and Shakespeare*, Salzburg Studies in English Literature, Salzburg: Universität Salzburg, 1979.

James I, *Minor Prose Works of King James VI and I*, James Craigie and Alexander Law (eds.), Edinburgh: Scottish Text Society, 1982.

Jenkins, Harold (ed.), *Hamlet*, Arden Shakespeare, London: Methuen, 1982.

Jones, Ann Rosalind, *The Currency of Eros: Women's Love Lyric in Europe, 1540–1620*, Bloomington: Indiana University Press, 1990.

Jones, Ann Rosalind, and Stallybrass, Peter, "The Politics of *Astrophil and Stella*," *SEL* 24 (1984), pp. 53–68.

"Fetishizing Gender: Constructing the Hermaphrodite in Renaissance Europe," in Julia Epstein and Kristina Straub (eds.), *Body Guards: The Cultural Politics of Gender Ambiguity*, New York: Routledge, 1991.

Jones, Kathleen, *A Glorious Fame: The Life of Margaret Cavendish, Duchess of Newcastle, 1623–1673*, London: Bloomsbury, 1988.

Kelso, Ruth, *The Doctrine of the English Gentleman in the Sixteenth Century*, Gloucester, MA: Peter Smith, 1964.

Kermode, Frank (ed.), *The Tempest*, Arden Shakespeare, London and New York: Routledge, 1954.

Kernan, Alvin B., *The Playwright as Magician: Shakespeare's Image of the Poet in the English Public Theater*, New Haven and London: Yale University Press, 1979.

Knapp, Jeffrey, *An Empire Nowhere: England, America, and Literature from Utopia to The Tempest*, Berkeley: University of California Press, 1992.

Knight, G. Wilson, *The Crown of Life: Essays in Interpretation of Shakespeare's Final Plays*, London: Oxford University Press, 1947.

Koestenbaum, Wayne, *Double Talk: The Erotics of Male Literary Collaboration*, New York and London: Routledge, 1989.

Lake, David J., *The Canon of Thomas Middleton's Plays: Internal Evidence for the Major Problems of Authorship*, London: Cambridge University Press, 1975.

Laqueur, Thomas, *Making Sex: Body and Gender from the Greeks to Freud*, Cambridge: Harvard University Press, 1990.

Lawless, Donald S., *Philip Massinger and His Associates*, Ball State Monograph no. 10, Muncie, IN: Ball State University, 1967.

Leech, Clifford (ed.), *The Two Gentlemen of Verona*, Arden Shakespeare, London and New York: Methuen, 1969.

Lewalski, Barbara, *Writing Women in Jacobean England*, Cambridge: Harvard University Press, 1993.

Lindenbaum, Peter, "Education in *The Two Gentlemen of Verona*," *Studies in English Literature* 15 (1975), pp. 229–44.

"Milton's Contract," in Martha Woodmansee and Peter Jaszi (eds.), *The Construction of Authorship: Textual Appropriation in Law and Literature*, Durham: Duke University Press, 1994, pp. 175–90.

Loewenstein, Joseph, "Plays Agonistic and Competitive: The Textual Approach to Elsinore," *Renaissance Drama* 19 (1988), pp. 63–96.

"The Script in the Marketplace," *Representations* 12 (1985), pp. 101–14; rpt. in Stephen Greenblatt (ed.), *Representing the English Renaissance*, Berkeley: University of California Press, 1988, pp. 265–78.

Long, William B., "Bookkeepers and Playhouse Manuscripts: A Peek at the Evidence," *Shakespeare Newsletter* 44 (1994), p. 3.

"Stage Directions: A Misinterpreted Factor in Determining Textual Provenance," *TEXT* 2 (1985), pp. 121–37.

Mack, Phyllis, *Visionary Women: Ecstatic Prophecy in Seventeenth-Century England*, Berkeley: University of California Press, 1992.

Marcus, Leah, *Puzzling Shakespeare: Local Reading and Its Discontents*, Berkeley: University of California Press, 1988.

Marotti, Arthur F., " 'Love is not love': Elizabethan Sonnet Sequences and the Social Order," *ELH* 49 (1982), pp. 396–428.

Manuscript, Print, and the English Renaissance Lyric, Ithaca: Cornell University Press, 1995.

"Shakespeare's Sonnets as Literary Property," in Elizabeth D. Harvey and Katharine Eisaman Maus (eds.), *Soliciting Interpretation: Literary Theory and Seventeenth-Century English Poetry*, Chicago and London: University of Chicago Press, 1990, pp. 143–73.

Masten, Jeffrey, "Designing Sodomies" (review of Claude Summers [ed.], *Homosexuality in Renaissance and Enlightenment England: Literary Representations in Historical Context*, New York: Haworth, 1992, and Jonathan Goldberg, *Sodometries*), *Lesbian and Gay Studies Newsletter* (July 1993).

"My Two Dads: Collaboration and the Reproduction of Beaumont and Fletcher," in Jonathan Goldberg (ed.), *Queering the Renaissance*, pp. 280–309.

" 'Shall I turne blabb?': Circulation, Gender, and Subjectivity in Wroth's Sonnets," in Naomi Miller and Gary Waller (eds.), *Reading Mary Wroth: Representing Alternatives in Early Modern England*, Knoxville: University of Tennessee Press, 1991, pp. 67–87.

McGann, Jerome J., *A Critique of Modern Textual Criticism*, Chicago and London: University of Chicago Press, 1983.

"The Monks and the Giants: Textual and Bibliographical Studies and the Interpretation of Literary Works," in Jerome J. McGann (ed.), *Textual Criticism and Literary Interpretation*, Chicago and London: University of Chicago Press, 1985, pp. 180–99.

McKenzie, D. F., *What's Past is Prologue: The Bibliographical Society and the History of the Book*, Bibliographical Society Centenary Lecture, 14 July 1992, Hearthstone Publications, 1993.

McLaren, Angus, *Reproductive Rituals: The Perception of Fertility in England from the Sixteenth Century to the Nineteenth Century*, London and New York: Methuen, 1984.

McLuskie, Kathleen, " 'A maidenhead, *Amintor*, at my yeares': Chastity and Tragicomedy in the Fletcher Plays," in Gordon McMullan and Jonathan Hope (eds.), *The Politics of Tragicomedy: Shakespeare and After*, London: Routledge, 1992, pp. 92–121.

McMillin, Scott, *The Elizabethan Theatre and The Book of Sir Thomas More*, Ithaca: Cornell University Press, 1987.

McMullan, Gordon, *The Politics of Unease in the Plays of John Fletcher*, Amherst: University of Massachusetts Press, 1994.

Miller, D. A., *The Novel and the Police*, Berkeley: University of California Press, 1988.

Mills, Lauren J., *One Soule in Bodies Twain: Friendship in Tudor Literature and Stuart Drama*, Bloomington, IN: Principia, 1937.

Montaigne, Michel de, *The Essays of Montaigne*, trans. John Florio, with an introduction by George Saintsbury, 3 vols., London: David Nutt, 1892; rpt. New York: AMS, 1967.

Montrose, Louis A., "The Purpose of Playing: Reflections on a Shakespearean Anthropology," *Helios* 7 (1980), pp. 51–74.

Mowat, Barbara A., "Theatre and Literary Culture," in John D. Cox and David Scott Kastan (eds.), *A New History of Early English Drama*, New York: Columbia University Press, forthcoming, 1996.

Muir, Kenneth, "The Problem of *Pericles*," *English Studies* 30 (1949), pp. 65–83.

Mullaney, Steven, *The Place of the Stage: License, Play, and Power in Renaissance England*, Chicago and London: University of Chicago Press, 1988.

Murray, Timothy, *Theatrical Legitimation: Allegories of Genius in Seventeenth-Century England and France*, New York and Oxford: Oxford University Press, 1987.

Nehamas, Alexander, "The Postulated Author: Critical Monism as a Regulative Ideal," *Critical Inquiry* (1981), pp. 133–49.

"Writer, Text, Work, Author," in Anthony J. Cascardi (ed.), *Literature and the Question of Philosophy*, Baltimore: Johns Hopkins University Press, 1987, pp. 267–91.

Orgel, Stephen, "Prospero's Wife," in Margaret W. Ferguson, Maureen Quilligan, and Nancy J. Vickers (eds.), *Rewriting the Renaissance: The Discourses of Sexual Difference in Early Modern Europe*, Chicago and London: University of Chicago Press, 1986, pp. 50–64.

"The Authentic Shakespeare," *Representations* 21 (1988), pp. 1–25.

"What is a Text?," *Research Opportunities in Renaissance Drama* (1981), pp. 2–4.

(ed.), *The Tempest*, Oxford Shakespeare, Oxford and New York: Oxford University Press, 1987.

Oxford American Dictionary, New York and Oxford: Oxford University Press, 1980.

Pantzer, Katharine F. (ed.), *A Short-Title Catalogue of Books Printed in England, Scotland, and Ireland, and of English Books Printed Abroad, 1475–1640*, first compiled by A. W. Pollard and G. R. Redgrave, 2nd edition, rev. and expanded, London: The Bibliographical Society, 1976–91.

Parker, Patricia, *Literary Fat Ladies: Rhetoric, Gender, Property*, London and New York: Methuen, 1987.

Patterson, Annabel, *Censorship and Interpretation: The Conditions of Writing and Reading in Early Modern England*, Madison: University of Wisconsin Press, 1984.

Peckham, Morse, "Reflections on the Foundations of Modern Textual Editing," *Proof* 1 (1971), pp. 122–55.

Pequigney, Joseph, *Such is My Love: A Study of Shakespeare's Sonnets*, Chicago: University of Chicago Press, 1985.

Perry, Henry Ten Eyck, *The First Duchess of Newcastle and Her Husband as Figures in Literary History*, Harvard Studies in English IV, Boston and London: Ginn and Company, 1918.

Pittenger, Elizabeth, "Dispatch Quickly: The Mechanical Reproduction of Pages," *Shakespeare Quarterly* 42 (1991), pp. 389–408.

Pollard, Alfred W., *Shakespeare Folios and Quartos: A Study of the Bibliography of Shakespeare's Plays 1594–1685*, London: Methuen, 1909.

Shakespeare's Fight with the Pirates and the Problems of the Transmission of His Text, 2nd edition, revised with introduction, Cambridge: Cambridge University Press, 1920.

Potter, Lois, *Secret Rites and Secret Writing: Royalist Literature, 1641–1660*, Cambridge: University Press, 1989.

"Topicality or Politics? *The Two Noble Kinsmen*, 1613–34" in Gordon McMullan and Jonathan Hope (eds.), *The Politics of Tragicomedy: Shakespeare and After*, London: Routledge, 1992, pp. 77–91.

Price, Hereward T., "Shakespeare as Critic," *Philological Quarterly* 20 (1941), pp. 390–99.

Proudfoot, Richard, "Shakespeare and the New Dramatists of the King's Men," in J. R. Brown and B. Harris (eds.), *Later Shakespeare*, London: Arnold, 1966, pp. 235–61.

Quiller-Couch, Arthur, Introduction, in Arthur Quiller-Couch and John Dover Wilson (eds.), *The Two Gentlemen of Verona*, New Cambridge Shakespeare, New York: Macmillan, 1921.

Rackin, Phyllis, *Stages of History: Shakespeare's English Chronicles*, Ithaca and New York: Cornell University Press, 1990.

Reed, John Curtis, "Humphrey Moseley, Publisher," *Oxford Bibliographical Society Proceedings and Papers* 2 (1930), pp. 57–142.

Roberts, Jeanne Addison, "Ralph Crane and the Text of *The Tempest*," *Shakespeare Studies* 13 (1980), pp. 213–33.

Rose, Mary Beth, "Where are the Mothers in Shakespeare? Options for Gender Representation in the English Renaissance," *Shakespeare Quarterly* 42.3 (1991), pp. 291–314.

Rubin, Gayle, "The Traffic in Women: Notes on the 'Political Economy' of Sex," in Rayna Reiter (ed.), *Toward an Anthropology of Women*, New York: Monthly Review Press, 1975, pp. 157–210.

Said, Edward, *Beginnings: Intention and Method*, New York: Basic Books, 1975.

Saunders, J. W., "From Manuscript to Print: A Note on the Circulation of Poetic MSS in the Sixteenth Century," *Proceedings of the Leeds Philosophical and Literary Society* (1951), pp. 507–28.

Schachter, Marc, "Montaigne's 'Liberté volontaire' and the Discourse of Friendship," unpublished paper delivered at Modern Language Association of America Convention, Chicago, 1995.

Schochet, Gordon J., *Patriarchalism in Political Thought: The Authoritarian Family and Political Speculation and Attitudes Especially in Seventeenth-Century England*, Oxford: Basil Blackwell, 1975.

Schwartz, Murray M., and Kahn, Coppélia (eds.), *Representing Shakespeare: New Psychoanalytic Essays*, Baltimore and London: Johns Hopkins University Press, 1980.

Sedgwick, Eve Kosofsky, *Between Men: English Literature and Male Homosocial Desire*, New York: Columbia University Press, 1985.

Epistemology of the Closet, Berkeley: University of California Press, 1990.

Sisson, Charles J., "Shakespeare Quartos as Prompt-Copies, With Some Account of Cholmeley's Players and a New Shakespeare Allusion," *Review of English Studies* 18 (1942), pp. 129–43.

Smith, Bruce, *Homosexual Desire in Shakespeare's England: A Cultural Poetics*, Chicago: University of Chicago Press, 1991.

Smith, Nigel, *Literature and Revolution in England 1640–1660*, New Haven: Yale University Press, 1994.

Stallybrass, Peter, "Shakespeare, Milton and the Individual," paper delivered at the English Institute, Harvard University, 1990.

"Shakespeare, the Individual, and the Text," in Lawrence Grossberg, Cary Nelson, and Paula Treichler (eds.), with Linda Baughman, and with assistance from John Macgregor Wise, *Cultural Studies*, New York: Routledge, 1992, pp. 593–610.

"Worn Worlds: Clothes and Identity on the Renaissance Stage," paper delivered at the Center for Literary and Cultural Studies, Harvard University, November 1993.

Stallybrass, Peter, and White, Allon, *The Politics and Poetics of Transgression*, Ithaca: Cornell University Press, 1986.

Stone, Lawrence, *The Family, Sex and Marriage in England 1500–1800*, Abridged edition, New York: Harper, 1977.

"Social Mobility in England, 1500–1700," *Past and Present* 33 (1966), pp. 16–55.

Sundelson, David, "'So Rare a Wonder'd Father': Prospero's *Tempest*," in Murray M. Schwartz and Coppélia Kahn (eds.), *Representing Shakespeare: New Psychoanalytic Essays*, pp. 33–53.

Taylor, Gary, "A New Shakespeare Poem?," *Times Literary Supplement* (20 December 1985), pp. 1447–48.

"'Shall I die?' Immortalized?," *Times Literary Supplement* (31 January 1986), pp. 123–24.

Taylor, Gary, and Warren, Michael (eds.), *The Division of the Kingdoms: Shakespeare's Two Versions of King Lear*, Oxford: Clarendon, 1983.

Thomas, Max, "Reading the Renaissance Commonplace Book: A Question of Authorship?" in Martha Woodmansee and Peter Jaszi (eds.), *The Construction of Authorship: Textual Appropriation in Law and Literature*, Durham: Duke University Press, 1994, pp. 401–15.

Townshend, Aurelian, *Tempe Restor'd*, in Cedric C. Brown (ed.), *The Poems and Masques of Aurelian Townshend with Music by Henry Lawes and William Webb*, Reading: Whiteknights Press, 1983.

Traub, Valerie, "The (In)Significance of 'Lesbian' Desire in Early Modern England," in Jonathan Goldberg (ed.), *Queering the Renaissance*, pp. 62–83.

Trevor, Doug, "Authoring Renaissance Translations: Marie de Gournay and John Florio," unpublished essay.

Turner, Robert K., Jr. (ed.), *A King and No King*, Regents Renaissance Drama Series, Lincoln: University of Nebraska Press, 1963.

van den Berg, Sara, "Ben Jonson and the Ideology of Authorship," in Jennifer Brady and W. H. Herendeen (eds.), *Ben Jonson's 1616 Folio*, pp. 111–37.

Waith, Eugene M., *The Pattern of Tragicomedy in Beaumont and Fletcher*, New Haven: Yale University Press, 1952.

(ed.), *The Two Noble Kinsmen*, Oxford Shakespeare, Oxford and New York: Oxford University Press, 1989.

Wall, Wendy, *The Imprint of Gender: Authorship and Publication in the English Renaissance*, Ithaca: Cornell University Press, 1993.

Wallis, Lawrence B., *Fletcher, Beaumont and Company: Entertainers to the Jacobean Gentry*, New York: Octagon, 1968.

Warner, Michael, "New English Sodom," in Jonathan Goldberg (ed.), *Queering the Renaissance*, pp. 330–58.

Weimann, Robert, "History and the Issue of Authority in Representation: The Elizabethan Theater and the Reformation," *New Literary History* 17 (1986), pp. 449–76.

Wells, Stanley, "Introduction," in Gary Taylor and Michael Warren (eds.), *The Division of the Kingdoms: Shakespeare's Two Versions of King Lear*, pp. 1–22.

Whigham, Frank, *Ambition and Privilege: The Social Tropes of Elizabethan Courtesy Theory*, Berkeley: University of California Press, 1984.

Williams, Raymond, *Keywords: A Vocabulary of Culture and Society*, New York: Oxford, 1976.

Woodmansee, Martha, "The Genius and the Copyright: Economic and Legal Conditions of the Emergence of the 'Author,'" *Eighteenth-Century Studies* 17 (1984), pp. 425–48.

Woolf, Virginia, "*ANON.*," *Twentieth-Century Literature* 25 (1975), pp. 382–98.

   A Room of One's Own, San Diego: HBJ, 1929.

Zitner, Sheldon P. (ed.), *The Knight of the Burning Pestle*, The Revels Plays, Manchester: Manchester University Press, 1984.

Index

Cambridge Studies in Renaissance Literature and Culture

General editor
STEPHEN ORGEL
Jackson Eli Reynolds Professor of Humanities, Stanford University